The Cruel Science

Animal Research from Aristotle to the 21st Century

David Irving

The Cruel Science
Animal Research from Aristotle to the 21st Century

SHOWALTER PRESS
New York, USA

First Published by Showalter Press in 2014

ISBN-13: 978-1500436063

All Rights Reserved.
Address all inquiries to
Showalter Press
3 Hanni Avenue
Sidney, New York 13838

Table of Contents

In loving memory of
Laurence G. Irving and Adeline Thomas Irving

Preface

A close investigation of animal research offers compelling insights into the need for developing new attitudes in the way people traditionally regard animals. For most people, animals exist as a source for food, clothing, occasional entertainment, and/or serving as household pets. With the growing societal awareness of the profound impact the human/animal connection has for the future welfare of the planet and even for human survival, however, it has become imperative for trying to find a new way of thinking about animals that focuses on just how important they really are to human beings. Most people today, for example, have at least a vague idea that cruelty is somehow involved in the production of the food they consume that comes from factory farms. Still, far too little consideration goes into what the production of cruelty-based foods means for every individual and, collectively, for the world.

The connection of the consumption of animal protein (flesh foods and dairy foods) to the killer diseases has by now been well established. Added to this problem, the production of meat and dairy products is expected to double in the next 35 years to feed an expanding population that will increase from seven billion to nine billion people.[1] Already the waste animals leave behind finds its way into the earth contaminating the groundwater that seeps into our streams and rivers or escapes via enormous stockpiles of manure which decomposes into the atmosphere as methane gas responsible for 18% of the greenhouse gasses contributing to global warming. It has also now been estimated that livestock used for food occupies around 38 percent of the entre ice-free land surface of the earth.[2] With trends like these, it is not difficult to foresee that if the expansion of livestock is not stopped it will eventually occupy most of the ice-free land surface of the world. Little imagination is required to envision the kinds of conflicts among nations to which a scenario like this could lead, including the waging of wars to compete for enough land space for human survival.

It is no exaggeration to assert that the attitudes people have about animals will be a key ingredient in the future welfare of the world. Already it has become crucial for human beings to reject attitudes that condone the mistreatment of the nonhuman animal population of the earth, such as required to produce animal foods, not only because it cannot be divorced from the destruction that follows but because of its profound impact on the human mind. Animal research is quite naturally one of the featured topics in the debate for here an examination quickly unearths a series of questions such as what part does animal research play in engendering the disrespect toward animals that makes the mistreatment of animals on factory farms tolerable? How much does animal research contribute to the violence that is leading human beings down a path toward self-destruction? In what ways does subjugating animals and using them against their will impact human character, and how significant is human character for the survival of the human species? These are serious questions for which serious people are trying to find answers. One of the biggest questions of all is whether animal research should be accepted or whether it should be rejected.

Quotations

The world stands at a parting of the ways and those who suffer know this with deeply anxious hearts. One way leads to destruction. It is the way of the tolerance of cruelty, if not the active engagement in it. It is the way of hunting for sport, the way of vivisection, the way of killing for self-adornment, the way of killing animals for food, the way of making slaves of animals without thought for their happiness and well-being....The other way leads to salvation. It is the way of harmlessness, the way of recognition of brotherhood with all creatures, the way of tenderness and compassion, the way of service and not of selfishness."

— George S. Arundale (author of Mt. Everest, a Spiritual Attainment)

To my mind the life of a lamb is no less precious than the life of a human being. I should be unwilling to take the life of a lamb for the sake of the human body. I hold that, the more helpless a creature, the more entitled it is to protection by man from the cruelty of man.

— Mahatma Gandhi

Chapter 1

Animal Research – An Overview

In today's world human beings offer only a few protections to the many species of animals with whom they have some kind of interaction. Cats and dogs have won enough favor to at least count on prohibitions from being slaughtered for food, that is, in most places in the Western world. But in countries like Argentina, Brazil, China, Korea, Peru, Switzerland, and Vietnam, animals cannot even depend upon this safeguard. In South Korea some people kill cats and dogs by torturing them in ways that can cause the animals as much pain as possible. This group believes that feeding on dogs who have been tortured will increase their sexual potency. They string dogs up and beat them with bricks, stones, and rods for long periods of time as the dogs defecate and urinate over themselves. Their cruelty knows no bounds as they hit cats repeatedly in the head with hammers, put them in bags, beat them against the earth, and then boil them alive all because they also believe that a tonic made from a cat that has been cooked according to this formula will cure rheumatism and neuralgia.[1,2]

Just as in the United States, acts of cruelty toward animals in South Korea are not sanctioned by the majority of the people who raise their voices in protest when such deeds are brought to their attention. But that does not stop the annual slaughter of two million cats and dogs for the meat trade every year in South Korea. Business like this is enough of an incentive for the government to look the other way, ignoring the laws that prohibit eating cats and dogs.

Most countries claim that they do not permit overt cruelty to animals, including the United States. Even so, human beings continue to find ways to mistreat animals in the most sadistic and bizarre ways imaginable, no matter what protections are offered by their system of government. In America, institutional cruelty to animals is freely permitted as long as it is connected to some economic interest, as in the case of the routine killing of livestock by cruel methods in the production of animal foods on factory farms. Further cruelty is encouraged in scientific inquiry where animal researchers are given free license to experiment upon almost any kind of animal they choose in almost any way they wish with little or no supervision. Evidence for this claim is not difficult to obtain by simply observing the kinds of experiments the National Institutes of Health (NIH) habitually funds. At the University of California San Francisco, for example, a researcher received public tax dollars to sew the eyes closed of 22 newly born kittens, implant chemical pumps into their heads so that he could inject drugs through a port into their craniums, force them to stay awake by means of a motorized floor, paralyze them in preparation for brain recordings, reopen their eyes, cut off the tops of their skulls, and then prop them up in front of a television screen to measure their brain activity. This scientist has collected millions of dollars from the taxpayers to conduct experiments like these upon kittens and cats and has made the amazing discovery that "cats' brains do not develop normally when their eyes are sewn shut."[3]

Just how did the idea originate that nature intended for human beings to subjugate animals in such cruel ways? Contrary to anthropologic misinformation that dominated most of the 20th century, today's anthropological research, unburdened by species bias ("speciesism"), reveals that human beings have not always courted some form of aggressive and combative relationship with animals.[4] The general disrespect and indifference toward animals that is prevalent today only began to grow in human consciousness some ninety thousand years or so ago in the long seven million year history of humankind. That happened when humans managed to reverse their role as prey hunted by predator animals to becoming predatory hunters of prey. With the accomplishment of this feat they began to pursue hunting on a large scale.[5]

Today, a might-makes-right attitude about animals is implanted firmly in the human consciousness. With humans, life is a miracle as displayed in marvelous photographic images from inside the womb choreographing the life of the human fetus from the

2

moment of conception to birth. The lives of nonhuman mammals, on the other hand, are relatively unimportant. They get no credit because they too possess a beating heart, blood that circulates through their bodies, lungs that breathe, a brain that thinks, and a biological system that feeds itself and procreates just like human beings. Humans are miracles created by God. Animals are things and who knows or cares much how they were created. Miracle? Not possible! Miracles apply only to humans.

The idea that human beings stand head and shoulders above all other life forms which have just one function, to serve human beings, is a belief that starts at birth and continues until death. Children learn by parents, family members, neighbors, teachers, schools, social and religious institutions, and their government, that animals are inferior and suitable for subjugation. The message plays like a continuous mantra in the mind over and over, night and day, year after year, and decade after decade. But for those who do begin to probe their relationships with other species, it doesn't take long to recognize that the way humans treat animals lies at the very core of some of the major problems facing the world. Clearly, human beings stand at the brink of a looming catastrophe, and disrespect and condescension toward other species is one of the principal contributing factors.

Animal researchers have ridden the wave of indifference toward other species with great success from the time animal research first began over 2300 years ago, using it as the rationale for conducting experiments upon animals in any way they wished. Inflicting pain and suffering upon animals without constraint, they often devised—and still do— the most brutal kinds of experiments. Because only a few weak laws existed that protected animals prior to the 20th century, there were no consequences to pay. Animals, innocent though they were, had no voice to protest the cruelty that was inflicted upon them.

As the world forged ahead, a few conscientious citizens did raise their voices in protest whenever they learned what was going on inside animal research laboratories. But animal researchers countered that there were no moral imperatives when it came to using animals to benefit human beings. These researchers were largely successful in convincing the public that it was perfectly normal to experiment on animals even if it meant the animals had to suffer. This was an acceptable condition, they insisted, that was required in order to advance human knowledge and find cures for human disease. And though anesthesia did not exist until nearly 2300 years after animal research began, animal researchers managed to get society to buy into the assumption that pain was of little consequence where animals were concerned. If experiments did cause animals pain, they insisted, animals, unlike human beings, experienced pain only minimally—if at all. Public apprehension was also allayed by animal research assertions that animals did not have the capacity to reason and that pain could never be a consequence for animals which did not reason. Besides, the researchers adamantly maintained, not only could animals not reason, they were not even conscious beings so no logical reason existed for why people should be concerned about the suffering of an animal. Finally, above the entire ethic promoting animal research hung the maxim which by then had become a part of everyday thinking, that all species on the earth were put here by God and nature for human use so that all other considerations mattered little.

With arguments such as these to bolster their work, animal researchers experimented upon animals in any way they wished and ignored all protests. In the 16th century they even gave public demonstrations in which they cut open pregnant animals to toy with the mothers' babies while the leaders of the church looked politely on. (See chapter 6.)

As is common in today's animal research laboratories, many of the early animal experiments were unnecessary and done just to satisfy the curiosity of the researchers. Robert Boyle (1627-1691) and Robert Hooke (1635-1703), for example, two British animal researchers experimenting at the Royal Society in London, invented a tubular-shaped vacuum air pump for the society into which they could put animals like mice, cats, birds, and snakes. The pump could be used in two different ways. Withdrawing the air caused the animals to suffocate quickly in the vacuum this created. Or, the animals could be left to slowly suffocate in the air that was available in the tube. From these kinds of experiments they deduced that not only did animals need air to live, but that it should be fresh air.[6] Animal researchers have been drawing self-evident conclusions like this from their work ever since. Such was the case, for example, with the experimenter at the University of San Francisco described above who sewed the eyelids of kittens closed. In like manner, an experimenter at the University of Wisconsin got $500,000 from the Department of Justice to electrocute pigs with Taser guns to try to determine whether or not stun guns were safe. This unnecessary experiment could easily have been done using follow-up studies of Taser victims.[7]

In today's world the term "duh research" has been coined to describe animal experiments like these which provide self-explanatory answers. At the National Institute of Mental Health, for example, researchers recently castrated monkeys to show that castrated monkeys were more subordinate and less dominate than monkeys who had not been castrated.[8,9] An experiment like this rightly deserves a "duh" rating. Few people, other than animal researchers themselves, believe that the NIH should fund these kinds of experiments with taxpayer dollars.

Though animal research got off to a stuttering start requiring over 1700 years before it began to get into full swing, once underway, the idea that animals were creatures without consciousness put on earth just for humans to use, was the rationale the researchers used to justify their work. These ideas influenced the general public either directly or as a validation of prevailing societal standards in which cruelty to animals was tolerated as a part of everyday life. In mid-18th century London, for example, societal cruelty found vivid expression in bloody spectacles in which animals were forced to fight against each other at cockfights or baiting sports in which an animal, such as a dog, tethered to a stake, was pitted against another animal—a bull, a bear, a raccoon, or a monkey.[10] These were popular entertainments all across England attended by both aristocrats (men and women) and an audience drawn from a frenzied public. Spectators at baiting events waged bets and cheered and hooted and hollered and salivated with great gusto to watch animals being forced to tear each other apart, behaving much as though they belonged on a page torn from a book on the coliseum games of ancient Rome.[11]

The miserable treatment of animals in scenes of daily life like these were not confined to England during the 18th and 19th centuries. Transport and work horses with festering sores and ribs easily visible through emaciated bodies were common sights along the streets broad and narrow of European towns and cities.[12] A glimpse of the kind of brutality transport animals endured is offered through the striking portrayal of a street scene in Fyodor Dostoievsky's novel *Crime and Punishment*. There the Russian novelist describes the boyhood experiences of his protagonist, Raskolnikov, who had often seen little peasant horses "straining their utmost under a heavy load of wood or hay, especially when the wheels were stuck in the mud or in a rut. And the peasants would beat them so cruelly, sometimes even about the nose and eyes, and he felt so sorry, so sorry for them that he almost cried, and his mother always used to take him away from the window."

In one of the most unforgettable scenes in literature, Raskolnikov dreams of a scene in which a boisterous, thick-necked peasant with a fleshy face, Mikolka, surrounded by several of his tavern mates and a drunken, whooping tavern mob, begins to repeatedly whip and beat a thin little sorel mare to make her pull a cartload of 8 drunken, uproarious peasants. Crying out that the mare is his property so that he has the right to beat her, Mikolka slashes the unfortunate horse in the eyes with his whip and then crushes her with a wooden shaft before bludgeoning her to death with a crowbar.

Dostoievsky drew the scene from his own memory when he was a fifteen-year old boy and had witnessed a government courier beating a peasant carriage driver on the back of the head who, having no authority of his own, avenged his humiliation by whipping the lead horse of his carriage.[13] The author described it as a "disgusting scene" that he could never forget.[14]

The beating of horses in *Crime and Punishment* was an apt description of what all too often became reality for transport animals during those times to which we pay token tribute today with the phrase "no need to beat a dead horse." Beaten without mercy sometimes until their skulls were crushed or their eyes were knocked out, horses and mules were commonly driven until they dropped and then were sold to the slaughterhouse where they often starved to death before being slaughtered.[15] These societal crimes did not go completely unopposed by concerned citizens. Among the notables who expressed their outrage were Henry Fielding, who threatened a fistfight with a coachman for mistreating his horse, the reportedly effeminate John Keats, who in 1819 fought a butler's son for bullying a kitten, and Charles Dickens who in 1838 "spoke out heatedly in court against a lout whom he had witnessed savaging his horse."[16]

It should not be overlooked, that whereas animal researchers, as scientists, had the opportunity to show a humanitarian side by rising in defense of helpless animals during periods of overt cruelty toward other species, such as with transport animals, like Fielding, Keats, and Dickens did, they chose instead to partner with the cruelty by abusing, exploiting, mistreating, and killing animals on the research table. The same kind of partnership holds true in today's world where overt cruelty is demonstrated daily on factory farms, on fur farms, in circuses, at rodeos, in zoos, at blood sports events (i.e., cock fighting), and in hunting and trapping activities. Animal research dines at the same table.

Opposition to animal research materialized slowly. It was not until the early 19th century that the gradual growth of animal rights organizations marked a more focused and organized approach for fighting back against animal cruelty. (See chapter 7) It started in England in Liverpool in 1809 with the short-lived Society for Preventing Wanton Cruelty to Brute Animals. This was followed by the founding of the Society for the Prevention of Cruelty to Animals (SPCA) established in London in 1824. Queen Victoria, an animal lover who joined the society in 1835 when she was still a Princess, bestowed the prefix "Royal" to the society in 1840 after she had become Queen. It was thereafter known as the Royal Society for the Prevention of Cruelty to Animals (RSPCA).[17] The American Society for the Prevention of Cruelty to Animals (ASPCA) was founded in America in 1866.[18]

Not to be overlooked, in 1847, a new organization related to animal rights also started up in Britain called the Vegetarian Society It was followed in 1850 by its counterpart in the United States which named itself the American Vegetarian Society. The latter held its opening convention in New York City where the members adopted a series of Sentiments and Resolutions which included the statements that if anyone would "...return to Paradise and purity, to mental and physical enjoyment, he must...abstain from the killing and eating of animals as food..." and that "...cruelty, in any form, for the mere purpose of procuring unnecessary food, or to gratify depraved appetites, is obnoxious to the pure human soul...."[19]

The animal rights movement gathered strength over the ensuing generations until the last quarter of the 20th century when it exploded into the powerful animal rights movement that exists today. But any advantage that might have accrued to animal rights activists due to their increase in numbers was offset to a considerable extent by the enormous growth of the animal research industry that in the meantime had ballooned into a multibillion dollar enterprise.

Buoyed by their social status and acceptance by the public, animal researchers made increasingly boastful and exaggerated claims extolling the benefits and accomplishments of animal research. At the same time, they ignored or deliberately sidetracked suspicions that their work may have sometimes produced disastrous results, such as the creation of the AIDS epidemic. Rather convincing evidence also exists which suggests that the Salk vaccine may be responsible for having already cost millions of deaths from cancer with many more still to come. [See chapter 10].

Conducting their experiments under the umbrella of science, animal researchers today wear the mantle of scientific respectability. This has helped to brush aside critics as irrelevant cynics and troublemakers whose anthropomorphic sympathies work against the better interests of science and society. Armed with prestige and respect, animal researchers have managed to keep much of the public on their side.

The animals rights movement, however, has kept pace often alerting the public about what goes on behind the closed doors of animal research laboratories. Because of their work, a growing segment of the population in the 21ˢᵗ century is far less willing to accept exaggerated assertions about the successes of animal research, nor do people any longer accept so readily the unproven hypotheses that animals experience only the most minimal pain and possess no consciousness. Charges by the animal research industry that people who object to animal research are just misguided bleeding hearts are also far less persuasive, and the animal rights movement has forced many of the excuses offered for animal experiments to walk the plank.

People in today's world are far more inclined to want to know the facts. What about those AIDS claims? Could animal research really have played a role in its creation even to the extent of causing the epidemic? Could people inoculated with the Salk vaccine really have been given a deadly simian cancer virus responsible for some ten million deaths? Animal research proponents have tried to sweep such claims under the rug. But these kinds of questions deserve to be examined independently without obstruction in order to determine if they have any basis in fact.

The justification for animal research was born from the concept that all nonhuman species on the planet are not rational beings and therefore are designed to be subservient to human beings in meeting their needs no matter what those needs might be. The negative human attitudes toward animals [out of which animal research originated] only began developing with the advent of large scale hunting operations some ninety thousand years ago, as referred to above. This was the time when Homo sapiens were refining the language skills they had begun to acquire some sixty thousand or so years before that.[20] One hundred and fifty thousand years later, human history had arrived at that part known as the ancient Greeks. This is where the story of animal research begins.

Chapter 2

The Sacrificial Greeks: the Significance of Animal Sacrifice to Animal Research

The Greeks are paramount to any discussion about animal research because animal research began with them. It evolved from the practice of animal sacrifice, a fixture of life that was firmly implanted in the culture of ancient Greece, the same that produced Aristophanes, Euclid, Euripides, Plato, Ptolemy, Socrates, Sophocles, and Aristotle. The Minoans, for example, who occupied the Isle of Crete for over a thousand years from 2700 BC to 1500 BC, sacrificed animals as evidenced by sacrificial basins they left behind, though nothing survives that would indicate they practiced human sacrifice.[1] On the Grecian mainland, the Mycenaeans (1600 – 1100 BC) carried on the tradition until their collapse, after which Greece entered a period referred to as the Dark Ages (1200 – 800 BC). This did not mark the end of animal sacrifice, however, which continued as shown by a human/nonhuman burial site found at Lefkandi on the Isle of Euboea, the second largest of the Greek islands. The site dates to about 1000-950 BC and contained the skeletons of a man, a woman, and four horses, with the humans being buried in a separate burial shaft from the horses. The man's remains were found in a bronze jar the rim of which was decorated with scenes of archers hunting animals. Two of the horses held bits in their mouths, and all four appeared to have been sacrificed.[2] (These kinds of burials are also reminiscent of ancient Paleolithic burials of people with animals dating back 100,000 years.)

For the next 300 years, from 800 to 500 BC , during the so-called Archaic period in Grecian history, the Greeks were busy forming city states of which Sparta and Athens are the ones most remembered today. But the people continued to practice animal sacrifice as portrayed in their religious rituals in which they sacrificed domestic animals to the gods by burning and eating then at ritual banquets. Banquets with sacrifices and prayer are a constant feature in Homer's *Iliad* (750 BC) In his *Odyssey* (725 BC), Eumaeus sacrifices a pig and prays for his master. Odysseus offers a ram to Zeus.

By the time the period of the Classical Greeks arrived (510 – 323 BC)—the period of Socrates, Plato, and Aristotle—the concept of animal sacrifice was deeply rooted in the Grecian culture. This is apparent also from the many plays of Euripides (480-406 BC) which involved either animal or human sacrifice, or both [though historians believe it is questionable whether actual human sacrifice took place during this time; in fact, doubt has been cast on whether the ancient Greeks really practiced human sacrifice.[3]]. Examples of sacrifice are found in the plays of Euripides like Bacchae, Electra, Iphigenia, Hecabe, Heraclidae, Orestes, and Phoenician Women.[4] The popularity of animal sacrifice during this period is also on display on the frieze of the Parthenon (constructed between 447 and 438 BC) that runs around the inside of the colonnade. It portrays a procession of people leading sacrificial animals to a gathering of gods which are seated to greet them.[5]

This is the atmosphere out of which animal research was conceived. At this point in time, human beings had been sacrificing animals since at least the burgeoning of the very first civilization in Sumer (5700-1763 BC). Early civilizations also practiced human sacrifice including, beside the Sumerians, those founded by the Ethiopians, the, Assyrians, the Babylonians, the Britons, the Canaanites, the Carthaginians, the Chinese, the Celts, the Danes, the Egyptians, the Etruscans, the Indians, the Persians, the Phoenicians, and the Scythians. Animal sacrifice is also a constant feature of the Old Testament stories of Moses—though not human sacrifice—as he led the Israelites to the promised land. Moses lived in the 13th century BC to sometime in the early 12th century.

Sacrifice was a major force unifying ancient cultures and a path by which the ancients sought guidance and answers about life and death. It stood as a means for inventing and establishing a relationship to the universe and its mysteries though it required indifference to the suffering of the victims being sacrificed, animal or human, and often involved bizarre, ritual killings. Diodorus Siculus, the Greek historian who lived from 90 – 21 BC, described how the Celts liked to "kill a man by a knife-stab in the region above the midriff, and after his fall they foretell the future by the convulsions of his limbs and the pouring of his blood."[6] Julius Caesar is said to have been repulsed by the barbarity of such Celtric rites, though apparently home-grown cruelty was not nearly so loathsome to the great Emperor since the Romans purportedly were quite expert at killing the same barbaric Celts in Gaul by cutting off their hands and feet and leaving them to bleed to death.[7]

It should be noted, in any event, that the Celts and the Romans seem to have liked to exaggerate each other's failings, and whether the Celtic rites which so outraged Caesar ever really happened have been called into question. Not in question is the cruelty practiced by the Romans in the killings in the Coliseums which included, beside humans beings, animals such as lions, tigers, bears, bulls, leopards, giraffes, deer, hippos, rhinoceroses and crocodiles all of which were tormented, stabbed, and gored to death. [8] Nor was Caesar repulsed by the practice of haruspicy, a method of divination in which animals were sacrificed so that the meaning of natural events such as lightning strikes or the flight of birds could be foretold. The divination was accomplished by examining the livers of the sacrificed animals. It was Titus Vestricius Spurinna, a haruspex [one who practices haruspicy], who warned Caesar to beware of the Ides of March after conducting a haruspectomy.[9]

The concept of the sacrifice of animals and humans is an invention of the mind. This must be true because the archaeological evidence reveals that it is a later creation of human endeavor.

Once it dawned on humans that the ritualistic sacrifice of their fellow human beings was not in their best interests, they mostly stopped doing it. The same was true for animal sacrifice, though it would continue into late antiquity (the 2nd to 8th centuries AD) before humankind finally drew the curtain on these chapters of superstition to a close. The means to its end in the Mediterranean world may have happened primarily through the role Christian thinkers played. It has been pointed out that whereas animal sacrifice had "dominated the ritual landscape of ancient Greek, Roman, and Jewish religion for millennia...this situation changed drastically in the fourth and fifth centuries AD, corresponding to the rise of Christianity."[10] Some Christians believe that early Christians were anxious to rid themselves of the cruelty of animal sacrifice and so exchanged the practice for the spiritual path to God taught by Jesus consisting of prayer and the love of God and one's fellow human beings. Jesus paved the way when he said: "I require mercy, not sacrifice."[11]

Even so, neither human sacrifice nor animal sacrifice have been completely erased from human activity. The sacrifice of human beings has continued in various instances over the centuries and can be found on occasion even today, for example, in muti (medicine) witchcraft killings in South Africa where some people believe the sacrificed body parts of children or old people will help them become rich and powerful.[12] As for animals, in the Cuban Santeria religion sacrificial rites are conducted not only in Cuba but wherever Santeria is observed, including in the United States. Animal sacrifice also goes on in some villages in Greece. In Nepal, around 250,000 animals are sacrificed to the goddess of power, Gadhimai, every five years in a Hindu festival that demands the sacrifice of rats, pigeons, pigs, roosters, goats, lambs, and other animals including 10,000 buffalo. The buffalo are hemmed in by a walled enclosure. There they are chased and decapitated by men wearing red bandanas and arm bands, viewed by a cheering crowd eager to observe the slaughter.[13]

In spite of occurrences like these, it would appear for the most part that the human race can congratulate itself for having eradicated human and animal sacrifice as a way of life. Yet upon closer investigation, and quite apart from the illustrations cited above, it seems that both human sacrifice and animal sacrifice have survived into contemporary times by simply appearing in different guises. A branch of animal sacrifice had already gone underground after the 3rd century AD where it remained in abeyance until its reemergence in the 16th century, as we shall see.

The key to the recognition of human and animal sacrifice in today's world is found in how sacrifice is defined. Archaeologist

Dr. Mike Parker-Pearson notes that human sacrifice is a method invented by human beings for exchanging life for death in order to achieve a specific result they believe will be favourable to humans.[14] He identifies human sacrifice as being either altruistic or coerced and cites capital punishment as an example of coercion sacrifice carried out for the purpose of cleansing and restoring order from the disorder created by capital crimes. Christianity, on the other hand, provides an example of altruistic sacrifice where Jesus allowed himself to be sacrificed to save humankind. Some Christians refer to Jesus as being the sacrificial lamb of God.

Examples of altruistic human sacrifice in modern times include the on-going suicide bombings in the Middle East committed in an effort to obtain a political and religious objective. During the Vietnam war several people poured gasoline over their bodies and then lit a match to themselves in an effort to bring that war to a close. More recently, 26 year-old Daniel Shaull, described by his father as a genius on a quest to bring peace and justice to the world, set himself on fire outside Nicholas Ungar Furs in Portland Oregon. He died in this act of self-immolation to protest the cruelty of the fur trade. To date the furrier remains open.[15]

Animal research provides the most perfect example of the practice of animal sacrifice in today's world. Behind locked doors animal researchers work away at their stated objective of serving the greater cause of humankind by doing research they insist benefits human beings. Nobody would dare claim, nevertheless, that animal research is an altruistic endeavor. This is an occupation that provides the researchers with lucrative careers, employment stability, peer prestige, and elevated social standing. In the remote past in the prehistory of the ancient world, the sacrifice of animals (and humans) also provided the shamans and priests conducting the sacrificial rites with the same kinds of benefits: lucrative careers, employment stability, peer prestige, and elevated social standing.

The Greeks are credited with giving the world democracy, philosophy, literature, and art, along with significant contributions in mathematics, music, astronomy, and architecture. But their belief in animal sacrifice evolved into animal research and set the stage for its proliferation and gradual increase and escalation into the enormous industry that today sacrifices millions of animals every year in a way that far exceeds any aspirations the ancient Greeks may ever have entertained or even imagined possible. In the United States alone, a study done by the Animal and Plant Health Inspection Service of the United States Department of Agriculture, estimated that between 25 and 30 million animals are used to experiment upon annually.[16] However, other figures put the number as high as 100 to 200 million which must be far more accurate.[17],[18] It is estimated, for example, that approximately 40 million genetically engineered animals are used worldwide just in the study of human diseases.[19] In any event, at 25 to 100 or 200 million animals experimented upon annually, just how extensive animal research really is begins to register. Worldwide, scientists have experimented upon billions of animals in just the last 20 years alone.

Simply put, animal sacrifice is still alive and well in the Western world in the form of animal research where animals are ritualistically sacrificed by the millions every year for the stated purpose of accomplishing certain industry-defined societal objectives which animal researchers claim means trying to find cures for human disease. Providing societal benefits is the same reason for which pagan societies engaged in the practice of animal sacrifice with as little thought for the suffering inflicted upon the animals to be sacrificed as animal researchers show for the animals they sacrifice today. The ideas and the practice is traceable to the ancient Greeks.

The inference can hardly be avoided that animal research is a vestige of archaic, barbaric rites that in any form constitutes cruelty to animals. The affects of cruelty on the human character and the linkage of animal cruelty to the serious problems that loom ever larger as a threat to human existence must become matters for serious concern if the Homo sapiens species is to survive no matter what health benefits animal researchers claim their work provides for society — a claim, incidentally, for which the evidence is flimsy at best.

The image that human beings create about themselves for themselves is of enormous significance. More and more people are

committing to changing that image from one where human indifference toward animals is the prevailing norm to one in which
human respect for life in all its manifestations is the dominant
feature. Many reasons exist for why this is the best state of mind for
the future welfare of human beings. Not least among them is that it
empties the mind of the images of living creatures being sacrificed,
which is another step toward reducing the violence that occupies
the human mind in the world today.

Chapter 3

Aristotle, Patron Saint of Animal Researc4

By the time human beings first decided to cut open animals to look inside a living creature, the custom of sacrifice was a part of the everyday thinking of classical Greece so that the use of animals to meet human needs was firmly entrenched in the consciousness of the people. It would be difficult to determine with any certainty who was the first person ever to cut into a living animal, or for that matter, to dissect a dead animal. Alcmaeon of Croton, (510? BC) has been credited with being the very first vivisector, (a person who operates on (vivisects) living animals for investigative purposes), though whether he deserves the distinction is questionable. He was a medical writer and the first to consider that the brain was the central organ of sensation and thought, a theory that Plato (429-347) accepted. Alcmaeon may also have had some association with the legendary philosopher/mathematician Pythagoras (570-490) and was distinguished enough for Aristotle to write a book about him. In any case, it is possible that Alcmaeon excised the eyeball of an animal in order to study whether vision was connected to the brain.[1] Yet, even if he did perform the excision (the Latin term used to describe the excision was "exsectionem" from "exsectio" = cutting out), no evidence exists to show that he carried it out on a live animal.[2] It could just as easily have been done on a dead animal and would have been, consequently, a dissection, not a vivisection. Some scholars even question Alcmaeon's role in the event entirely, though it has been pointed out that tracing the optic nerve to the brain could have helped him conclude that the brain controlled the senses.

Democritus (ca 460 – ca 370 BC), a philosopher known for his work on atomic theory and considered by some to be the father of modern science, is also reported to have vivisected animals. But

17

the reports are based on stories handed down from 17th century sources for which no facts exist to verify whether the stories are true or accurate.[3]

After Democritus, however, a philosopher followed who not only dissected animals but came as close as possible to conducting vivisections without actually doing it. This was Aristotle (384 – 322 BC). His name is familiar to everyone. A student of Plato and the teacher of Alexander the Great, Aristotle focused on morality and aesthetics, logic and science, and politics and metaphysics in his studies. Scholars around the world ever since have acknowledged him as being one of the most important philosophers in the history of Western civilization whose work has profoundly influenced the thinking of the Western world. Pertinent to this discussion, he also made a major impact on Christian theology in the middle ages that still resonates today in the kind of relationships people have with animals. (See chapter 5)

Aristotle believed in the existence of an "unmoved mover of the universe, a supra-physical entity, without which the physical domain could not remain in existence."[4] Though not moving, this "unmoved mover" was the mover of all things in order to achieve perfection which is a state of pure actuality [being].[5] Fascinatingly enough, this viewpoint is similar to teachings associated with Buddhism such as the concept of the "void" where form is emptiness and emptiness is form. The 14th century so-called "mystic" priest, Meister Eckhart, expressed a similar understanding when he wrote: "For in this breaking through I perceive what God and I are in common. There I am what I was. There I neither increase nor decrease. For there I am the immovable which moves all things."[6] (Schopenhauer compared Eckhart to Buddha and noted that the spirit of the development of Christianity was nowhere so perfectly and powerfully stated as in the writing of German mystics like Meister Eckhart.)[7]

As for life on earth, Aristotle believed in an ordered hierarchical world arranged by nature in which every living thing had a fundamental essence inherent to what it was and the actions and activities in which it engaged. Humans stood at the apex of the hierarchy. Below humans came the world of animals followed by the vegetable world, and at the bottom, the world of inanimate objects. All form was unified by four elements which had to originate from basic primary matter which was unlimited. Above all stood God consisting of pure form and pure intellective soul.[8]

Aristotle believed in the concept of soul, however, his belief differed considerably from the way people traditionally regard the soul today. For him, every living thing was unified by a soul including plants, whose nutritive soul took in nutrition. This plant soul governed embryology and growth. Animals and humans both possessed a higher, sensitive soul by means of which they could move and perceive and which ruled the basic instincts. Humans also possessed a rational soul which gave them intelligence and the power to reason which was absent in animals. This soul governed the intellectual, conscious mind.[9],[10] But while organic objects, animals, and humans were unified by a soul, inanimate objects were different. By Aristotle's concept, a rock is not destroyed when it is split in two because it does not possess an internal principle of unity. Split a human being in two, however, and the internal unity on which that person depends is destroyed.[11] Inanimate objects like rocks or water were scattered across the universe so that a lake (or an ocean) is really only part of the whole of water. They have no fundamental unity. Living objects (plants, animals, and humans), on the other hand, were unified into distinct wholes.

The soul for Aristotle was neither a material part of the body nor a part separate from the body. Rather it was a set of capacities and abilities that could not exist without the body that a living thing possessed.[12] The goal of life was to be in harmony with this set of capacities and abilities and to strive for perfection in that endeavor. This was the path to happiness.

For Aristotle, rationality was the factor that sharply differentiated the human animal from the nonhuman animal. This division and the interpretation that followed after Aristotle's death has led to a belief system in which nonrational animals are defined as being separate and expendable, to be used in any way humans desire. Proponents of this theory concede only marginal respect for animals, if at all, which they believe is reserved for the rational animal—human beings. Being nonrational and incapable of thought, nonhuman animals have no rights except as the rational human animal decides to grant them.

It has taken centuries to arrive at a point where the bias in the human mind against animals created by this rational/ nonrational hypothesis can be addressed. Today, animal cognition scientists have established that thought processes are at work inside the brains of animals just as they are in humans. And while many contemporary philosophers of mind still cling to the Aristotelian hierarchical concepts, some are beginning to reevaluate these theories in light of present day knowledge. Harvard Professor of Philosophy, Matthew Brendan Boyle, summed up the new outlook as follows:

> According to a tradition reaching back at least as far as Aristotle, human beings are set apart from other terrestrial creatures by their rationality. Other animals, according to this tradition, are capable of sensation and appetite, but they are not capable of *thought*, the kind of mental activity associated with the rational part of the soul....For, the tradition holds, the presence of rationality does not just add one more power to the human mind; it transforms all of our principal mental powers, placing us in a different order of being from the one to which dumb brutes belong. Although the historical roots of this tradition run deep, I think it is fair to say that many contemporary philosophers regard it with suspicion.... For whatever we mean by calling our minds "rational," surely this must be compatible with a recognition that the human mind is one kind of animal mind, which has arisen through the same sorts of evolutionary processes that also produced the minds we call "nonrational." And our increasingly detailed sense of the psychological, behavioral, and neurophysiological similarities between ourselves and other animals, and of the ways in which we "rational" creatures frequently think and choose on pa-

20

tently nonrational principles, only adds to the pressure to see the specialness of our minds as a matter of degree rather than one of kind.[13]

As is sometimes the case with brilliant thinkers and creative people, Aristotle did not exercise the independence of mind to analyze, understand, and go beyond the customs and traditions of his own times in certain respects. For example, in his view, men were superior to woman, who he regarded as some kind of incomplete or deformed man; animals were to be used however humans saw fit, including for sacrifice, food, and labor; and he also believed that wars were justified. Aristotle saw slavery as a natural condition for people who became slaves, and that these slaves were well-suited for serving their Greek masters even though he regarded slaves as being barbarians.[14],[15]

Aristotle's beliefs about slaves compels comparisons with other famous proponents of slavery who have made a major impact on the world like Thomas Jefferson and George Washington. (Twelve U.S. presidents held slaves including Jefferson and Washington.) Whenever unfavorable actions attributed to them related to slavery come to light, excuses can be and often are made to protect their reputations such as that they were just a product of their times who lived without the benefit of present day hindsight. But men like Alexander Hamilton and Benjamin Franklin were contemporaries, yet both were abolitionists. This was a choice that was also open to Jefferson and Washington. And the abolition movement was in full swing during the lives of all of the slave-holding U.S. Presidents so that none of them can be excused on the grounds that they were just swept along with the current of their times. Besides, exceptional insight and understanding is expected of exceptional people, a category to which Jefferson and Washington clearly belong. The acceptance of the institution of slavery by twelve United States Presidents added to the dynamic that would eventually require a civil war and the deaths of 600,000 people plus the wounding and injuring of 2,000,000 more in order to resolve the conflict. Jefferson and Washington might have made a significant difference had they stood against slavery, or had Jefferson insisted that when he wrote the words "all men are created equal" in the U.S. Constitution that he meant for those words to apply to everyone, including African Americans, the Chinese, and the Native American people of the plains.

Dissenters against animal sacrifice were around in Aristotle's day too, so excuses are not available for his failure to recognize that animal sacrifice was cruel, or, for that matter, that the way humans related to animals could profoundly influence the direction of the future of the world. His own student, Theophrastus (371-287 BC), who took his place as the head of the Lyceum (Aristotle's school in Athens), thought that "animal sacrifice displeased the gods" and that "vivisection and meat eating were inhumane."[16] Plato, Aristotle's teacher, who was, reportedly, a vegetarian, wrote in his Republic how his famous mentor, Socrates (469-399 BC), promoted a vegan diet and further detailed Socrates' argument that feeding on cattle could lead to war.[17, 18] Pythagoras, too, may well have been a vegetarian who believed in kindness toward animals.[19] Aristotle would not have failed to have been aware that some of his contemporaries and immediate predecessors were thinking outside the box about matters like animal sacrifice, war, and consuming animals. He chose, however, to remain inside the box.

Just as the pro-slavery words, attitudes, and actions of the slave-holding American presidents played their role in creating the momentum that lead to the civil war, the same standard must be applied to Aristotle. His acceptance of status quo values like animal sacrifice and his beliefs, attitudes and actions toward nonhuman species played a significant part in forming a general state of consciousness from which objectionable practices would take root and spread, such as animal research and vivisection.

Aristotle's view about animals was consistent with a culture in which animal sacrifice was nearly as common as everyday shopping. It was so ordinary, in fact, that commentators of the times made little effort to describe it so that later historians had to piece together what animal sacrifice was all about from depictions on vases and from the writings of the Greek poets and a few references by various historians of the period.[20]

In Aristotle's day, priests, kings, warriors, and ordinary people were all qualified to offer sacrifice to the gods. They could even make bloodless offerings with foods like grains or cakes. But those who could afford it would sacrifice an animal such as a goat, a sheep, a pig, or a member of the poultry family. The sacrifice of larger animals, like an ox, however, was a luxury that only a minority of supplicants could afford.[21] Animal sacrifice also benefitted the average person who had a taste for meat but could not afford it in that they could sometimes get the leftovers from animal sacrifices to take home to eat.

The Greeks offered sacrifice for many different reasons. Someone who believed that they had offended a god might offer sacrifice to put them back in good graces with the god. Or if someone wanted to be purified from an "avenging spirit," they could sacrifice an animal.[22] The historian Xenophon (430-350 BC), a pupil of Socrates, described how he sacrificed a pig so that his travels would go well.[23]

At the sacrifice a procession of worshipers adorned themselves with garlands and draped the animal to be sacrificed with ribbons as they proceeded festively but reverently to the altar. If any animals had horns, the supplicants gilded the horns with gold. Musicians were also sometimes invited to join the procession, often a flute player, who could be male or female. A virtuous girl carried a sacrificial basket filled with barley or cakes beneath which the sacrificial knife was concealed. It had to be hidden, because if the animal knew of its impending doom it might become terrified and begin to fight and try to escape. If that happened, it would be taken as a bad omen. Someone also carried a vessel of water for the priest who would sprinkle the sacrificial area, the alter, the supplicants, and the sacrificial animal, which might also be offered water to drink. Water sprinkling was most important because it would cause the animal to make a movement that could be taken as a nod signaling that the animal had agreed to be sacrificed. At the point of sacrifice, the supplicant suddenly removed the knife from the sacrificial basket, still keeping it concealed, then swiftly cut a few hairs from the animal's forehead, throwing them on the ritual fire atop the alter. This indicated that the animal was no longer pure and could be sacrificed. The animal was then lifted over the alter and the supplicant slit its throat. As blood flowed down the alter it was collected in a vessel and poured over and around the alter. At that moment the women present uttered a high-pitched cry to mark the passage from life to death. Afterwards the sacrificed animal was roasted and eaten at the site, though at times it could be taken away to be eaten elsewhere if the supplicant wished. [24],[25],[26]

Animal sacrifice was a messy affair. It involved "dung, urine, blood, the ash and fat from burning and cooking, the oil of anointing and basting, the wine and other fluids of libation, and the dispersed and burned remnants of grain, pastry, and other offerings."[27]

A ritual like that described above raises many ethical questions. How can it not be cruel to deceive an innocent and unsuspecting animal and then seize it from behind to slit its throat? And what better words than pagan and/or barbaric should be used to describe the celebration that followed such messy rites of deception mixed with dung, urine, and blood? Just what kind of character does it build in the human mind over time to engage in activities like these especially in terms of retaining respect and appreciation for the life force that is inherent in all living creatures?

The trickery involved in deceiving an innocent animal to take away its life in such a display of superstition and ignorance was not a matter of concern for most scholars like Aristotle who accepted it as being perfectly normal just like the majority of Greeks living at the time. But surely the capacity to reason, which Aristotle believed constituted the major difference between animals and humans, was absent during these pagan feasts. Reason demands the ability to go beyond societal norms, common prejudices, and the influences of a society's conditioning on the individual.

Given the extent to which animal sacrifice was going on around him, it must not have caused Aristotle much concern to begin dissecting animals from the standpoint of morality. Any conflicts would have arisen from the strong taboos against mutilating the body that existed in his day.[28] Aristotle's goal, however, was to learn about human anatomy, and he took note of the obvious anatomical similarities between human and nonhuman animals. The more he could learn about the internal workings of the body of an animal, the more he would understand nature and how it worked in human beings.

It was unpleasant, offensive, foul-smelling work to cut open and sort through the flesh and organs of a dead creature.[29] As distasteful as it was, it had to be done if knowledge was to be advanced. And increasing knowledge and the search for perfection were requirements of the philosophy Aristotle espoused as a way of life. Thus he embarked on the path of dissecting animals.

Besides dissection, Aristotle also conducted experiments on living animals, and he may also have engaged in vivisection as indicated by his description of this experiment.

> In all animals alike, in those that have a chest and in those that have none, the apex of the heart points forwards, although this fact might possibly escape notice by a change of position under dissection.[30]

Here, even though he uses the word dissection, it seems odd that the position of the heart would change position under the stationary conditions in which dissection occurs.

In any case, Aristotle's came as close to vivisection as he could possibly come without actually vivisecting an animal. That becomes clear from the following description. Noticing that the blood vessels of emaciated humans caused their blood vessels to stand out, Aristotle thought that if this condition could be replicated in animals, the vascular system might be easier to study. The best way to accomplish that was to emaciate an animal by starving it and then strangle it to death.[31] The animal could then be dissected. As Aristotle described it:

> Now since...observation is difficult, it is only in strangled animals which have been previously emaciated [by starvation] that it is possible adequately to discover the facts [concerning blood vessels], if one makes the subject one's business.[32,33]

The suffering this would cause an animal was obviously not a concern for Aristotle. Considering that animal sacrifice was going on around him all the time and that he had no hesitation in starving an animal in order to emaciate it, to strangle an animal to death so that he could dissect it must have caused him little anxiety. The obvious question that people ask today is why Aristotle did not think it was cruel to starve an animal to the point of death and then murder it by strangulation no matter what the cultural norms of the times may have been.

Aristotle's anatomical work with dissection combined with his animal experiments and his far-reaching influence qualifies him as a serious contender for being the most important animal researcher in the history of animal research. The rationale that emerged from the procedures and principles upon which he relied is the same that animal researchers have employed ever since to justify their work. It constitutes a kind of canon of values that offers animals researchers a refuge against ethical doubts that may arise in the course of their work. During the latter 18th century, for example, when many animal researchers began to seriously question the morality of their experiments because of the suffering it imposed upon animals, this rationale was there to rely upon as a trusted defense for their work. The thesis as taught by Aristotle is that humans, being rational, are superior to animals, which are not rational, and that being superior, humans have the right to use animals in any way they desire. This might-makes-right approach has governed animal research ever since and has pervaded society in all aspects of how people treat animals.

Though a credo like this may be modified overtime, at least in outward appearance, in order to withstand complaints raised by opponents of animal research—for example, today's universities are required by law to establish standards of care in conducting animal research—in essence it remains the foundation upon which animal research rests just as it served as the foundation that gave birth to the animal experiments of Aristotle. It is this framework that has helped to make cruelty toward animals in research laboratories acceptable in the centuries that followed Aristotle's work.

Peasants who tied cats to the tops of their heads in the Middle Ages and ran full speed to squash the cats against a wall just for fun were not born to be cruel. They grew up with cruelty as sanctioned behavior that was part of a long heritage dating back centuries into the past. Similarly, animal research was born out of cruel practices which can be sequentially connected to the past starting with large scale hunting in the Paleolithic era some ninety thousand years ago followed by the invention of warfare some seventy-six thousand years later leading to the enslavement of nonhuman and human animals some five to eight thousand years or so ago that resulted in animal sacrifice and human sacrifice. It was at this link in the chain that animal research appeared on the world stage in ancient Greece a little over some twenty-three hundred years ago.

The disrespect for animals which the Greeks had absorbed from pagan sacrificial traditions was the foundation upon which animal research was created. Simply put, animal research was born out of pagan violence and has played a substantial role in the continuation of violence as an acceptable norm for human behavior. That role can be defined as making cruelty to other species respectable and creating cultural attitudes toward animals that defines them as insignificant and expendable. These attitudes have played a major part in undermining the health of the people of the earth and the planet itself which is the condition in which the world finds itself today.

Chapter 4

The Great Assumers

Following on Aristotle heels, the next two individuals to conduct animal experiments were Herophilus (330 – ca. 260 B.C.), born just eight years before Aristotle's death, and his younger rival, Erasistratus (304 – 245 B.C.), both of whom worked in Alexandria. They could hardly have escaped Aristotle's influence whose reputation was still on the ascendancy in Alexandria during their lifetimes.[1] Erasistratus, who became famous as a physician, also had a direct link to Aristotelian theory through his teacher Metrodorus who happened to be Aristotle's son-in-law. Herophilus, who has been called the father of anatomy by some, was guided by the work of Hippocrates (460 – 377 BC) but was well acquainted with the work of Aristotle and accepted, for example, the philosopher's theory that "the defining difference between men and women was that males possessed greater heat and that therefore women did not produce seed to contribute to conception."[2] This was also one of the theories behind Aristotle's belief that men were superior to women.

Like Aristotle, Herophilus and Erasistratus both dissected animals. They were also the first Greek physicians to dissect the human body, but not the first ever in the history of humankind. Susruta, a Hindu surgeon, had already practiced dissection and the removal of cataracts from human corpses before trying the procedure on live patients in 1000 BC, around 700 years earlier.[3] The goals of Herophilus and Erasistratus, however, extended much further. They also vivisected animals, especially Erasistratus who performed many experiments on living goats, pigs, and oxen.[4] Still, for these two physicians, animal anatomy provided insufficient data for a comprehensive understanding of human anatomy. They wanted the real thing and so they appealed to the king for permission to vivisect human beings who had been condemned to death for criminal deeds.[5] By this time, the prohibitions that applied in Aristotle's days against opening the human body had ebbed, and the king granted their request.

Fortified by their ambitions and ideals, Herophilus and Eristratos proceeded to vivisect their fellow human beings, albeit not without heavy criticism. Most people thought it was cruel "to cut into the belly and chest of men whilst still alive…and that too in the most atrocious way," as the Roman historian Cornelius Celsus (25 BC-50 AD) would later describe their work. Especially when the knowledge "sought for with so much violence, some can be learnt not at all, others can be learnt even without a crime."[6] Still, Herophilus and Erasistratus had the tenor of the times on their side. Criminals, slaves, and enemies of war "were not highly valued," and slaves were even tortured in the courts to obtain information.[7] The prevailing attitude can be discerned from Aristotle who wrote:

> …the art of war is a natural act of acquisition, for the art of acquisition includes hunting, an art which we ought to practice against wild beasts, and against men who, though intended by nature to be governed, will not submit; for war of such a kind is naturally just.[8]

This quote also reveals how hunting as an acceptable form of human activity had become so ingrained in the human consciousness that it occupied a cherished place in the mind of even one of the greatest intellectual giants of human history. Aristotle, rather obviously, took for granted that hunting was a natural occupation for humans. Like every other human past and present who has ever believed this idea, he could only have arrived at the conclusion by assuming it to be true. But assumption is not truth. And, besides, the archaeological evidence proves that every human being who has ever believed that hunting is an activity in which human beings naturally indulge because it is their nature, including Aristotle, has been badly mistaken. Early humans were not hunters, though several highly regarded anthropologists of the 20th century and their supporters succeeded for a while in convincing the world that they were. The facts reveal, to the contrary, that all species of humans prior to Homo sapiens survived mostly on a plant-based diet, and this includes Homo sapiens, who did the same for the first 160 to 180 thousand years of their existence on earth. They made the switch to meat only about 70 to 90 thousand years ago after they had made large scale hunting a new feature of their way of life.[9]

One philosopher who did not resort to assumption in defining what the relationship of human animals to nonhuman animals should be, was Michel de Montaigne (1533-1592) who counseled:

> *Presumption* is our natural and original disease....Tis by the same vanity of imagination that [man] equals himself to God, attributes himself divine qualities, and separates himself from the crowd of other creatures.[10] [Author's emphasis.]

For Montaigne, humans denied that other species possessed "soul, and life, and reason" out of human arrogance and vanity.[11] Sigmund Freud took the same position when he wrote:

> ...in the course of his development toward culture man acquired a dominating position over his fellow-creatures in the animal kingdom. Not content with his supremacy, however, he began to place a gulf between his nature and theirs. He denied the possession of reason to them, and to himself he attributed an immortal soul, and made claims to a divine descent which permitted him to annihilate the bond of community between him and the animal kingdom.[12]

Fortunately, the vivisection of human beings as practiced by Herophilus and Erasistratus did not catch on and would not happen again until the 20th century when both the Nazis and the Japanese Imperial Army engaged in the practice.

Herophilus and Erasistratus belonged to a medical sect known as the dogmatists who believed that the dissection and vivisection of animals was necessary for acquiring a knowledge of human anatomy. They were opposed by another medical sect known as the empirics who thought that vivisection was unnecessary and immoral and that medical practice should not be the cause of suffering and death.[13] The empiricists would win the battle, at least in the short run, and after the days of Herophilus and Erasistratus animal research and animal vivisection, like human vivisection, came to a halt. For the next four hundred years it remained in abeyance. It was then during the 2nd century AD that the Roman physician Galen (130-210 AD) stepped onto the world stage. Today he is ranked alongside the top physicians the ancient world of medicine had to offer like the Greek physician Hippocrates (460-377 BC), Galen's idol, and the Arabian physician Ibn al-Nafis (1210-1288 AD).

Galen was well acquainted with the work of Aristotle, enough so that he could write:

> It is not astonishing that Aristotle made several errors in anatomy, as, for example, in believing that the hearts of large animals had three chambers. He was not an expert in dissection…[14]

Galen, however, would make his own mistakes. He based his anatomy of the uterus on dogs, the kidneys on pigs, and the brain on cows and goats.[15] It is only fair to note, however, that in his day Roman law prohibited the dissection of a human corpse.

Like Aristotle, Galen was a product of his times whose predisposition toward animal research can be identified with the world that was going on around him. Well educated in medicine at Alexandria, the greatest medical center of antiquity, and a physician for the Emperor Marcus Aurelius, Galen spent his early career as both a physician and a surgeon for gladiators. It is not difficult to imagine the brutality that he must have witnessed and the gore he must have been required to either treat or observe. Such experiences may well have contributed to the callousness that easily qualifies him as one of the top ten cruel animal researchers of all time, at least prior to the 20th and 21st centuries when thinly disguised sadism became the functioning norm for many animal researchers.

Advising his students to cut "without pity or compassion," the cries of an animal being vivisected were meaningless to Galen as was the "unpleasing expression of the ape when it is being vivisected."[16] He described with frightening pitilessness how an animal ceased breathing and crying out if the thorax was cut in a certain way, but how by covering the wounds, the experimenter could cause the animal to resume breathing and crying out. In a similar manner, his experiments showed that cutting the spinal cords of pigs, goats, and apes to certain degrees would produce corresponding degrees of paralysis. Galen was thoroughly at home cutting the nerves of animals and relished vivisecting the brain of an ape so that he could stimulate it to produce different effects on the body.[17]

Like Aristotle, Galen thought that animals existed on a lower level. He did not believe they experienced pain to any significant degree. Referring to an operation on the thorax of an animal, Galen wrote that "it is surely more likely that a nonrational brute, being less sensitive than a human being, will suffer nothing from such a wound."[18] The reader should note the use of the word "nonrational," rationality being the divider that separated humans from animals which, as we have seen, is what Aristotle taught. Note also how "nonrationality" is linked to the absence of pain. To Galen, "nonrational" creatures experienced no pain. Pain was reserved for "rational" humans. In addition, note the use of the word "unlikely." In reality, Galen had no idea of how "likely" or "unlikely" an animal experienced pain. He just "assumed" that pain for animals was "unlikely" because he wanted this to be true. Today, it is well documented that animals can experience considerable pain and that Galen was badly mistaken. And finally, the reader should note that Galen felt compelled to explain that his experiments caused no pain to the animals he experimented upon, indicating the strong possibility that he entertained doubts about

32

the premises upon which he was relying to justify his experiments.

To assume an idea is true and to know an idea is true are two separate things. Hippocrates wrote that to believe [assume] one knows is ignorance. To actually know is science. Galen's idea that animals felt little if any pain must be called what it was: ignorance.

The belief that animals feel no pain has provided animal researchers with the means for placating members of the public who worried that the work being undertaken by vivisectors was cruel. It would permeate the public consciousness and become widely accepted and continues to this day. The author of this book first experienced the concept when, as a boy, local townspeople where he grew up assured him that the squealing and screaming of pigs he heard being castrated without anesthesia in the farmer's barn across the street had nothing to do with pain because pigs, being animals, felt nothing. As a young boy, the author did not know that the idea was an ancient one traceable all the way back to Galen and that it was untrue.

Fortunately, not everyone accepts ancient ideas that in their greatest depth are as absurd as they are on the surface. Many animal researchers over the centuries presumed only to varying degrees while some did not presume at all simply because their own experiments proved that animals did indeed experience considerable pain and were conscious, intelligent beings. (See chapter 11 for a discussion of animal consciousness.) Nevertheless, the number of scientists across time who have accepted these ancient ideas asserting that animals possessed no consciousness and did not experience pain, for which there has never been any logical or scientific basis, is astonishing, especially when the ideas are presented as being unbiased and objective. Even more astounding is that the belief continues today as we shall discover in examining the work of a present-day philosopher/theorist on animal mentality. (See chapter 13.) That animal researchers would rely upon these theories for centuries and use them as a rationale to perform cruel experiments upon innocent animals without ever testing the truthfulness of the hypothesis is another of those failings born of presumption—which Montaigne termed a disease.

While Aristotle was the first animal researcher of real significance, Galen was the father of modern biological research who set the standards for animal testing and vivisection. His work would be translated into Latin and Arabic and his theories would be studied for centuries.

Galen belonged to that class of individuals who, when it came to knowledge about animal consciousness and behavior, could correctly be called "The Great Assumers." Whenever they wanted something to be true, they just assumed it to be true and proceeded on those grounds. This is a major theme that traverses the entire history of animal research. It is as prevalent with animal researchers in modern times as it was in the ancient world of Aristotle and Galen.

Chapter 5

Calling All Christians:
How the Church Fathers Imposed a Doctrine of
Cruelty to Animals On the Christian Faith

No one picked up on vivisection immediately after Galen's death, and animals were granted a reprieve for the next 1300 years before the arrival of the next animal researchers. In the meantime, the underlying philosophy that provided the rationale for Galen and for the vivisectors who would follow was being assimilated and disseminated by the early Christian church fathers as they busied themselves constructing an infrastructure of values upon which animal research would depend when it reemerged in the 16th century. The church leaders had become familiar with Greek philosophers like Plato, Pythagoras, and Socrates, and some had come under the spell of Aristotle's monotheistic, hierarchical system in which humans were regarded as "rational" whereas animals were distinguished by their "nonrationality."[1] These ideas found a home in the Christian Church and became a way of thinking about animals that stands in sharp contrast to most Biblical scripture that refers to animals.

The appearance of Aristotle's rational/nonrational hypothesis as a determinant of status in the hierarchy of "being" even crept into the New Testament in two instances. *The Second Letter* of *Peter* states:"These people, however, are like *irrational* animals, mere creatures of instinct, born to be caught and killed."[2] Mirroring *The Second Letter of Peter*, the following scripture in *The Letter of Jude* makes a similar comparison: "But these people slander whatever they do not understand, and they are destroyed by those things that, like *irrational* animals, they know by instinct."[3] [Emphasis by author.]

The Christian church took Aristotle's hierarchical classification of life forms and species division and incorporated these concepts into the Christian belief system. The question that Christians never seem to have stopped to ask over the past 2000 years, is whether this kind of thinking corresponds to what their leader, Jesus, taught. Instead, they permitted the rational/nonrational hypothesis of Aristotle to enter the Christian mainstream without seriously consulting New Testament scripture for purposes of comparison where the words and actions of Jesus and, for that matter, Biblical scripture in general, tell a far different story in relation to animals than the hierarchical principles laid out by Aristotle.

Two of the early church fathers prominent in setting the direction the Christian church would take were St. Paul (10 - c. 61-68 AD) and St. Augustine (354 - 430 AD). Both would influence how Christians would come to think about animals, though for entirely different reasons.

I

A Mistaken Attribution to the Apostle Paul

Paul, known also as Saul, went further in championing the path that Jesus set than anyone else among the early church fathers. (See Appendix for a few facts about Paul's life.) He makes quite clear that a new world lies ahead in which the old laws dictated in the Old Testament should meld into the new values of love and compassion proclaimed by Jesus.

A good illustration of the differences between the old and the new lies in the following example. According to the law of the Old Testament prophet Moses, women and men could be stoned to death for various sexual offences. But when the scribes and Pharisees brought a woman who had been caught in the act of committing adultery before Jesus for his opinion on whether stoning to death was a suitable punishment for the offense, which was what Moses commanded, Jesus said: "He that is without sin among you, let him first cast a stone at her."[4] When the woman's accusers could not meet Jesus' challenge they soon departed. Jesus then turned to the women and told her that he did not condemn her but that she should "go and sin no more."[5]

Paul understood perfectly this new teaching that Jesus brought to the world. In regard to racial and ethnic divisions, human slavery, and the subjugation of women, for example, Paul wrote the following where the "law" refers to the law of Moses and the Old Testament:

> Now before faith came, we were imprisoned and guarded under the law until faith would be revealed. Therefore the law was our disciplinarian until Christ came, so that we might be justified by faith. But now that faith has come, we are no longer subject to a disciplinarian, for in Christ Jesus you are all children of God through faith…There is no longer Jew or Greek, there is no longer slave or free, there is no longer male and female; for all of you are one in Jesus Christ." [6]

Statements like these represented a radical departure from the way of life in ancient times to a more expansive and universal (and democratic) way of thinking and living as taught by Jesus. Two thousand years later, however, the full transition from the old to the new still remains to be fully accomplished within the Christian community, The Christian Church continues to struggle to rid itself of some of the old traditions that preceded the arrival of Jesus. For example, male chauvinistic attitudes toward women still prevail in some Christian communities, though in others the transition has been more fully accomplished.

Whatever Greek writings may have influenced Paul in regard to animals might be impossible to determine, but he had to have been familiar with Greek customs and traditions having grown up in the city of Tarsus whose culture at the time was Greek. There Paul was well educated and a student of the rabbi Gamaliel in the study of law. (Gamaliel, unlike Paul, spoke out in support of Christians.) Until his conversion Paul also belonged to the

Pharisees, a fundamentalist group dedicated to upholding the law and persecuting Christians. (see Appendix)

Paul made a statement about animals that has influenced Christian attitudes toward animals ever since though surely this was not his intention. At the time he had traveled to the ancient city of Corinth where he preached that it was the duty of Christians to provide compensation for those who preached in the name of Jesus, even though he renounced his own personal right to receive money for his work. In making his argument, Paul referred to one of the laws written by Moses which stated: "You shall not muzzle an ox while it is treading out the grain."[7] This was a command intended to protect the oxen from farmers with an overly materialistic side. When the oxen treaded out the grain it became separated from the husk and the oxen would then eat some of the grain as they worked. Muzzling the oxen prevented them from eating the grain and increased the yield for the farmer.

Moses' law was intended to assure that the oxen could share equally in the labor that produced the grain. (Many people interpret the passage as a show of God's concern for the welfare of oxen.) But after stating the scripture that "You shall not muzzle an ox while it is treading out the grain," Paul then interrupted reciting the scripture and asked: "Is it for oxen that God is concerned? Or does he not speak entirely for our sakes?" And Paul then answered his own question: "It was indeed written for our sake, for whoever plows should plow in hope and whoever threshes should thresh in hope of a share in the crop."[8]

Unwittingly or not, Paul had just asked the never before asked question: Who is God concerned about, the ox or the farmer, and, by extension, does God really care anything about animals compared to humans? Seizing upon Paul's answer, the church has used it to proclaim that God is indifferent to the fate of animals because he was not concerned with what happened to the ox but rather with what happened to the farmer. A closer examination of Paul's comment, however, reveals that Paul did not say this. Remember, in reply to his own question "Is it for oxen that God is concerned? Or does he not speak entirely for our sakes?" Paul answered: "It was indeed written for our sake..." But here he stops and makes no attempt to back up his own statement to show why the law was "written for our sake." Instead, he creates an analogy. "...for whoever plows should plow in hope and whoever threshes should thresh in hope of a share in the crop." This statement is a non sequitor that is unrelated to Paul's question and answer of whether God was concerned for the oxen. In fact, there is no suggestion in this scripture itself that the farmer is in any danger of not receiving his share of the crop. Paul's reply to his own state-ment "Indeed it was written for our sake" is a complete disconnect. It does, however, serve as an analogy intended to convince the Corinthians that they should support their Christian ministers and not "muzzle" them from earning a livelihood. The analogy com-municates that those who work for their labor deserve the fruits of their labor so that if the farmers were required to permit their oxen to eat some of the grain, the Corinthians too—by extension—should permit those who preached to them on behalf of Christianity to eat some of the grain [in order to be compensated for their labor]. This has nothing to do with whether or not God was concerned with the oxen. What Paul really says here is that "You shall not muzzle *a Christian preacher* while he is *preaching* [treading out the grain []...for whoever plows [the Christian preacher] should plow [peach] in hope and whoever threshes [the Christian preacher] should thresh [preach] in hope of a share in the crop [earning money from his preaching]." Clearly, this must be the case because Paul immediately follows up with the question: "If we have sown spiritual good among you, is it too much if we reap your material benefits?" To suggest that Paul made any argument whatsoever that it was "for our [human] sake" that God was concerned in not muzzling the oxen because God had no concern for the oxen, is to suggest something that Paul did not say. It also is apparent that Paul had no interest in backing up his contention that it was for "our sakes" that God muzzled the oxen. If that had been his desire, he would have explained it. His only goal was to show the Corinthians that they needed to be willing to compensate their preachers because the preachers deserved to be paid for their work, not to declare that God was indifferent to the fate of animals. But the church fathers picked up on Paul's reply in order to claim that it proved that God had no concern for the ox and only cared for the welfare of the farmer. And by extension, they claimed that since God was not concerned about the ox, he was unconcerned about all animals the world over past, present, and forever. According to this line of thinking, Paul's statement proved that God was indifferent to the fate of animals and that all animals on earth were put here for the sole purpose of serving human beings. That is a preposterous claim for which no support exists other than to insist, like all the Great Assumers who have ever lived, that it is true.

That the Christian church took this position becomes evident in the words of Thomas Aquinas (1224-1284(5), one of the greatest of the theologian/philosophers in the Christian world whose work we will discuss in further detail momentarily. Aquinas said, in reference to this verse by Paul, "...it matters not how man behaves to animals, because God has subjected all things to man's power...and it is in this sense that the Apostle [Paul] says that God has no care for oxen, because God does not ask of man what he does with oxen or other animals." As we have seen, however, Paul did not say that "God has no care for oxen," and to add, as Aquinas did, that Paul said the reason God had no care for oxen was "because God does not ask of man what he does with oxen or other animals" is to manufacture nonexistent words for Paul which he did not say and to invent a meaning which he did not intend.

Aquinas was not alone. When queried about the passage, Martin Luther (1483-1586), to whom the founding of the Protestant faith is credited, made a joke at the oxen's expense: "Does God care for oxen? No, of course not. Because oxen can't read. It was written for us, not for the oxen." [9]

John Calvin (1509-1564), the founder of the Presbyterian Church, expressed a similar stand in making a case against animals. In the process, he also expressed the ancient idea that the only real reason for being kind to animals is because it teaches kindness toward humankind.

> But what Paul actually means is quite simple: Though the Lord commands consideration for the oxen, He does so, not for the sake of the oxen, but

rather out of regard for men, for whose benefit even the very oxen were created. Therefore that humane treatment of oxen ought to be an incentive, moving us to treat each other with consideration and fairness. As Solomon put it in Proverbs 12:10 A righteous man regardeth the life of his beast: But the tender mercies of the wicked are cruel.' You should understand, therefore, that God is not concerned about oxen, to the extent that oxen were the only creatures in His mind when He made the law, for He was thinking of men, and wanted to make them accustomed to being considerate in behaviour, so that they might not cheat the workman of his wages. For the ox does not take the leading part in ploughing and threshing, but man, and it is by man's efforts that the ox itself is set to work. Therefore, what he goes on to add, 'he that plougheth ought to plough in hope' etc., is an interpretation of the commandment, as though he said, that it is extended, in a general way, to cover any kind of reward for labour.[10]

Calvin has even gone so far in this passage to say that God created the oxen [hence all animals], for human use ("for whose benefit even the very oxen were created"). But the creation story in the Bible related to the creation of the world of animals as stated in the book of Genesis does not say that God created the animals for human benefit. It simply says the following:

And God said, "let the waters bring forth swarms of living creatures and let birds fly above the earth across the dome of the sky." So God created the great sea monsters and every living creature that moves, of every kind, with which the waters swarm, and every winged bird of every kind. And God saw that it was good. God blessed them saying, "Be fruitful and multiply and fill the waters in the seas, and let birds multiply on the earth." And there was evening and

41

there was morning, the fifth day. And God said, "Let the earth bring forth living creatures of every kind: cattle and creeping things and wild animals of the earth of every kind." And it was so. God made the wild animals of the earth of every kind, and the cattle of every kind, and everything that creeps upon the ground of every kind. And God saw that it was good. [11]

The creation story in Genesis does not comport with Calvin's belief and assumption that God created animals for humankind's benefit or, for that matter, anything else. Genesis simply states the solitary value attributed to God's work which is that the creation of the animal world was "good." It stops there.

When God was finished creating the animals, he gave humankind "dominion" over all the animals he had created, as stated in Genesis 1:28.[12] Aquinas alluded to this dominion above in his own terms when he said: "God has subjected all things to man's power." But giving "dominion" is far different than saying that God created the animals for human benefit or subjected them to man's power. "Dominion" means that God entrusted his precious creation of the animal kingdom to the care of humankind. That humankind has often abused that dominion with their power is one of the tragedies of life to which human beings have fallen victim by abusing their power over the animal kingdom. Today humans are paying for that abuse through human disease and damage to the earth created by their mistreatment and torture of animals.

Calvin's contention that God created animals for the benefit of human beings is the same erroneous contention by which most Christians live today. It is a contention, however, that the Bible—regarded by many Christians as the word of God himself—does not support.

Because modern Christianity is a Judeo/Christian religion, founded on both the Old and the New Testaments, it is easy enough to understand the tendency to think that God was indifferent to the fate of animals based on the instructions God gave to Moses and Moses gave to his people in the Old Testament to slaughter animals as offerings, including oxen and lambs, and that if grain were to be offered that frankincense should be put on it.[13] But apparently the Lord changed his mind 700 or so years later when he said to the prophet Isaiah that "whoever slaughters an ox is like one who kills a human being; whoever sacrifices a lamb, like one who breaks a dog's neck; whoever presents a grain offering, like one who offers swine's blood; whoever makes a memorial offering of frankincense, like one who blesses an idol. These have chosen their own way, and in their abominations they take delight." When we look for guidance from the Bible as to how Christians should live today, in comparing the law of Moses to the new way of living Jesus brought to earth, it is well to keep in mind the admonition found in the Gospel of John that "The law indeed was given through Moses; grace and truth came through Jesus Christ."[14]

Certainly Jesus supplemented the words of Isaiah just quoted when he said: "I desire mercy, not sacrifice."[15]

Further support for Isaiah's position over the law of Moses in regard to animal sacrifice lies in that Isaiah is the prophet who foretold the coming of Jesus. :Moreover, God as the creator of the universe surely has the power to change his mind if he so chooses, and in the book of Exodus God did change his mind: "And the Lord changed his mind about the disaster that he planned to bring to his people."[16] In the book of Genesis, God also allowed Abraham to bargain him down from fifty to ten over how many righteous persons needed to be found in the city of Sodom for him not to destroy the city.[17] These passages describe a flexible God in his relationships with human beings. In the wake of the position both Isaiah and Jesus took about animal sacrifice, the sacrifice of animals as practiced by Moses and his followers cannot be used to suggest that God was indifferent to the welfare of animals nor can it be used to justify the abuse of animals in today's world. God obviously had different intentions for how his creation would practice their dominion over the animal kingdom once his son arrived on the earth.

Paul's words about muzzling the ox were misinterpreted and have echoed down the corridors of Christian history right to the present time fortifying the Christian bias against animals. This is unfortunate and also a disservice to Paul because Paul offered no indication that he thought in these terms. On the contrary, to the very same Corinthian community which he advised to pay their preachers living wages for preaching about Jesus, he spoke the following words revealing his acceptance and appreciation of the glory of God's creation of the universe and the individual species with which God populated the earth. "But God gives…to each kind of seed its own body. Not all flesh is alike, but there is one flesh for human beings, another for animals, another for birds, and another for fish. There are both heavenly bodies and earthly bodies, but the glory of the heavenly is one thing, and that of the earthly is another."[18] Paul makes no attempt to indicate that God placed a hierarchical value on his creations like Aristotle did. Rather, Paul just takes note of their differences without placing a value or a judgment on those differences and notes that they are all a gift from God.

Conceptions that separate humans from other animals in various ways that imply sympathy and concern for humans but deny rights and feelings for animals are consistent with Aristotle's influence, but not with the Bible as illustrated in both the Old Testament and the New Testament, including Paul's description of earthly bodies just described. In the Old Testament, for example, the third chapter in the book of Ecclesiastes concludes with the following lines:

> I said in my heart with regard to human beings that God is testing them to show that they are but animals. For the fate of humans and the fate of animals is the same; as one dies, so dies the other. They all have the same breath, and humans have no advantage over the animals; for all is vanity. All go to one place; all are from the dust, and all turn to dust again. Who knows whether the human spirit goes upward and the spirit of animals goes downward to the earth? So I saw that there is nothing better than that all should enjoy their work, for that is their lot; who can bring them to see what will be after them?[19]

Many Biblical verses stress a positive association between humans and animals. In the book of Exodus (whose authorship is attributed to Moses by some scholars but questioned by others), passages like the following express an outlook that not only do animals have certain rights but that humans are obligated to help them achieve those rights. "When you see the donkey of one who hates you lying under its burden and you would hold back from setting it free, you must help to set it free." And Moses also counseled: "Six days you shall do your work, but on the seventh day you shall rest, so that your ox and your donkey may have relief..."[20] Here the command to rest is not for the benefit of the farmer but for the benefit of the farm animal which also adds strength to the argument that God's concern was for the oxen, not the farmer, in the scripture commanding that the farmer should not muzzle the oxen treading out the grain.

In the book of Deuteronomy, also attributed to Moses, Moses exhibits the same kind of concern: "You shall not plow with an ox and a donkey yoked together."[21] Plowing with two dissimilar animals could cause greater hardship for one of the animals, in this case the ass who is smaller and whose steps are shorter so that the greater burden would fall on it. Many people interpret this scripture to be another of those passages which show God's mercy for animals.

In Psalms 145:9 and 16 the author, David, notes that God's compassion extends equally to humans and all living creatures. "The Lord is good to all, and his compassion is over all that he has made...You [the Lord] open your hand, satisfying the desire of every living thing." Likewise, referring to God in Psalms 36:6, David notes that "...you save humans and animals alike, O Lord."[22]

In concurrence with the above verses, Proverbs 12:10, to which John Calvin referred, also tells of the need for humans to be concerned for the wellbeing of their animals, warning that to be cruel to them is evil. "The righteous know the needs of their animals, but the mercy of the wicked is cruel."[23]

And in Genesis 49:5-7, Jacob castigates his sons Simeon and Levi for their cruelty against humans and animals: "May I never come into their council; may I not be joined to their company—for

45

in their anger they killed men, and at their whim they hamstrung oxen. Cursed be their anger, for it is fierce, and their wrath, for it is cruel!"[24]

The above scripture was not written by people who regarded animals as mere things to be used by humans however they desire. The words and the tone convey respect and a deep appreciation of the lives of animals. The authors of these words reveal a comprehension that like humans, animals have been created by God and that God cares for all his creatures, not that he is indifferent to their treatment.

In the New Testament in the book of Luke, Jesus does not regard animals as mere objects either. He refers to them with the same kind of respect and compassion. "Are not five sparrows sold for two pennies? Yet not one of them is forgotten in God's sight."[25] So while the people who lived in the time of Jesus may have become accustomed to placing little value on minor animals such as sparrows, just as they do today, Jesus tells us that the sparrows are precious to God who keeps them in his sight. Moreover, the same passage in the book of Matthew reads: "Are not two sparrows sold for a farthing? Yet not one of them will fall to the ground apart from your Father."[26] Here Jesus says the sparrows are protected and belong to God's kingdom even in death. Do these words not mean that animal, like humans, also have a heavenly destiny?

In a different setting, Jesus' portrays the same sense of concern farmers had for the animals under their dominion in Old Testament days and gave notice that animals have rights that had to be observed in his times as well. "Does not each of you on the sabbath untie his ox or his ass from the manger, and lead it away to water?" And he asked: "Which of you having a son or an ox that has fallen into a well, will not immediately pull him out on a sabbath?"[27] Here Jesus shows that when in harm's way, a human being and an animal are equal in their need for human intervention and assistance and stand above the dictates of human-made law that would prohibit offering assistance on the sabbath.

Jesus compares the spirit of humans to animals when he refers to a sinner as a sheep "gone astray."[28] And he compares the maternal instinct of human mothers to protect their offspring

46

equally to that possessed by animals when he says: "…how often have I desired to gather your children together as a hen gathers her brood under her wings…"[29] What would Jesus have to say about the brutal ways in which chickens are treated on factory farms in today's world? Would he condone eating these chickens or their eggs?

John the Baptist compared the inner quality of Jesus with the gentleness of a sheep when he referred to Jesus as the "Lamb of God."[30] And when Jesus was baptized by him, the scripture tells us that "just as he [Jesus] came up from the water, suddenly the heavens were opened to him and he [John] saw the Spirit of God descending like a dove and alighting on him. And a voice from heaven said, 'This is my Son the Beloved, with whom I am well pleased.'"[31] John does not hesitate to voice his opinion that the spirit of God himself is like a gentle, peaceful dove. And who was John the Baptist? According to Jesus, "Truly I tell you, among those born of women no one has arisen greater than John the Baptist."[32] Jesus thus has enjoined his followers to seriously ponder the reflections of John.

In concluding the discussion of trying to determine how Paul felt about animals, it is highly pertinent to point out that he would not have been unfamiliar with Old Testament scripture that made positive statements about animals in relation to God such as those listed above. Paul also would have known scripture in which God stated his intentions for establishing a covenant with human beings where peace prevails in an environment that includes a close association with and respect for animals in which equality between humans and animals prevails. For example, in the Book of Hosea, in the second chapter, God speaks about how he will one day make a new covenant with Israel. "I will make for you a covenant on that day which will include the wild animals, the birds of the air, and the creeping things of the ground; and I will abolish the bow, the sword, and war from the land; and I will make you lie down in safety."[33] Paul must have been acquainted with this verse because he refers to this second chapter of Hosea in his own letter to the Romans where he says: "As indeed He [God] says in Hosea." Paul then quotes from the second chapter of Hosea right after the scripture just quoted where Hosea described God's future covenant with humankind that includes the animal kingdom.[34] So Paul had to have been familiar with God's intentions for making a covenant with the people and the animals in which war and its weapons are abolished and peace is established. To suggest that Paul would teach that God was indifferent about the treatment of animals, as some of the Christian Church fathers have done, is to ignore the kind of evidence presented above and also as provided by Paul in relation to Hosea.[35] Paul gave no indication anywhere in his writings that he believed God was indifferent to the treatment of animals, and to make a case that he did is to attribute a false teaching to him that he did not make.

II
A Mistaken Attribution to Jesus

Few Church Fathers have had greater influence on Christianity than the highly respected theologian/philosopher St. Augustine. A brilliant thinker, he was influenced by Bishop Ambrose of Milan (who baptized him), Greeks like Virgil and Aristotle, and the Roman philosopher and statesman, Cicero. Founder of the doctrines of Original Sin and Just War, Augustine has been credited as one of the main figures merging the "Greek philosophical tradition" with the "Judeo-Christian religious and scriptural traditions."[36] His influence has extended to people like Boethius, John Scottus Eriugena, Bernard of Clairvaus, St. Anselm, Thomas Aquinas, Descartes, Martin Luther, John Calvin and philosophers like Schopenhauer, Kierkegaard, and Nietzsche, to which, in more recent times, may be added the names of such philosophers, theologians and church leaders as Ludwig Wittgenstein, John Piper, and Pope Benedict XVI.

In contrast to St. Paul, the influence the Greeks had on Augustine is not difficult to determine. Augustine studied the writings of the classical Greeks when he was a youth and was familiar with the books of the Platonists and with Greek esoteric ideas.[37] He refers to the Greeks in his writings like *The Trinity* and his *Confessions* in which he described his introduction to Aristotle's *Categories* and its influence on him:

> And what did it profit me that, when I was scarcely twenty years old, a book of Aristotle's entitled *The Ten Categories* fell into my hands? On the very title of this I hung as on something great and divine, since my rhetoric master at Carthage and others who had reputations for learning were always referring to it with such swelling pride. I read it by myself and understood it.[38]

The *Categories* has been described as "the backbone of Aristotle's own philosophical theorizing...an unparalleled influence on the systems of many of the greatest philosophers in the western tradition."[39] This passage also reveals how highly and widely Aristotle was respected and studied by the members of the clergy in Augustine's day.

Besides the welcome influence Aristotle's *Categories* had on him, his influence on Augustine can also be seen in Augustine's categorization of life forms into three tiers: those that exist (stone), those that live (plants and animals), and those that possess intelligence (human beings).[40] The parallel to Aristotle's hierarchy of being is obvious in regard to form in nature, as previously referred to, and consisting of inanimate objects (rocks, water); organic objects (plants); animals; and humans.

It is apparent that Augustine understood and absorbed Aristotle's system of hierarchy categorizing different life forms into primary groupings. This included Aristotle's ranking of animals as being nonrational. In his *The City of God*, Augustine expressed his belief that animals are nonrational when he wrote that God "did not wish the rational being, made in his own image, to have dominion over any but irrational creatures, not man over man, but man over the beasts."[41] As Augustine put it, in referring to scripture which we will discuss in more detail momentarily, any belief that considered animals and humans to be equal was the "height of superstition."[42] Further, he stated that "there are no common rights between us and the beasts and trees." Moreover, he also wrote that "we can perceive by their cries that animals die in pain, although we make little of this since the beast, lacking a *rational soul*, is not related to us by a common nature."[43] [Emphasis by author.]

In order to justify his position, Augustine turned to the gospel story of Jesus and the swine told in Mark 5:1-20 from which he tries to project his own negative attitudes about animals onto Jesus. [Nearly the same story is told in Matthew 8:31, but Augustine describes the story as told in Mark.] In this story, Jesus supposedly ordered the demons possessed in a man to enter a herd of 2000 swine which then ran into the sea where they drowned. Augustine wrote the following description about this event:

> Christ himself shows that to refrain from the killing of animals and the destroying of plants is the height of superstition, for judging that there are no common rights between us and the beasts and trees, he sent the devils into a herd of swine and with a curse withered the tree on which he found no fruit....Surely the swine had not sinned, nor had the tree.[44] [The story of the curse and the withered tree is found in Matthew 21:19-22.]

Is it true, as Augustine said, that Jesus judged "that there are no common rights between us and the beasts and trees" so that it would require superstition to justify not drowning 2000 swine in the service of humankind? Christians, if they are to be true to themselves, must inquire whether or not Augustine tried to impose his own biases against animals upon Jesus with these statements. Nowhere in the words of Jesus as given in the Bible does Jesus say that he has judged that humans and animals share no common rights. And he also does not hint in that direction. Quite contrary to Augustine's analysis, which he made with no supporting scripture, Jesus' advised that humans and animals both deserve assistance equally if they are in harm's way, as noted earlier.[45] This is a "common right," quite contrary to what Augustine said. And, in terms of the comparison of humans with other animals, as also

50

discussed, while Jesus told his disciples that they were worth more than "many sparrows," this was preceded by his words that God kept his eye on the sparrows. The point that Jesus sought to make was that if God cared for the sparrows surely he cared even more for humankind. This indicates that Jesus believed God cared deeply for nonhuman animals and was not indifferent to their welfare as Augustine sought to impute to him by referring to this miracle story about the swine. Jesus himself never spoke an unkind word about animals.

Augustine's analysis of the miracle story of Jesus and the swine is a reflection of his own unsympathetic attitude toward animals which surely is connected to Aristotelian thought. It is not farfetched to suggest that the influence of Aristotle's hierarchical system of being on Augustine played a part in the uncharitable way in which Augustine described Jesus as being indifferent to the killing of animals. Had he chosen, Augustine could have portrayed Jesus in a humanitarian light with scripture to back it up. For example, he might have pointed out the correlation between the statements Isaiah and Jesus made in reference to animal sacrifice that stand on the side of animals, not sacrifice. Or he might have referred to the time when Jesus entered the temple and "overthrew the tables of the money changers and the seats of them that sold doves."[46] He could also have taken note of other scripture descriptive of the life of Jesus that reflected a positive association with animals including John the Baptist referring to him as the Lamb of God or that Jesus was born in a manger where animals such as oxen, donkeys, sheep, and cows were likely present. Instead, Augustine chose to emphasize scripture that tells a miracle story about Jesus in which Jesus supposedly was responsible for 2000 pigs running into the sea where they drowned to death—not exactly a pretty picture. And it has the unfortunate effect of suggesting that Jesus was indifferent to the lives of animals. Whatever one chooses to believe about this miracle story of the demons and the swine, one factor seems clear: it does not match the character of Jesus in his relationship with animals as portrayed in any other part of the New Testament.

Augustine's acceptance of Aristotle's hypotheses that animals are nonrational, mindless creatures contributed to the creation of a tradition within the Christian Church that has caused and continues to bring great harm to innocent animals around the world and to the followers of the Christian faith who have accepted a way of life that is indifferent to the suffering of other species. It places a limitation on the most important characteristic of the Christian faith: love and compassion. As Jesus described in his own words, God's care covers not just humans, but animals too, even the little sparrows about whom God cares so deeply that he will not allow even one to not one to fall to the ground apart from God himself.

The important question Christians have yet to ask themselves, is whether they are truly pursuing the path to God laid out by Jesus if they ignore this important aspect of Jesus' teachings: his feelings and thoughts about nonhuman species.

III
The Spread of Aristotelian Thought

After Augustine, Aristotle's influence continued to spread in the expanding Christian world through translations of his work on logic into Latin by Anicius Manlius Severinus Boethius (ca. 480–524 or 525),who also translated the work of other Greek philosophers. Boethius wanted to hand down the great Greco-Roman culture to other generations and might have contributed more had he not got caught up in political machinations involving King Theodoric the Great, whom he served, and who had him imprisoned and then brutally executed for treason.[47] Boethius' translation of Aristotle was the only major one available in Europe until the 12th century.

One of the persons the Boethius translation reached was St. Anselm (1033-1109), an important Christian theologian/philosopher heavily influenced by St. Augustine— "the blessed Augustine," as he called him. The influence that Aristotelian ideas exerted on Anselm in relation to animals directly or indirectly is discernible in Anselm's comment concerning the issue of rationality as providing an acceptable division between humans and animals.

...every animal can be understood without reference to rationality, and no animal is from necessity rational....But no man can be understood without reference to rationality, and it is necessary that every man be rational.[48]

Once again, it appears that Aristotle's hierarchical concept in relation to the rationality of humans vs. the nonrationality of animals has made an impact on one of the church fathers.

Another important figure in the Catholic Church during these times was St. Francis of Assisi (1182-1226) who, in contrast to the other church fathers, is often praised for his kindness to animals. St. Francis loved all of life including the rocks and stones, the flowers ad trees, the sun and the planets, the elements themselves, and all sentient creatures.[49]

It was during St. Francis' lifetime that a kind of Aristotelian Renaissance began. Previously, the collected works of Aristotle had been available only in Byzantium in the East while the West had to be content with the Boethius translations. But during the 12th century, Aristotle's collected works were translated from Hebrew and Arabic into Latin and soon made their way into the European universities. The overall reaction was overwhelming as scholars rushed to embrace Aristotle's philosophy of nature in which all of nature operated in a harmonious, hierarchical system with man at the top of the ladder.[50] The rationalist Spanish Muslim scholar and philosopher Averroes (1126-1198) also wrote explanatory commentaries to almost all of Aristotle's works in an attempt to show that philosophy and religion could get along together. These commentaries made a major impact on some of the Medieval Christian theologian/philosophers.

For Christianity, the resurgence of Aristotelian thought at first elicited the fear that it posed a challenge to the Christian faith. In reaction, the Church considered banning Aristotle's work. But Albert the Great (1193/1206-1280), who has been called one of the most universal thinkers of the Middle Ages, labored to reconcile the differences between faith and reason to which the church objected. He had studied Aristotle extensively and set for himself the monumental task of paraphrasing all the known works of Aristotle (which he also did for Boethius and several other philosophers and theologians).[51]

One of the major works of Aristotle's which became immensely popular and to which Albert turned his attention was Aristotle's *De Animalibus* (On Animals), consisting of three treatises, *History of Animals, On the Parts of Animals*, and *On the Generation of Animals*. These treatises were assembled together in nineteen books.[52] By midcentury *De Animalibus* had become a regular part of the Arts faculty at the University of Paris.

Albert began writing commentaries on *De Animalibus* sometime between 1356 and 1360, finishing in 1363. The work became highly popular. An accompanying work has also survived (though lost until 1922) titled *Questions Concerning On Animals*. This is a report about what Albert taught his students in regard to Aristotle's books on animals in Cologne, Germany in 1358 transcribed by a student who attended the lectures. It was later edited by Albert himself. The depth and breadth of the questions, which cover all 19 books of Aristotle's *De Animalibusd* in 509 pages, offers an indication of just how seriously Albert studied and was influenced by Aristotle's work on animals.[53]

One of the questions Albert posed was whether brute animals are differentiated according to habits. (Habits in this context meant character traits and behavior characteristics such as fortitude, gentleness, generosity, and chastity.) Albert replied to his own question as follows: "Habits exist in a rational being....But brute animals do not participate in reason." [54] Albert then argues that animals do have good habits (character traits) but not in the way humans have them, rather they have them in an imitative way and "this is how the Philosopher understood it." [55] The Philosopher, of course, is Aristotle.

Just as Albert strove to unite faith and reason, this would also become one of the dominant and lifelong themes in the work of another 13th century theologian, Thomas Aquinas, referred to earlier in connection with the Apostle Paul's "oxen" analogy and for whom the philosophy Thomism is named[56] His influence on Christian thought would grow to exceed even that of Albert's. The modern Church considers him to be one of the greatest theologians and philosophers of the Middle Ages and, as with Albert, has placed him among the Catholic saints. Aquinas' writings are still recommended for acquiring a solid foundation in theology today.

As a youth, Aquinas was influenced by Averroes from whom he became acquainted with the work of Aristotle. When he was twenty-one, Aquinas turned to Albert for instruction. In Albert, Aquinas found a teacher whose views on Aristotle coincided with his own and Albert soon came to regard Aquinas as an equal. Working together, the pair succeeded in bringing Aristotelian thought more firmly into the Christian fold.[57] The two would continue their productive relationship as colleagues until the untimely death of Aquinas in 1274(5) at the approximate age of fifty-one. [58]

It may be safely said that Aquinas was Aristotelian through and through. He was fascinated by Aristotle's "pre-Christian" ability to comprehend nature in such depth, and to him, Aristotle's "Unmoved Mover" was synonymous with God. Like Albert and many of the scholars of his times, he referred to Aristotle as *The Philosopher*, and like *The Philosopher*, Aquinas also adopted a hierarchical view toward animals. He thought that the only reason for being kind to animals was because if people were cruel to animals they might treat other people cruelly, a viewpoint also expressed in the 16th century by John Calvin, as noted earlier, and many others.[59] Were it not for that prohibition, for Aquinas, humans should have been able to treat animals in any way they chose.[60] (To many people even today, this is the only reason for showing any kindness toward nonhuman animals.)

The influence of Aristotle on Aquinas in relation to animals is clearly visible from the following passage, part of which was quoted earlier:

> There is no sin in using a thing for the purpose for which it is. Now the order of things is such that the imperfect are for the perfect...things, like plants which merely have life, are all alike for animals, and all animals are for man. Wherefore it is not unlawful if

men use plants for the good of animals, and animals for the good of man, as *the Philosopher* states. ...it matters not how man behaves to animals, because God has subjected all things to man's power.[61]

This is the position that has been adopted by the Christian church, both Catholic and Protestant, that has been carried forward to the present. The question that must be asked of this passage, is how Aquinas determined for what "purpose a thing is," which, in regard to animals, was to be at the service of humankind as humans desired. The answer, rather obviously, is that he copied the idea from Aristotelian ideology and believed in it because, like all the other "Great Assumers," he assumed it to be true. From an Aristotelian point of view, Aquinas stated it perfectly in terms of how animals should be treated: "...it matters not how man behaves to animals, because God has subjected all things to man's power."

Aristotle must also be asked how he arrived at the decision that the purpose of animals was to use them in the service of mankind. And for him the answer lies equally in that he "assumed" it to be true since no logical or factual explanation other than assumption exists to show that animals were nonrational creatures put on earth for humans to use however they liked. Certainly, as illustrated, the Bible does not assume it, nor has science ever proved it or even been asked to prove it, though today animal cognition scientists are proving just the opposite at their own discretion.

Aristotle was a product of his times, as we have seen, who accepted societal norms like animal sacrifice and slavery both of which led in the direction of creating assumptions such as that animals are to be used however humans decide they want to use them, including for food, sacrifice, and animal research.

IV
The Meaning of the Aristotelian Hierarchy of Being for the Christian Church

The mixture of Greek and Christian thought synthesized in the early church and discussed here has produced a "speciesist" brew that Christians have been drinking ever since.[62] Speciesism— prejudice against animals—functions like the other "isms" such as racism or sexism in that it postulates the proposition that one group is superior over another based on differences as perceived and defined by the self-proclaimed superior group which seeks to impose their belief on everyone else. Martin Luther, John Calvin, Thomas Aquinas, Albert the Great, St. Anselm, St. Augustine, , and Aristotle were all speciesists. St. Francis was the notable exception among the church fathers discussed. He did not proselytize against other species, and while he may not have denounced the speciesist attitudes that have contributed so much to societal violence and the brutalization of animals in today's world, as some critics would have liked, he possessed a sense of compassion that was lacking among the other Christian theologian/ philosophers who imposed limitations upon their own compassion through their hierarchical, speciesist outlook on animals.

It is love and compassion like that possessed by St. Francis which lie at the very core of Christianity. It stands in direct opposition to the speciesist worldview that withholds kindness and compassion from animals. This is the Aristotelian, nonChristian worldview adopted by the Christian church which has continued through the centuries until the present time. It has so permeated the thinking of the church that in the 19th century, Pope Pius the IX would not even permit a Society for the Prevention of Cruelty to Animals in Rome to form on the grounds that it might cause people to think they had some obligation toward animals.[63]

The attitudes of Christians toward animals make it easy for Christians to accept the abuse of animals in every circumstance in which they are abused whether in animal research laboratories, on fur farms, on factory farms, through hunting and trapping, or in blood sports, circuses, rodeos, and zoos. Considerable responsibility for the enormous health and ecological problems facing the people of the world today must be laid at the doorstep of the way humans treat animals and this includes Christians. And though it is a subject most Christians would prefer to ignore, there is no escaping that animal consumption is a major contributor to the poisoned atmosphere and water resources of the earth upon which people depend for survival. This is a major cause of cancer, heart disease, stroke, diabetes, Alzheimer's disease, and many other deadly conditions.

According to the World Christian Encyclopedia, about 2 billion Christians are living today.[64] With the world population now standing at 7 billion people, Christians comprise nearly one-third of all living people. Their attitudes toward animals and how they treat them, including eating them, has enormous consequences for the world. For example, it takes 3.25 acres to produce the food for one person consuming the average American diet of animal and plant foods. Without animal foods, only 1/6th of an acre is required. It has been estimated that only 5% of the land currently devoted to food production in the world would be needed to produce the world's food if everyone stopped eating animal products. This means that an enormous percentage of the land now used for livestock could be returned to forest or grasslands if 2 billion Christians stopped consuming animals and much of the poverty in the world could be eliminated.

Christians must begin to ask themselves, does a speciesist mindset really help to live in ways that realize Christian ideals? Does speciesism represent the true Jesus and should it be a philosophy that is acceptable to Christians? Is speciesism right for the world? What is its impact on the poor? What will it mean for the future?

In the Old Testament book of Hosea, as referenced before, God states that he plans to make a new covenant with animals and the people of Israel.[65] The book of Isaiah also foretells God's plan for a future kingdom in which humans and animals will peacefully coexist.

The wolf shall live with the lamb, the leopard shall lie down with the kid, the calf and the lion and the fatling together, and a little child shall lead them. The cow and the bear shall graze, their young shall lie down together; and the lion shall eat straw like the ox. The nursing child shall play over the hole of the asp. And the weaned child shall put its hand on the adder's den. They will not hurt or destroy on all my holy mountain, for the earth will be full of the knowledge of the Lord as the waters cover the sea.[66]

Also referring to humankind's future relationships with other species, the book of Job tells people not to hate their tribulations because a far better world lies ahead in which they "shall be in league with the stones of the field, and the wild animals shall be at peace with you."[67] Clearly, the knowledge from God as revealed by Hosea, Isaiah, and Job includes the message that animals have inherent rights and equal rights. In God's future world, people will treat all animals with respect, kindness, and understanding. This should serve as the foundation for interactions between human and nonhuman animals in the present day world, and this is one of the most significant messages the Bible conveys.

The church leaders in today's world have no intention of bringing the chapter of speciesism in the history of Christianity to an end, and they have little interest in debating the topic. But speciesism is about cruelty, brutality, injustice, and the killing of the innocent. These are nonChristian values which are not in harmony with the Christian message of love and compassion taught by Jesus. It is up to Christians generally, individually, and collectively, to do what their leaders will not do and that is to reject the speciesist beliefs laid down by the early church fathers many centuries ago.

Jesus brought a far different message to the earth than the hierarchical belief system in which animal sacrifice played such a large part as in the days of Aristotle or the time of Moses. Jesus expressed the difference in his message that put love and compassion above all other human values. As Jesus said:

You shall love the Lord your God with all your heart, and with all your mind. This is the greatest and first commandment. And a second is like it: You shall love your neighbor as yourself. On these two commandments hang all the law and the prophets.[68]

Christians who hunt and believe in killing animals for food like to claim that the commandment "thou shalt not kill" brought down from the mountain by Moses only applies to humans because God commanded Moses to slaughter animals for sacrifice. But this does not account for the evolutionary aspect of human consciousness exemplified by Isaiah's denunciation of sacrifice or the arrival of Jesus on earth who said:

"I desire mercy, not sacrifice."[69]

Jesus came to the world to change the world and he did. His footprints upon the earth marked a new era of love and compassion and the fulfilling of ancient laws through love. With his arrival, the old world began its transition to a new world, though the conversion still continues today and has often been delayed as people from every corner of the earth struggle to understand how to implement peace on earth. The job goes on but can never be completed until impediments like the cruelty of speciesism and the willing slaughter of animals give way to compassion.

Christianity has at its center charity, kindness, understanding, love, standing up to evil, and, of course, compassion. These are the Christian values people use when they relate to other people. Christians have been conditioned, however, to withdraw compassion in their relationships with animals beyond a few exceptions like household pets. But compassion is part of the essence of the message Jesus brought to earth. It can only be experienced in its fullness with the rejection of all limitations imposed upon it by Aristotelian hierarchical thinking and through an understanding that all living beings deserve the love and compassion taught by Jesus Christ.

60

Chapter 6

The Divide Widens

During the period in which the early church was formulating its belief system about animals, Galen's work on anatomy continued to be taught in the universities. Yet it would be close to 1000 years after his death before physicians resumed an interest in dissection or vivisection. The first dissections happened at the University in Salerno where a Professor of Anatomy, Copho of Salernum, wrote a text on anatomy based on the dissection of a pig around 1150 AD. A second text from an unknown author followed ten to twenty years later.[1,2] These texts were used for study at the University. The Emperor Frederick II endorsed the work going on at Salerno by issuing a decree in 1241 proclaiming that all who wanted a license to practice medicine in Naples were required to have a knowledge of anatomy.[3]

Human dissections were prohibited by the Roman Catholic Church until the late 13th century when autopsies were allowed for legal reasons to determine the cause of death in criminal trials and to study epidemic diseases.[4,5] The urge for greater knowledge of anatomy was also in the air, and once the prohibitions on human dissection was lifted, others quickly followed. In 1316 Mondino de Liucci (1275-1326)—born near the time of Aquinas' death (1274(5)?)—conducted the first public dissection of a corpse at the University of Bologna. Gentile da Foligno (d.1348) followed up in 1341 by introducing dissection at the University of Padua which by this time was becoming the center for the study of anatomy.[6] Dissections were also conducted at the universities in Venice, Florence, Siena, Perugia, Genoa, Ferrara, Pisa, and the University of Montpellier in Southern France.[7,8] These dissections of human corpses were the first since the days of Herophilus and Erasistratus shortly after the death of Aristotle.

Classroom demonstrations of human dissections continued in the 15th and 16th centuries accompanied by an interest in dissecting animals. Two of the new dissectors of the era were Leonardo da Vinci (1452-1519) and Michelangelo (1475-1564) both of whom dissected humans and animals.[9] In 1533, the Catholic Church ordered an autopsy on conjoined twins Joana and Melchiora Ballestero to determine whether they shared the same soul. The autopsy showed that they each had their own heart and so it was decided they had separate souls.[10]

With the revival of an interest in comparative anatomy, Pierre Belon (1517-1564) dissected dolphins in 1551 (comparing them to fish) at Padua University which still retained its reputation as the foremost place to study anatomy.[11],[12] Belon, who was murdered in 1564 by unknown assailants, published a book in 1555 which included 161 illustrations printed from woodcuts of a variety of birds, a portrait of himself, and a skeleton of a man placed beside the skeleton of a bird to show the anatomic similarities between the two species.[13]

Andreas Vesalius (1514-1564), Realdus Columbus (1515-1559), Gabriele Fallopius (1523-1562), and Hieronymous Fabricius (1537-1619) all occupied the prestigious Chair in Anatomy At Padua University.[14] Fabricius, a confirmed Aristotelian and Galenist, even built an Anatomy Theater at his own expense so that he could conduct dissections on humans before an audience. Meanwhile, public dissections of animals soon escalated to include vivisections prompted in part by the 1531 rediscovery of Galen's *On Anatomical Procedures* and other work.

Vesalius and Columbus practiced vivisection and were especially eager to grandstand their skills before an audience. Both these anatomists cut open living female animals that were pregnant. The animals of choice were pigs or dogs. One such event occurred in which Colombus "cut open a pregnant dog, removed the puppies, and then hurt them in front of the mother." Though suffering tremendous pain, the mother tried to comfort her babies. Columbus noted that "the bishops and other clergymen in attendance were especially impressed by this display of motherly love." [15]

And here Columbus revealed one of the chief purposes of public vivisections, or so it was advertised: to inspire sympathy for the suffering of the animal which was supposed to teach a lesson in compassion.[16] How deeply the clergy sympathized with the poor mother in her painful demonstration of concern for her puppies, however, would be difficult to know. If they felt real compassion, the question naturally arises as to why they would attend such a spectacle without registering a protest or intervening in some way to prevent these displays of cruelty. It is safe to surmise that Columbus would not have greeted protests to his work with much enthusiasm.

The English physician William Harvey (1578-1657) studied in Padua with Fabricius. After he learned his skills he returned to London where he lived and worked. There he experimented on animals for the purpose of studying the circulation of the blood. Harvey was the first person since Galen to institute a systematic program of research based on the vivisection of animals, and his techniques would be widely studied.[17] Working methodically, he would tie an animal to a board, slice open its chest, cut an artery near the heart, and observe as the blood pumped out and the animal died.[18]

Like Columbus, and Vesalius, Harvey also liked to dissect and vivisect animals before an audience and gave public lectures in anatomy to show off his skills. According to one commentator, besides the "learned," his lectures were attended by "jacks-in-office [self-important petty officials], petty lordlings [insignificant lords], money-lenders, barbers and such like ignorant rabble, who, standing around open-mouthed, blab that they have seen miracles."[19] Nevertheless, public demonstrations like the ones Harvey performed were an effective means for conveying the vivisection story to public audiences which, similar to the ancient Romans, were open to having their instincts for cruelty titillated.

Like all anatomists of his era, Harvey did his work without mitigation of the pain for the animals he vivisected. Anesthesia in the form of ether and chloroform would not be discovered until near the mid 19th century, ether being the first to be employed in a human operation in 1846. Even after the use of anesthesia became accepted practice, it was used on animals only sparingly and sporadically right through the late 19th century.[20] This means that nearly every animal experiment conducted from Aristotle to the 20th century was done with no relief for pain and suffering for the animals used in the experiments.

While some animal researchers were uncomfortable with vivisection because it obviously caused pain and suffering to animals, they could still fall back on the rationalization that the world was composed of a hierarchical system in which animals were distinctly separate and different, suitable as objects to be controlled and used however humans wished. But then in the 17th century, the 23 year-old French philosopher, mathematician, and scientist René Descartes (1596-1650), originator of the phrase "Cogito, ergo sum" (I think, therefore I am), added another dimension to animal research which helped to alleviate any guilt an animal researcher might feel for his work. Descartes had a new world view to put forward before his contemporaries in which the entire universe consisted of one huge mechanical process.[21] His vision brought the concept of "soul" into the picture in an original, new manner which created an even wider gulf between humans and animals. This could only mean bad news for the animals and much more cruelty in the future.

Before Descartes, as handed down from the Greeks, people generally believed that all living things possessed a soul and were part of a larger world soul to which everything belonged. The soul might be seated in some particular place, but it "permeated all parts of the body." [22] These kinds of concepts were also taught in the Medieval cathedral schools and universities.[23] Aristotle, as noted, believed that plants, animals, and humans all possessed a soul. But now René Descartes was adding a new chapter to the discussion.

Attributing his discovery of his new cosmos to a vision he claimed he had received from the Mother of God [Mary, mother of Jesus], he worked out different theories including the concept of the separation of mind and matter.[24] He felt that "the mind cannot be doubted, but the body and material world can [so that] the two must be radically different."[25]

In Descartes' new universe, all "things," including the human body, were to be regarded as mechanical objects that operated like clocks or automata according to mathematical principles. In contradistinction to such a mechanical world, the rational human mind stood singularly alone. This was the prize that God had given to humankind and only to humankind. It was immaterial and incorporeal. You couldn't touch it. You couldn't smell or taste it. You couldn't see it. You couldn't feel it. Nor could you hear it or pour it into a flask. Yet this invisible mind was real. "Cogito, ergo sum" proved the reality of the mind, and this is what Descartes called the rational soul. To Descartes, soul and thought were synonymous.

The difference between the rational soul of Descartes and many of the philosophers, church leaders, and physiologists who preceded him, was that for the latter the soul was contained in or connected with the body. The Greek philosopher Empedocles (495-435 BC) believed the soul was contained in the heart. To Aristotle, the human soul was a set of capacities and abilities, but he also thought, similar to Empedocles, that the heart was the seat of the soul.[26] Galen, following Plato's lead, thought that the soul was located in three parts and thought that "the presence of a network of nerves at the base of the ox brain" provided him with anatomical proof.[27] For Augustine and Aquinas, the soul was attached to the whole body.[28] William Harvey, on the other hand, thought that the soul was contained in the blood, a concept similar to one described by Moses in the Old Testament where blood is the receptacle for life.[29],[30] For Descartes, however, the mind (soul) was separate from the body and from nature which were mechanical in form. That theory created a problem, however, because if the body was just a mechanical object, where could the soul be located? Descartes had a solution. He allowed for the soul and the body to come together in one place and one place only. That place was the pineal gland which, as he discussed in works like *The Passions of the Soul*, he thought was a "double gland." For Descartes, this gland was filled with animal spirits and it controlled their flow. [Animal spirits can be thought of as meaning a kind of "basic mental energy and life force." For a fuller definition see Akerlof and Shiller in "Animal

Spirits."][31] Interestingly enough, it seems Descartes may have got the idea from Galen who stated that the function of the pineal gland was to control the flow of animal spirits. Also rather fascinating was the later addition to the discussion made by the 19th Century founder of Theosophy, Madame Helena Blavatsky (1831-1891), who declared that the pineal gland was an atrophied vestige of the eye of Shiva of the ancient Hindu mystics, the so-called Third Eye which opened into the psychic and spiritual domains.

Descartes' new dualistic theory of mind vs. matter, which became known as Cartesian dualism, marked a radical departure in the way people viewed themselves in relation to their concept of God, nature, and the universe and the manner in which they regarded other species. [The name Cartesian is derived from Cartesius, the Latin form of the name Descartes.] Whereas Aristotle's rational man and nonrational animal created a sharp divide between human beings and animals, for the followers of Descartes, the divide became and unbridgeable chasm.

The mechanical objects that populated the new universe proclaimed by Descartes required a change in beliefs about the soul if this philosophy were to succeed. Since mechanical objects did not think but merely functioned according to the operations of their inner mechanisms, according to Descartes, they could not possibly possess a soul.[32] This meant that the old belief system no longer applied. Henceforward, plants and animals were to be regarded as mechanical objects in the new mechanical universe. The idea that plants and animals possessed a soul or were part of a larger, world or universal soul could be discarded. Humans were to be the exclusive owners of that mysterious substance called the "soul." Animals, being mere mechanical objects, could not possibly possess one and further, being mechanical objects, also could not experience pain.

After Descartes, humans who behaved badly toward other species had no need to feel guilty or remorseful about any harm they caused to animals, though certain individuals of the past, like Galen, Colombus, and Harvey seemed to have already arrived at that state of mind. But for the future, the floor plan was available to anyone who wanted it. Descartes spelled it out when he wrote:

"thus my opinion is not so much cruel to animals as indulgent to human beings...since it absolves them from the suspicion of crime when they eat or kill animals."[33]

Killing animals in animal research laboratories could just as easily have been added to the statement as indicated by Descartes' own operations on animals dead and alive. He dissected the heads of animals in a futile search for "imagination" and "memory" and vivisected live dogs in order to study how the heart pumped blood. About an experiment on a dog, he said the following:

> If you slice off the pointed end of the heart in a live dog, and insert a finger into one of the cavities, you will feel unmistakably that every time the heart gets shorter, it presses the finger, and every time it gets longer it stops pressing it.[34]

The suffering of a dog, or any other animal, was not a consideration worth mentioning for vivisectors who aligned themselves with Descartes. His enthusiastic followers even declared that if a dog cried when it was beaten, that proved pain no more than a church organ was in pain when a key on the instrument was depressed to produce a sound. Since both were mechanical, both felt no pain.[35]

Animal researchers who so chose were now liberated to investigate animals as separate mechanical automata. Though this was still 200 years before the "discovery" of anesthesia these researchers had no hesitation in nailing a living dog to a wall by its paws and operating on it. A late seventeenth century eye-witness account of animal experiments described the suffering animals were forced to endure as mechanical objects at the Jansenist seminary of Port-Royal in France:

> They administered beatings to dogs with perfect indifference, and made fun of those who pitied the creatures as if they felt pain. They said the animals were clocks; that the cries they emitted when struck were only the noise of a little spring that had been

touched, but that the whole body was without feeling. They nailed poor animals up on boards by their four paws to vivisect them and see the circulation of the blood which was a great subject of conversation.[36]

The persons responsible for treating animals in this manner reasoned that no good God would allow human beings to be cruel to nonhuman animals. Therefore, if a human kicked a nonhuman animal it must be just a machine. Otherwise, God, being a just and good God, would not have allowed it to happen. It is small wonder that a few years later Voltaire (1694-1788), thoroughly repulsed and disgusted by the ignorance and cruelty of these kinds of "scientists," vented his rage at their obtuseness when he wrote:

> This dog, so very superior to man in affection, is seized by some barbarian virtuosos, who nail him down to a table, and dissect him while living, the better to shew you the meseraic veins. All the same organs of sensation which are in yourself you perceive in him. Now, Machinist, what say you? Answer me! Has Nature created all the springs of feeling in this animal, that it may not feel? Has it nerves to be impassible? For shame! Charge not Nature with such weakness and inconsistency.[37]

The term "Machinist" is an obvious reference to those who followed the "mechanistic" principles of Descartes. Voltaire was not the only one to be less than thrilled by the "barbarian virtuosos" during Descartes' day. An English philosopher told Descartes that his new theory about animals was "murderous." Other critics said that it went "against all evidence of sense and reason" and "contrary to the common sense of mankind."[38] Pierre Gassendi (1592-1655), a French philosopher, astronomer, mathematician and Abbot, argued against the Aristotelians and battled against Descartes, finding the idea that animals lack reason to be nothing but prejudice. "I restore reason to the animals," he wrote. "I find no distinction between the understanding and the imagination."[39] This was a distinction the Aristotelians made.

Descartes' mechanistic world challenged the authority of the ancient beliefs that animals and plants possessed a soul. The full usurpation of the throne was not accomplished overnight, however, and the subject continued as a topic of considerable and even acrimonious debate among the followers and adversaries of Descartes. In 1672, for example, Père Ignaz-Gaston Pardies (1636-1673), in spite of being a Cartesian himself, argued that animals possessed a material soul of an "intermediate third substance between extended matter and the non-extended rational soul of man."[40] He also thought that animals were capable of knowledge and emotions. The physician, anatomist, and architect Claude Perrault (1613-1688) also believed that animals possessed a soul, and in 1680, in regard to Descartes mechanistic theory, wrote rather humorously, if not derisively, in his *De la méchanique des animaux* that "you could put a female dog and a male dog side-by-side and they would produce another dog, but put two clocks side-by-side and they could remain there forever without producing another clock."[41]

The debate over whether or not animals possessed a soul continued to arouse considerable discussion in the 18th century. The Jesuit author Noël Régnault (1683-1763) wrote in 1732 that the animal soul existed someplace between brute matter and spirit.[42] And in the introduction to his *Histoire des insects* in 1734, Réne-Antoine Ferchault de Réaumur (1683-1757), a devoted Cartesian but an ardent lover of insects, wrote:

> But will we refuse all intelligence to insects and re-
> duce them to the simple state of a machine? Here is
> the great question of the soul of animals, debated so
> often since Descartes, and about which so much has
> been said since the debate began. All that we owe to
> the disputes which it engendered is that the two op-
> posing opinions both seem plausible, but it is impos-
> sible to demonstrate which of the two is right.[43]

[For a further discussion on the intelligence of insects, see chapter 13.]

When it came to the soul of animals, for Réaumur it was the supreme power who decided where to place intelligence, and that could include placing it in an insect if he so desired, or even in an oyster, no matter what Descartes had to say on the subject.

In the final analysis, at least up to the present time, those who proclaimed that animals possessed no soul have been the winners of the debate.

In Descartes' Day, his vision from the Virgin Mary was a good enough reason for a new breed of animal researchers to adopt and establish an entirely new world view in which the human species was allowed to beat the dog no matter how brutally on the grounds that animals were just mechanical objects. If it was good enough for Descartes, it was good enough for these animal researchers. These kinds of attitudes continue to prevail today with many vivisectors, including Nobel laureates who practice vivisection, as we shall see, who take the position that animals are mere things incapable of thought without feelings or consciousness, perfectly suitable for slicing open and taking apart in pursuit of their objectives.

Of course, many people thought Descartes' ideas were farfetched and many people rejected them. But the concept of soul as being the exclusive property of the human species is the theory of soul which dominates the thinking of the Western world today, and almost everyone who believes in an individual soul thinks that it is found inside the body in some undefined place. It is true that some followers of certain Eastern religions (e.g., Hindu, Islam, Jain, Sikh) believe that animals possess immortal souls. The Mormons also believe that afterlife extends to animals, and the Anglican church is generally "positive" on the issue. Most people, however, do not believe that nonhuman animals or other life forms possess a soul and survive death, and the concept of a world or universal soul, or that the body is a part of the soul rather than the soul a part of the body is utterly foreign to the Western mind. Yet, as noted earlier, Jesus said, in relation to the sparrows, that "not one of them will fall to the ground apart from your Father," an indication that animals are a part of something much larger than themselves who are protected even after death.[44]

The biggest difference between the world of centuries past and the new mechanistic universe of Descartes was that for the former the world was a living, breathing thing infused with the essence of soul that pulsated with the life force of nature. For the new mechanistic cosmos, however, all matter became an inert, dead thing that moved only according to the laws of mechanics just as surely as if it were a clock. Matter was distinct and separate from the mind and while it was still created by God, it was created through the intermediary of mathematics.

Descartes' influence on the world of science was relatively short-lived. His mechanistic theories about matter would soon be pushed aside by the Newtonian universe of atomic matter. And Sir Isaac Newton (1643-1727) did not believe in treating animals like mechanical objects. In fact, for Newton, who was a lover of cats and is said to have invented the cat door, the "injunction to love one's neighbor encompassed four-footed as well as two-footed neighbors."[45] Newton simply believed it was human duty to be merciful to animals. Even so, it was Descartes who succeeded in laying the foundations for today's mechanistic view in both physics and biology such as, for example, that the body is purely mechanical.[46] And scientists in today's world (as the public has frequently had occasion to observe) often walk around and talk like they are "disembodied minds."[47] The mechanistic view has also served to increase the gulf in the Western world—in fact, to help build an almost inviolable wall of separation—between human beings and other species that today plays a major part in how humans interact with animals. On the one side stand human beings, the possessors of a soul destined by God himself for eternity, but on the other side stands everything else including all nonhuman forms of life, the soulless possessors of nothing.

The sense of separation between human beings and the rest of nature in which humankind is a special, superior kind of soul-possessing entity was not unique to Descartes and he was not the first to express it. But the denial of the existence of the soul for everything that is nonhuman has helped to create a clear and decisive division separating humankind and nature in which humans have increasingly grown comfortable exploiting the material, "mechanical" world however they like. Humans think nothing of taking off the top of a mountain to get at its energy resources or of depleting the oceans of its sea life; nor do they hesitate to cut into and dismember living, breathing members of nonhuman species in animal research laboratories.

Opposition to vivisection was minimal in the 17th and 18th centuries and animal researchers increasingly fell dutifully in line swallowing without questioning the hypothesis that human animals and nonhuman animals were two separate entities, one superior because it possessed mind and soul, the other inferior because it possessed nothing. Animal researchers were thus liberated to exercise their dominion over all species in any manner they deemed would best serve their interests, no matter how cruelly that dominion might express itself.

The new mechanistic universe bequeathed to the world by the 17th century made a powerful impact on the lives of animals. It marked the beginning of the disintegration of the last remnants of general respect for animals dating back to the Paleolithic past and beyond. With the onset of the new way of perceiving the non-human species of the earth, any rights accorded to them were withdrawn as animals were demoted from the status of possessors of soul endowed with unique qualities and abilities by God himself to a slave class for the purpose of serving human needs and wishes.

Chapter 7

Animal Research in the 17th, 18th, and 19th Centuries and the Rise of the Protest Movement

Ten years after the death of Descartes' a group of animal experimenters formed a scientific club in London which they called the Royal Society. Here they cut open many animals dead and alive. This was where Robert Hooke and Robert Boyle invented their tubular-shaped vacuum air pump for suffocating animals. As described earlier, with this popular device they could withdraw the air, causing the animals to expire in the vacuum or leave the animals to suffocate in the air supply that was available in the pump. Researchers at the Royal Society were highly innovative. In one experiment they cut open the thorax and diaphragm of a dog, leaving its heart visible, and then kept the dog alive by pumping air into its windpipe through a bellows. The purpose was to determine whether it was the pumping of the lungs or the air itself the dog depended upon for life. As for the suffering caused by their experiments, the researchers could hardly have escaped knowing the extent to which they were abusing, tormenting, and murdering animals. Boyle himself noted that a viper was "furiously tortured" in a vacuum experiment.[1]

Bizarre and fantastic curiosity experiments have frequently been a part of animal research, and no constraints were put on experimenters at the Royal Society. There Richard Lower began siphoning the blood from one animal to another using sheep and dogs just to see what would happen. The animals in these experiments invariably died. Edmund King, who assisted Lower in the experiments, tried out his own version at his home in which he replaced the blood of a dog with a mixture of milk and sugar. He had a difficult time because the dog kept struggling, but when he stopped, King was able to complete the experiment. The dog vomited and lost the use of his limbs before he perished. King was able to report, nevertheless, that the dog "seemed to know when he was kindly spoken to." After the experiment the dog smelled "so foul it made the servants sick." [2]

Far from supporting Descartes' mechanistic theories about animals, laboratory research proved that animals were not mere clocks. They were sensitive, intelligent, highly communicative beings who suffered fear and pain and who responded to affection and love much the same way human beings do, by showing affection and love in return whether as household companion animals or out in the world someplace at home with their own kind. Buttressed by the addition of Cartesian mechanistic theories to the old justifications for animal research based on the nonrationality of animals, however, most animal researchers continued to regard nonhuman species as mere objects suitable for their use in any fashion they desired as animal research pushed ahead with little regard for the suffering of the animals.

In Italy, Marcello Malpighi (1628-1694) and Carlo Fracassati (d. 1682) cut open dead and living guinea pigs, cats, sheep, frogs, and birds and injected their lungs and pulmonary vessels with colored water in hit-or-miss efforts to understand how the lungs functioned. Problems arose because the colored water could not "easily" replace the blood in the pulmonary vessels without killing the animals. In one experiment, Fracassati injected a dog with hydrochloric acid, reporting that "the animal complain'd a great while...and observing the beating of his breast, one might easily judge, the dog suffered much."[3]

The idea that animals were just things suitable for obtaining knowledge about human anatomy was also beginning to ease into the public consciousness as evidenced in 1705 when the actress and playwright Susanna Centlivre (1673-1723) published a farce, *The Basset Table*, in which a "philosophical girl" cuts open her pet dove to see if it has a "gall." When challenged to account for her actions, the girl replies:

Why what did you imagine I bred it for? Can animals, insects, or reptiles be put to a nobler use than to improve our knowledge?[4]

The same kind of sentiments were evident in the public dissections and vivisections taking place in menageries and veterinary schools in Italy, Germany, England, France, and Holland at around the same time. They were attended by the upper classes for whom dissection and vivisection were exciting new games to play. These well-to-do citizens where only too eager to get in on the latest fad and happily paid top admissions to view dissections with an added fee for viewing the sexual organs as an encore.[5] Events like these slanted public sentiment in directions less favorable to animals as the objectification of nonhuman species burrowed further into the public consciousness.

Vivisection in the 18th century was performed by people who called themselves "anatomists" or "physiologists." With growing public acceptance, this group became increasingly confident that their experiments were justified. Physiologist Julien Legallois (1772-1814), who tried to prove that life was found not in the whole body but in the spinal cord, wrote that "experiments on living animals are among the greatest lights of physiology."[6] Johann August Unzer (1727-1797), a German physician, believed that the soul was located in the brain and that therefore higher animals possessed a soul; lower animals, which had no brain did not (insects, worms, jellyfish, sponges, etc.). Trying to prove his point, he decapitated dogs at the University of Halle in order to compare them to animal species without a brain.[7] Like many of his fellow physiologists, satisfying his curiosity took precedence over life itself. If that cost an animal to suffer that was too bad. Unzer grew nearly bellicose in proclaiming that animals had no rights and bragged that his research was a "murderous deed." He dared anyone to bring charges against him, so self-assured was he that the dogs upon whom he experimented were just things which he was free to decapitate as he liked. He described one experiment on a dog in a letter titled: "A letter to Mr. NN which is shown that it is possible to feel without head." But Unzer had his detractors, and this letter brought a scornful reply by Abraham Kastner, an opponent of vivisection, who wrote that "whether it was possible to *think* without head" certainly it was possible "to *write* without head." [8], [9]

At the Royal Academy of Sciences at Göttingen in Germany, the Swiss physician Albrecht von Haller (1708-1777) intentionally tested animals for responses to painful stimuli. According to him, he had no alternative other than to perform the "cruel torture" with chemical substances, heat, or the scalpel by "touching, cutting, burning, or lacerating" the part of the animal he wanted to test for what he called "irritability."[10] Touching could consist of either a regular touch, a slight touch, or a violent touch. As in today's world, Haller's curiosity-based experiments were done behind closed doors where nobody could see what he was doing.

Grotesque, curiosity-driven experiments reached their zenith for 18th century England when the country's most prominent zoologist and surgeon, the Scotsman John Hunter (1728-1793), implanted human teeth in fowls, grafted spurs onto their combs, and transplanted their genitals with those of the opposite sex.[11]

More reflective members of the public were deeply disturbed by the reports of the exceptionally cruel, curiosity experiments some of the physiologists were performing. The English poet Alexander Pope (1688-1744) sharply criticized his neighbor, Reverend Stephen Hales, for blood pressure experiments he had performed upon dogs, sheep, a horse, and a deer, in which he pierced an artery in their legs and bled them to death.[12] In responding to a query about Hales, Pope replied:

> Yes he is a very good man, only—I'm sorry—he has his hands imbrued with blood...Indeed, he commits these barbarities with the thought of its being of use to man. But how do we know we have a right to kill creatures that we are so little above as dogs, for our curiosity, or even some use to us?

Pope went on to point out that:

Man has reason enough only to know what is necessary for him to know, and dogs have just that too.[13]

The poet and writer Samuel Johnson (1709-1784) would
have concurred, attacking vivisectors in "The Idler," a weekly news
journal in which he published a series of essays, where he described
animal researchers as "inferior Professors of medical knowledge
(among whom was) a race of wretches, whose lives are only varied
by varieties of cruelty."[14] Upon learning that Reverend Hales was
working on decapitated frogs, Johnson, like Pope, took note of his
cruelty, referring to him as one of those doctors who "extend the art
of torture."

The animal research of the 18th and 19th centuries proceeded out of a general acceptance of the suffering of animals in the
laboratory and saw a continuation of experiments that were
exceedingly cruel. To observe how it affected circulation, the British
researcher Marshall Hall (1790-1857) crushed the brain and spinal
cords and other parts of the bodies of frogs and fish. In 1820, Pierre
Flourens, a French physiologist, removed large portions of animals'
brains and reported that they could still move but they were
reduced to nothing more than "complex machines." He did not
comment on the suffering of these "complex machines" kept alive
to observe their movement minus most of their brains. But these
gentlemen had little on François Magendie (1783-1855), another
Frenchman, who vivisected without hesitation. Some of his work
easily competes with Galen for the top cruelty award toward
animals of all times, at least prior to the 20th and 21st centuries.
Magendie "tortured animals in public, slicing into living flesh as if
it were a piece of mutton, as the bound beasts screamed in agony.
Men became sick to their stomachs and women fainted."[15] In order
to demonstrate the functioning of the facial nerves, Magendie
nailed a living greyhound to a table by its paws and ears with blunt
large spikes, to make certain the dog could not tear itself away, and
then performed his vivisection. He told his audience he would keep
the dog alive overnight so that he could operate on the other side of

the face the next day, and if the dog was quiet enough after that, he would cut into the torso to demonstrate how the heart and viscera functioned.[16] It cannot be overly stressed that this vivisection, like all vivisections of the times, was done without anesthesia.

For determined animal researchers, concerns about the suffering of research animals and other issues of morality was not important. They insisted that since animal research made a contribution to human anatomy, it was not only moral but immoral not to do it. Invoking the principle that whatever is good for human beings is justified helped in overcoming any anxieties and reservations that might creep in. So long as some benefit for humankind was intended, animals could be tortured and abused in the most execrable ways. Henri Duhamel Dumonceau (1700-1782), an animal researcher of the times, expressed the common attitude when he wrote that "each day more animals are dying in order to satisfy our appetite that the scalpel of the anatomist might sacrifice for the purpose of useful research, which is directed to the conservation of our health and the cure of diseases."[17]

For the general public, the acceptance of cruelty toward animals as being an element of human consciousness had become so ingrained in daily life that it was not easily remedied. When Richard Martin (1754-1834), an M.P. (Member of Parliament) in the British Parliament, proposed a law preventing the mistreatment of horses, the reaction in the chambers turned into an occasion for back-slapping joviality:

> ...when Alderman C. Smith suggested that protection should be given to asses, there were such howls of laughter that *The Times* reporter could hear little of what was said. When the Chairman repeated this proposal, the laughter was intensified. Another member said Martin would be legislating for dogs next, which causes a further roar of mirth, and a cry "And cats!" sent the House into convulsions.[18]

Martin would become one of the founders of the first organization against animal cruelty (the Society for the Prevention of

Cruelty to Animals (SPCA)) and was often referred to as Humanity Dick. Though it took years, he finally succeeded in getting a bill through the House of Commons, watered down though it was, that for the very first time made cruelty to animals a "punishable offense." It was called the Ill-Treatment of Cattle Act and was signed into law by the House of Lords and King George IV in 1822.[19],[20]

Asked on one occasion why he took the side of animals, Martin, who had been known in his youth for a special talent in dueling, is said to have responded: "Sir, an ox cannot hold a pistol."[21]

As vivisection increased, questions continued to mount sometimes even from a few animal experimenters themselves who were assailed by doubts. This included Haller who reported the inner turmoil he was experiencing from conducting his "irritability" experiments testing for pain when he wrote that "since the beginning of the year 1751, I have examined (in) several different ways, a hundred and ninety animals, a species of cruelty for which I felt such reluctance, as could only be overcome by the desire of contributing to the benefit of mankind."[22]

The President of the Berlin Academy of Sciences, Pierre-Louis Moreau de Maupertuis (1698-1759), opposed the mechanistic philosophy of Descartes because he thought that if doctors practiced cruelty to animals it could lead them to be cruel to people. But this was just a repetition of the same old argument made by John Calvin, Thomas Aquinas, and many others. It did not take into account the suffering of the animals being cut into or arguments about their rights such as that animals are more than mere things who also have an interest in the debate and who yearn to avoid suffering and death in the same manner as humans beings.

Another vivisector with a conflicted conscience was Alexander Pope's neighbor, the Reverend Stephen Hales. He had first begun vivisecting when he was in college at Cambridge University. A friend of his, William Stukeley (1687-1765), would catch stray cats and dogs around the university upon whom the two friends would experiment. But struck by pangs of conscience, Hales stopped experimenting on animals for 25 years, conceivably influenced by his neighbor, the poet Pope. Unfortunately, Hales resumed vivisecting again.

Other vivisectors continued to wrestle with the morality of animal testing. Christlob Mylius, a student at the University of Leipzig in the mid-18th century, and a friend of the previously mentioned antivivisectionist Abraham Kastner, debated the rights and wrongs of vivisection, but eventually decided that vivisection was necessary if "physiology" were to advance. If it had to be done, he thought, it was better to do it on nonhuman animals than on human animals. Mylius apparently did not give much thought to the possibility that it did not have to be done at all.

A few animal researchers in every period do become conflicted about their work to a degree sufficient enough to cause them to change direction. In Germany, the physiologist Johannes Peter Müller (1801-1858) began his career experimenting on animals until doubts caused him to switch to medical subjects that did not require animal testing.[23] Dr. Christian Barnard, who conducted the first human heart transplant in 1967, also had a change of heart about experimenting upon chimpanzees after the following incident occurred which he described in his book *Good Life, Good Death*.

> I had bought two male chimps from a primate colony in Holland. They lived next to each other in separate cages for several months before I used one as a donor. When we put him to sleep in his cage in preparation for the operation he chattered and cried incessantly. We attached no significance to this, but it must have made a great impression on his companion, for when we removed the body to the operating room, the other chimp wept bitterly and was unconsolable for days. The incident made a deep impression on me. I vowed never again to experiment with such sensitive creatures.[24]

The impression, however, was not deep enough for Barnard to vow to stop experimenting on animals altogether.

80

It is surprising that greater conflicts have not erupted within the ranks of the professional animal researchers. This could be in part because many would-be animal researchers investigate what it is all about before they ever begin and turn away from a profession based on cruelty in favor of a more humane way of living out their lives. Certainly, within the human mind the measure of right and wrong stands ready to sound an alarm when it confronts animals being mistreated. We have seen how Aristotle's student Theophrastus criticized animal sacrifice. Opposition to the mistreatment of animals was also recorded back in the 12 century when John of Salisbury (1150-1180) wrote down these words opposing the cruelty of hunting:

> Who more bestial than he who, neglecting duties, rises at midnight, that with the aid of dogs keen of scent, his active huntsmen, his zealous comrades, and his retinue of devoted servants, at cost of time, labor, money, and effort, he may wage from earliest dawn till darkness his campaign against beasts?[25]

In the 17th century, the Duchess Margaret Cavendish (1623-1673), a writer and an independent thinker, penned her thoughts about the way people treated animals in her world. She was married to a man who corresponded with Descartes and in whom Descartes even confided that he did not share "the opinion of Montaigne and others who attributed understanding or thought to animals."[26] Nor, as is clear from her words, would Margaret have agreed with Descartes. Today the lines from her famous poem "The Hare" are as meaningful as the day on which she wrote them:

> As if that God made Creatures for Mans meat,
> To gie them life and sense for man to eat;
> Or else for sport, or recreations sake,
> Destroy those lifes that God saw good to make;
> Making their stomacks, graves, which full they fill
> With Murther'd Bodies that in sport they kill.
> Yet man doth think himself so gentle, mild,

When he of creatures is most cruel wild,
And is so proud, thinks only he shall live,
That God a God like nature did him give,
And that all creatures for his sake alone,
Was made for him, to tyrannize upon.

Animal researchers who struggled with the ethics of vivi-section but took the side against the animals anyway because it supposedly benefitted human beings got little sympathy from the opponents of animal research. They sided with the famous 1780 declaration by the philosopher Jeremy Bentham (1748-1832) who wrote: "The question is not, 'Can they reason? nor Can they talk? But Can they suffer?'"[27] These words defeated many of the arguments made by the animal researchers and continue to make their impact even today. For Bentham, as with Cavendish, it was "tyranny" for humans to cause animals to suffer. Bentham was backed by other prominent figures like the philosopher John Stuart Mill (1806-1873). Significant, too, was the comment made by Victor Hugo (1802-1885) that "Vivisection was a crime."[28] He was elected as the President of the Société française contre la vivisection in 1883, two years before his death.

It must be noted, nevertheless, that for Bentham, as with many of the great thinkers and artists of their eras, like Benjamin Franklin, Arthur Schopenhauer, and Richard Wagner,[29] all of whom rejected humankind's speciesist way of thinking, he still continued to consume and to rationalize consuming animals.[30] All of these men did the same without regard to the suffering imposed upon the animals in the slaughterhouses which in those days were even worse than those in operation today.[31] A convincing cloud of doubt has also been raised about several other advocates for animals who lowered their standards of morality when it came time for dinner.[32] Fortunately, other voices spoke out committing totally to the struggle for the rights of animals including their right not to be slaughtered by human beings for food. One of those voices be-longed to the poet and progressive thinker Percy Bysshe Shelley. Philosopher and Physician David Hartley (1705-1757) was of like mind and wrote that "With respect to animal Diet, let it be considered, that taking away the Lives of Animals in order to convert them into Food does great violence to the principles of Benevolence and Compassion."[33] And John Tweedle (1769-1799), who died at the age of thirty of a mysterious fever, said that he was "persuaded we have no other right than the right of the strongest, to sacrifice to our monstrous appetites the bodies of living things, of whose qualities and relations we are ignorant."[34]

Beside criticizing animal researchers, adversaries of animal research managed to keep the focus on the cruelty and activities of some animal researchers in the public eye long after the researchers had passed on. In 1740, 50 years after the death of Boyle, a poem in the *Gentlemen's Magazine* in London compared the on-going torture of animals in the Boyle/Hooke vacuum air-pump with the Roman emperor Domitian (51-96 AD). [Domitian, known as a tyrant, executed even his "mildest critics" and insisted he be addressed as "master and god."[35]] Twenty years later in 1760 a public lecturer on anatomy and mechanics called the vacuum air pump experiments the "agonies of a most bitter and cruel death [that were] shocking to every spectator who [had] the least degree of humanity."[36]

Back in the same year in which Bentham had posited his famous declaration (1780), the esteemed German philosopher Immanuel Kant (1724-1804) had confidently written that "Animals are not self-conscious, and are there merely as a means to an end. That end is man."[37] Kant was 56 years of age at the time who, in spite of his speciesist outlook on life, at least conceded that he deplored excessive cruelty to animals. He had grown up in a society that was increasingly accepting vivisection as a legitimate practice and went along with the current of the times.

Kant and Bentham may not have been acutely aware of it, but the seeds for significant opposition to animal research were being sewn around them. The emergence of the beginnings of an organized animal rights movements first in Great Britain in 1824 with the founding of the SPCA (later the RSPCA) and then in the United States in 1866 with the inauguration of an SPCA in New York City, as well as the Vegetarian Society in Britain in 1847 and the American Vegetarian Society in New York in 1850, assured that criticism and opposition to animal research was established and would continue to grow. (See also chapter 1)

Had he been alive, "Humanity Dick" Martin would have been gratified at the rise of Frances Power Cobbe (1822-1904) in England, an Irish writer, early feminist, social reformer, suffragette, and antivivisectionist. Besides protesting against animal experiments in France and Italy in the 1860s, Cobbe and her circle, which had the support of Queen Victoria, published many articles and letters in the popular press and denounced the admiration British researchers had for Dr. Bernard, the famous vivisector. (See chapter 8) In November of 1875, together with Richard Hutton and Dr. George Hoggan, to whom she was introduced on the eve of his famous letter to the London Morning Post of February 1, 1875 (see chapter 8), she helped found and became the leader of what would become the largest and most powerful antivivisection organization in England, the Victoria Street Society. Its members included Cardinal Manning, Lord Chief Justice John Duke Coleridge (nephew of Samuel Taylor Coleridge), Alfred Tennyson, and Robert Browning. The President of the Society was Anthony Ashley Cooper, the Seventh Earl of Shaftesbury.[38]

In 1879, joining with Lord Truro, Shaftesbury unsuccessfully attempted to enact legislation to abolish vivisection altogether. Writing to Cobbe, he said:

> We are bound in duty, I think to leap over all limitations, and go in for the total abolition of this vile and cruel form of Idolatry; for idolatry it is, and like all idolatry, brutal, degrading, and deceptive. [39]

Cobbe met Charles Darwin in 1868. At first they got on well together and exchanged letters. Darwin praised an article Cobbe had written on the consciousness of dogs, calling it the "best analysis of the animal he had read." He sent Cobbe two of his own articles on the animal mind which included "The expression of the emotions in man and animals," published in 1872.[40] By 1875, however, the differences between the pair had become evident and fully visible. In response to a request by his daughter, Henrietta, to

84

sign an antivivisection letter sent by Cobbe, Darwin responded: "I certainly cannot sign a paper sent to me by Miss Cobbe, with her monstrous attack against Virchow."[41] (Rudolf Virchow was a renowned German scientist and vivisector.) On April 18, 1881 Darwin and Cobbe began a notable exchange of letters in The Times of London which started off with a letter Darwin wrote to the Times responding to a letter from Swedish Physiologist Frithjof Holmgreen in support of vivisection.

> I know that physiology cannot possibly progress except by means of experiments on living animals, and I feel the deepest conviction that he who retards the progress of physiology commits a crime against mankind.

Upon reading the letter, Cobbe responded in The Times the very next day with her own letter titled "Mr. Darwin on Vivisection." There she stated that this philosophy [the evolution philosophy] "overestimated the scientific advance of physiology, and did not take into account the disappearance of the sentiments of compassion and kindness implied in this process." She asked: "What shall it profit a man if he gain the whole world of knowledge and lose his own heart and his own consciousness?" On April 23rd Cobbe continued her train of thought with these lines to The Times:

> It is impossible for a man to devote his life to such a practice without experiencing a growing ardour for scientific curiosity and a corresponding recklessness and callousness respecting the suffering which the gratification of that curiosity may involve.[42]

Remarkably, Darwin himself detested cruelty to animals. He was critical of training methods used on circus dogs, imposed heavy fines for mistreatment of farm animals in his role as a local magistrate, and co-authored a manifesto with his wife, Emma, to stop the use of steel traps to capture animals for their fur.[43] Darwin never performed an experiment on an animal during his lifetime and in *The Descent of Man* wrote:

> In the agony of death a dog has been known to caress his master, and everyone has heard of the dog suffering under vivisection who licked the hand of the operator; this man, unless he has a heart of stone, must have felt remorse to the last hour of his life.

The vivisector to whom Darwin is thought to have referred was François Magendie himself.

For Cobbe, considering the innate sense of kindness she observed in Darwin in respect to animals, his support of vivisection must have seemed tragic. As she noted:

> Mr. Darwin eventually became the center of an adoring *clique* of vivisectors who (as his biography shows) plied him incessantly with encouragement to uphold their practice, till the deplorable spectacle was exhibited of a man who would not allow a fly to bite a pony's neck, standing before all Europe as the advocate of vivisection.[44]

Darwin was, in reality, repulsed by vivisection and confessed that it made him "sick with horror." But whereas Cobbe "vehemently condemned" vivisection, when it came to having to make a choice, Darwin defended vivisection in the name of "scientific progress," saying that it was justified for "real investigations on physiology; but not for mere damnable and detestable curiosity."[45]

The action that Cobbe, Hoggan, Lord Truro, the Earl of Shaftesbury and others in their circle took marked substantial progress in opposing vivisection and animal research. They promoted legislation and published antivivisection literature in the Victoria Street Society's periodical the Zoophilist. They were not alone. A magazine called The Home Chronicler also kept the public informed about the cruelty of experiments the physiologists were performing and published articles such as "Dr. Wickham Legg's Experiments on Cats."[46]

Antivivisection petitions, press editorials, and public condemnation of vivisection created a platform from which the antivivisectionists could launch a meaningful battle against the English vivisectionists. On the antivivisection side stood the Victoria Street Society, the London Anti-Vivisection Society, the Society to Abolish Vivisection, notable figures like Charles Dickens and Thomas Carlyle, and the support of a large block of middle-class women. On the vivisection side stood prominent scientists and physiologist like Charles Darwin, Thomas Huxley, John Burden Sanderson, the Physiological Society, the Association for the Advancement of Medicine by Research, and the powerful British Medical Journal.

Cobbe and the Victoria Street Society contacted members of the House of Lords favorable to their position who succeeded in putting through a bill in Parliament to regulate vivisection, the Anti-vivisection act of 1876.[47] In its original version, which followed the plan the Victoria Street Society promoted, the act would have prohibited all experiments on horses, dogs, and cats, and would have required complete anesthetizing of all animals experimented upon. Just before the bill was set for passage, however, the person in charge, Lord Carnarvon, had to take an emergency leave because of his wife's sudden illness and subsequent death which gave the medical profession time to convince the Home Secretary to water down the bill.[48] The final version of the act did require licensing of all vivisectors and that all animals experimented upon must be anaesthetized and killed immediately upon the conclusion of the experiment, but it also permitted experiments on dogs, cats, horses, mules, and asses to be conducted without anesthesia if they were necessary for the success of the experiment.[49]

Queen Victoria, who sought to have antivivisection legislation and stronger laws against animal cruelty enacted, also made her voice heard in the vivisection debate, referring to vivisection as a "disgrace to humanity and Christianity." She had a letter written to vivisector Joseph Lister asking him to stop vivisecting, When the Victoria Street Society charged physiologist David Ferrier (1843-

1928) of vivisecting without a license, the Queen addressed the Home Secretary, Sir William Harcourt, as follows[50]

> Windsor Castle, November 25, 1881. There is, however, another subject on which the Queen feels most strongly, and that is this horrible, brutalising un-christian-like vivisection. That poor dumb animals should be kept alive as described in this trial is *revolting and horrible*. This *must* be stopped. Monkeys and dogs—two of the most intelligent amongst those poor animals who cannot complain—dogs, "man's best friend," possessed of more than instinct, to be treated in this fearful way is *awful*. She directs Sir Wm. Harcourt's attention most strongly to it. It must really not be permitted. It is a disgrace to a civilized country.

David Ferrier was a prominent physiologist and a Fellow of the Royal College of Physicians. He was charged with "perform[ing] experiments, calculated to give pain to two monkeys, in violation of the restrictions imposed by the Anti--Vivisection Act..."[51] The charges resulted from Ferrier's desire to measure physiological responses to electric brain stimulation on monkeys following up on the work of German scientists Gustav Fritsch and Eduard Hitzig. But anesthesia dulled the responses Ferrier expected. In order to get around the problem he waited until the monkeys came out of the anaesthesia and then continued the experiments on the monkeys in an unanesthetized state instead of killing them. This was a requirement for all vivisectors according to the provisions of the Anti-Vivisection act, unless they had applied for and received a special certificate. Ferrier's experiments came to light in August of 1881 when he invited attendees at the International Medical Congress in London to examine his work which had been challenged by a German physiologist, Friedrich Goltz. Cobbe and the people at the Victoria Street Society learned what was going on and examined the Home Office records which revealed that Ferrier had never applied for the special certificate to continue experimenting upon animals after they had recovered from anesthesia.[52] This was the evidence Cobbe needed to bring charges against Ferrier for violating the Anti-Vivisection Act.

The trial became a cause célèbre pitting the antivivisectionists against the British scientists and their supporters. The latter wanted to assert their independence from any restraints on their work and prove that Ferrier was innocent. The British Medical Association even paid his legal fees. The penalty for the offense was only a fine of £50, but Cobbe hoped to use the trial to put the cruelty of Ferrier's vivisection squarely in the public eye and hold him accountable to the law.[53] At trial, however, Ferrier was able to show that Gerald Francis Yeo, a Professor of Physiology at Kings College London, was the person who actually performed the surgery on the monkeys and that Yeo had applied for and received the special certificate. Though Ferrier participated in the experiments which he led, because he had not done the surgery there was no legal case to be made against him and the charges were dismissed.

The battle may have been lost but the war against vivisection raged on including a continuing fight against Ferrier. In an 1885 publication titled Professor Ferrier's Experiments on Monkeys' Brains" published by the Victoria Street Society, the author described how Ferrier and Yeo had caused monkeys to go blind by cauterizing their brains with a "red hot wire," and then watched the animals run around crashing into furniture in "mortal dread" of their "tormentors." The article went on to say that "Professor Ferrier was acquitted at Bow Street, [but] . . . there is a larger tribunal before which both he and his colleague must appear."[54]

This early face-to-face confrontation pitting the antivivisectionists against the forces of vivisection was a precursor to the many battles that would follow especially after the explosion of the animal rights movement nearly a century later. The new animal rights movement was still in its infancy in the days of Cobbe and the Victoria Street Society. Their efforts and those of like-minded associates was not enough to turn aside the tide of public opinion that was firmly set in the minds of the educated class and the general population. People still believed that nonhuman animals were suitable for use in the service of humankind in any manner human beings desired. The new movement was growing in strength nevertheless and would eventually challenge every justification for animal research that animal researchers had ever made as people with progressive minds and compassion in their hearts joined to challenge the concept that cruelty to animals was an acceptable means for survival, the belief system upon which humans had been relying for centuries with very little protest and which still survives today.

Chapter 8

A Dark and Foreboding Place
The Transition from the Study of Anatomy to
the Search for the Cure for Disease and Beyond

Prior to the 20th century, animal research was done primarily to try to acquire greater knowledge about the anatomy of the human body and how it worked. Searching for cures for disease was not a part of the process to any significant degree. By the turn of the 20th century, however, animal research had entered a new phase where the search for cures for human disease would become the primary focus of animal research. It had already begun with the work of the French physiologist Claude Bernard (1813-1878), a vivisector who believed that pain was a necessary adjunct to animal experimentation. Bernard stressed the view that scientists were a superior breed of people with the right to vivisect animals "wholly and absolutely."[1] His own mentor was the brutal Francois Magendie, profiled briefly in chapter 7.

From Magendie, Bernard learned his craft well. Known as *The Prince of Vivisectors*, Bernard led the way in furthering a reliance on animal models for the study of disease and the view that animal research was an appropriate medium for finding a cure for human health problems. His book *Introduction to the Study of Experimental Medicine* championed vivisection and was widely studied by physiologists and students of physiology in Europe and in America. In Great Britain, scientists traveled to France to study Bernard's techniques as well as those of Magendie.

Students from the United States also traveled abroad to study with Bernard. Among these was John Call Dalton (1825-1889), a teacher of physiology at the College of Physicians and Surgeons in New York City. He may have been the first physiologist to use vivisection in his classes in the United States upon completing his study with Bernard in 1850. Later he wrote that Bernard had "placed the science [of physiology] on its true footing, and has indicated the only true course, that of experimenting on living or recently killed animals."[2]

Francis Donaldson, (1823-1891), another American who studied with Bernard in Paris, wrote the following portrait of one of Bernard's classrooms.

> It was curious enough to see walking about the amphitheatre of the College of France dogs and rabbits, unconscious contributors to science, with five or six orifices in their bodies from which, at a moment's warning, there could be produced any secretion of the body, including that of the several salivary glands, the stomach, the liver and the pancreas.[3]

It should not be forgotten that these animals walking around oozing secretions from man-made wounds were not anaesthetized before those wounds were inflicted upon them, nor were the animals afforded any easement for their continued suffering during the remainder of their experimentally determined life spans.

A retired naval officer, Dr. George Hoggan (1837-1891), became an assistant to Bernard, the experience of which led him to join forces with Frances Power Cobbe in founding the Victoria Street Society to fight against vivisection. He described his experience of being inside Bernard's laboratory in a letter to the London Morning Post of February 6, 1875 as follows:

> In that laboratory we sacrificed daily from one to three dogs, besides rabbits and other animals, and after four months experience I am of the opinion that not one of those experiments on animals was justified or necessary. The idea of the good of humanity was simply out of the question, and would have been laughed at, the great aim being to keep up with, or get ahead of one's contemporaries in science, even at the

price of an incalculable amount of torture needlessly and iniquitously inflicted on the poor animals. During three [military] campaigns I have witnessed many harsh sights, but I think the saddest sight I ever witnessed was when the dogs were brought up from the cellar to the laboratory for sacrifice. Instead of appearing pleased with the change from darkness to light, they seemed seized with horror as soon as they smelt the air of the place, divining apparently their approaching fate. They would make friendly advances to each of the three or four persons present, and as far as eyes, ears and tail could make a mute appeal for mercy eloquent, they tried it in vain. Even when roughly grasped and thrown on the torture-trough, a low complaining whine at such treatment would be all the protest they made, and they would lick the hand which bound them till their mouths were fixed in the gag, and they could only flap their tail in the trough as their last means of exciting compassion. Often when convulsed by the pain of their torture this would be renewed, and they would be soothed instantly on receiving a few gentle pats. It was all the aid and comfort I could give them, and I gave it often. They seemed to take it as an earnest of fellow feeling that would cause their torture to come to an end—and end only brought by death....Hundreds of times I have seen when an animal writhed in pain, and thereby deranged the tissues, during a deliberate dissection; instead of being soothed, it would receive a slap and an angry order to be quiet and behave itself. At other times, when an animal had endured great pain for hours without struggling or giving more than an occasional low whine, instead of letting the poor mangled wretch loose to crawl painfully about the place in reserve for another day's torture, it would receive pity so far that it would be said to have behaved well enough to merit death, and as a reward would be killed at once by breaking up the medulla, or "pithing," as this operation was called. I have often heard the professor [Bernard] say, when one side of an animal had been so mangled, and the tissues so obscured by clotted blood, that it was difficult to find the part searched for, "Why don't you begin on the other side?" or "Why don't you take another dog? What is the use of being so economical?" One of the most revolting features in this laboratory was the custom of giving an animal on which the professor had completed his experiment, and which still had some time left, to the assistants to practice the finding of arteries, nerves, etc., in the living animal, or for performing what are called fundamental experiments upon it—in other words, repeating those which are recommended in the laboratory handbooks...Having drunk the cup to the dregs, I cry off, and am prepared to see not only science, but even mankind, perish rather than have recourse to such means of saving it. I hope that we shall soon have Government inquiry into the subject, in which experimental physiologists shall only be witnesses, not judges. Let all private vivisection be made criminal, and all experiments be placed under Government inspection, and we may have some clearing-away of abuses that the Anatomy Act caused in similar circumstances.[4]

Hoggan's letter created an uproar. According to Cobbe, it provoked reactions of horror and aversion in English readers, generating a wave of protests.[5] Back in France, Bernard made no effort to ignore the critics. He had already defended his position ten years earlier in his book *An introduction to the study of experimental medicine* where he wrote: "Have we the right to make experiments on animals and vivisect them? As for me, I think we have this right, wholly and absolutely. No hesitation is possible; the science of life can be established only through experiment, and we can save living beings from death only after sacrificing others."[6]

The cellars of France where the animals were kept while they waited to be experimented upon were miserable, dark, unhealthy places and were provided by an impecunious College of Medicine to its faculty, which included Dr. Bernard.

One person who clearly agreed with Dr. Hoggan's assessment of the famous vivisector's experiments was Bernard's wife, Marie Francois Martin. A wealthy woman whom Bernard is thought to have married to support his work, she reproached her husband for his cruelty to animals and separated from him in 1870 because of it.[7] Marie was joined by her two daughters, much to her husband's dismay, and they became dedicated antivivisectionists, founding the first antivivisection society in France. The trio of women took in stray dogs from the streets of Paris and did their best to rescue "experimental animals, especially dogs." [8] One of Bernard's daughters would eventually use part of her inheritance to found a hospital for dogs and cats in an effort to make up for what she regarded as the crimes of her father.[9]

Bernard admitted that his research was mostly curiosity driven. "The experiment itself supplies me with the key questions," he said.[10] The novelist Silas Weir Mitchell (1829-1914), who became famous for his novels and for a rest cure, studied with Bernard for a year in 1850 and remembered these words his teacher spoke. "Why think when you can experiment. Exhaust experiment and then think."[11]

For Bernard cruelty toward animals was a necessity for the benefit of human beings.

> Experiments on animals, with deleterious substances or in harmful circumstances, are very useful and entirely conclusive for the toxicity and hygiene of man. Investigations of medicinal or of toxic substances also are wholly applicable to man from the therapeutic point of view.[12]

Bernard had no respect for animals and was a pioneer guru of vivisection for the scientists of the 20th century who would follow. He made animal experimentation a part of the scientific method but did not subject the foundation or the rationale for animal experiments to scientific testing, that is that animals were suitable subjects for experimentation because they were nonrational, nonfeeling creatures who experienced little pain. The assumption that this was true was good enough for him. By the time of his death in 1878 Bernard was the most famous physiologist in the world. He was given a national funeral in France.

In the same year of Bernard's death, the German Robert Koch (1843-1910), who in 1882 would discover the bacteria that caused tuberculosis, was busy inoculating animals with different substances in order to produce various infections in them in his studies on wound infection.[13] The next major impetus for using animals in the study of medicine, however, would come in 1885 from a competitor of Koch when, after five years of work on the project, Louis Pasteur (1822-1895) developed a vaccine for rabies.

Pasteur was well acquainted with the work of Bernard and had known him personally during his life. In fact, Bernard had participated in one of Pasteur's experiments in which Bernard "took some blood from a dog." Pasteur and Bernard had also worked together in 1865 when a cholera scare hit Paris. But it was in the following year that the close friendship between the two scientists would become a matter of public record which would reveal how united they were in their beliefs in animal research, though, as shall become evident, the pain inflicted upon unconsenting animals was disturbing to Pasteur.

Bernard had taken ill from a serious, life-threatening gastric condition for which his doctors could find no cure. Concerned for the health of his friend, Pasteur wrote a review of Bernard's work and achievements for the Moniteur Universel, a newspaper which placed an emphasis on literature, science, and art. The tribute appeared in the November 7, 1866 issue of the Moniteur and was titled "Claude Bernard: the Importance of his Works, Teaching and Method."[14]

In the review Pasteur described Bernard's famous book on animal experiments, *Introduction to the Study of Experimental Medicine*, as follows:

Nothing so complete, so profound, so luminous has ever been written on the true principles of the difficult art of experimentation....This book will exert an immense influence on medical science, its teaching, its progress, its language even.

As for his friendship with Bernard, Pasteur had this to say:

I might have spoken of the man in everyday life, the colleague who has inspired so many with a solid friendship, for I should seek in vain for a weak point in M. Bernard; it is not to be found. His personal distinction, the noble beauty of his physiognomy, his gentle kindliness attract at first sight; he has no pedantry, none of a scientist's usual faults, but an antique simplicity, a perfectly natural and unaffected manner, while his conversation is deep and full of ideas.

By the time Pasteur was putting the finishing touches on his review, however, Bernard had started to recover. After informing the reader that Bernard was on the mend Pasteur added these reflections:

May the publicity now given to these thoughts and feelings cheer the illustrious patient in his enforced idleness, and assure him of the joy with which his return will be welcomed by his friends and colleagues.

Bernard received the homage the next day and was thrilled. He wrote to Pasteur as follows:

My dear friend, I received yesterday the Moniteur containing the superb article you have written about me. Your great praise indeed makes me proud, though I feel I am yet very far from the goal I would reach....In the meanwhile it is a very precious encouragement to

97

me to be approved and praised by a man such as you. Your works have given you a great name, and have placed you in the first rank among experimentalists of our time. The admiration which you profess for me is indeed reciprocated; and we must have been born to understand each other, for true science inspires us both with the same passion and the same sentiments.

While the two joyous scientists embraced each other exulting in their friendship and congratulating each other for their contributions to science, Bernard's dogs waited in the miserable, dark cellars unaware of the fate that would soon befall them once Monsieur Bernard had fully recovered from his illness. It is safe to conclude that unlike Monsieur Pasteur, they were not attracted by Bernard's "gentle kindliness."

Perhaps it was from observations of the vast distance in understanding between humans and animals as portrayed by the scene just described that prompted the Nobel Prize winner in literature, Isaac Bashevis Singer, to famously proclaim: "In relation to animals, all people are Nazis; for the animals, it is an eternal Treblinka."[15]

Rabies is an ancient disease contracted by the bite of an animal infected with the disease that dates back more than 2000 years. The disease attacks the central nervous system including the spinal cord and the brain. It has never posed a threat for most individuals, and few people are ever bitten by a rabid animal. But in the 19th century, there was no cure for the disease and attacks did occur. In London, for example, 29 rabies deaths were reported in just the first few weeks of 1877.[16] A bite from a rabies-infected animal meant seizures, paralysis, and hallucinations followed by certain death. Being attacked by an insane animal with its teeth barred and hypersalivating was a fearsome image to contemplate and everyone was familiar with the disease and its symptoms. At this point in his life, Pasteur had already made several important discoveries and was well known to the public for inventing the procedure that would eventually bear his name, "pasteurization." He had conducted the first pasteurization test with Claude Bernard

98

in 1862. But the rabies vaccine Pasteur developed in 1885, which proved effective in treating a 9 year old boy, roused the public's imagination anew. The country showed its gratitude by showering Pasteur with even greater fame. By the turn of the 20th century, hardly a city in France did not have a street named after Louis Pasteur.

In developing his rabies vaccine Pasteur conducted experiments such as injecting tissue from rabies-infected cow brains into the heads of rabbits.[17] But it was not his first incursion into animal testing. By the 1860s he was already using dogs in experiments to develop sterile techniques for dressing wounds, and between 1878 and 1883 used animals in working on an anthrax vaccine for cattle, a cholera vaccine for chickens, and a swine fever vaccine for pigs.[18]

In order to understand Pasteur in relation to animal research it is necessary to take note of the kind of scientific environment into which he was thrust and the personality he brought to the workplace as he battled for success.

Unlike Dr. Bernard, Pasteur was far from enamored of vivsecting animals. On the contrary, he was reportedly squeamish about performing animal experiments and would not do some of them. He was certainly aware that animals had to endure considerable pain in his experiments which he sought to mitigate. This is apparent from the suggestion he made to the Academie of Sciences in 1874 that they conduct an experiment using animals for the purpose of "demonstrating the evil influence of ferments and protoorganisms in the suppuration of wounds" and that in this experiment that they should use chloroform. [Chloroform as an anesthesia, along with ether, was being used in surgical procedures beginning from around the mid 19th century.]

> I would make two identical wounds on the two symmetrical limbs of an animal under chloroform…. Finally, I should like to cut open a wound on an animal under choloroform…[19]

Here Pasteur revealed the same moral concerns about subjecting animals to unwanted painful experiments that some of his vivisecting predecessors had expressed in the 18th century. Like them, Pasteur, also forged ahead because he was convinced of the benefit to human beings his work accomplished in spite of misgivings for the cruelty his experiments inflicted upon innocent, unconsenting animals.

To whatever extent Pasteur may have pondered the morality of vivisection he must have quickly set it aside. It would not have been easy for any serious scientist to question vivisection to any significant degree in the middle of the highly charged battles for success in which scientists contended in the mid to late 19th century in Europe. Further, Pasteur was not averse to competing vigorously in support of his work or to the recognition and fame that came his way, as revealed in his letters showing a side that was "unabashedly ambitious and opportunistic."[20] Unrestrained and aggressive in pressing his points of view, Pasteur so insulted an 80-year-old surgeon over his surgical procedures, that the surgeon challenged Pasteur to a duel. In another public fight, Pasteur charged that an experimental error by the veterinary school of Turin had undermined confidence in his vaccine. The school denied the charge and accused Pasteur of being like a "duelist who challenges all those who dare to contradict him….but who has the habit of choosing the weapons and of obliging his adversaries to fight with their hands tied." [21]

One of Pasteur's competitor's for the spotlight in the development of the anthrax vaccine was Robert Koch. Pasteur tended to minimize Koch's contributions, though they were necessary for his own success in developing his vaccine. (Both Koch and Pasteur were credited with the development of the germ theory of disease.)[22] During the 1880s the two scientists engaged in a rancorous public debate arising from personal rivalries over who deserved credit in developing the anthrax vaccine. Chauvinistic grudges related to the Franco-Prussian War of 1870-1871 may also have played a part.[23] Pasteur blamed Koch and his pupils for a multitude of errors arising from their inexperience while the Koch side claimed that Pasteur's procedures produced contaminated vaccine cultures for anthrax.

In 1881 Pasteur gave a public demonstration of his anthrax vaccine in which he used two groups of animals, each consisting of 24 sheep, a goat, and 6 cows. He vaccinated one of the groups with the anthrax vaccine. Later he injected both groups with live anthrax. All animals in the vaccinated group survived, but in the second group, the 24 sheep and the goat died within two days. The 6 cows survived but were noticeably sick. While the demonstration was a public relations success, when it came time to report the results for his anthrax and cholera vaccines to the Academie de Médicine, Pasteur is thought to have deliberately withheld some information pertaining to the "degree of protection of the vaccine."[24] Such an "oversight" could have resulted from the combative atmosphere in which Pasteur found himself engaged.

The competitive fight for results and recognition in the scientific battles of Louis Pasteur and his opponents in the late 19th century overshadowed the suffering of animals who were sacrificed to test the theories over which these battles were fought. At this point in the history of humankind, animals had been shuffled far down the ladder of status to where few people expressed any opposition to the confinement of these animals in the dark and barren cellars of animal researchers without consideration for the animals' welfare. For those researchers who did feel any compassion, such as shown by Louis Pasteur's instructions to use chloroform in his wounds suppuration experiments, that sympathy was smothered by the competitive atmosphere that had developed among scientists in late 19th century Europe. This was the feature that would continue to expand as the primary controlling factor in animal research in the 20th and 21st centuries as scientists vied for top money grants, prestigious awards that many hoped would lead to the Nobel prize, and peer recognition. It has served to keep animals in their niche, each lost in a monochromistic background of millions of other indistinguishable living creatures available for instant use by animal researchers who, with their patron universities, biomedical research institutions, private medical facilities, and other institutions compete for huge sums of money doled out by the NIH and other government agencies.

For people who, like Claude Bernard, believe that animals were designed to be experimented upon in animal research laboratories without mercy for the benefit of humankind, the animal research industry serves as a model of scientific achievement that expresses medicine's highest standards and ideals. For those who believe that this industry amounts to little more than a money-producing machine fed by innocent animals and run by materialists seriously constrained in their capacity to comprehend the profound unity of life, it represents a dark and foreboding place where the light of true scientific reason has never shone.

Chapter 9

The New Era
A Portrait of Animal Research as it Exists Today

The push for medical knowledge supplied by animal research as promoted by animal research champions like Claude Bernard alongside the animal experiments of scientists such as Louis Pasteur and Robert Koch (and by Physiologists in England and other parts of Europe) was the first salvo launching a new age in animal research that would grow into the huge animal research industry of the 20th century that is still on display today. The ensuing research in 1907 of Paul Ehrlich (1854-1915) in which he used animals en masse in developing the drug Salvarsan 606 to treat syphilis, the worst sexually transmitted disease in the history of humankind prior to AIDS, signaled that the history of animal research centered around the study of anatomy had drawn to a close.

One of the most striking features that distinguished animal research in the new age from the past was the significant increase in the number of animals experimented upon. Pasteur had already used hundreds of animals in developing his rabies vaccine and Magendie was reported to have used 8,000 dogs in experiments investigating the Englishman Charles Bell's theory of nerves.[1] Then Ehrlich who, incidentally, was a close friend of Koch, used thousands of mice in developing his drug Salvarsan 606 for the cure of syphilis.[2] This was the trend. By the mid-twentieth century, Jonas Salk and Albert Sabin were using millions of monkeys in developing their polio vaccines.

Animal research from the 20th century forward has been marked by a huge expansion of government supported animal research projects. Crafted largely for the benefit of universities, private medical facilities, biomedical research institutions (AIDS, toxicity, and primate research facilities, etc.), the government, and the corporate world of pharmaceutical companies and other special interests, government funded animal research today is "socialism" at its best costing the taxpayers billions of dollars every year. Whereas at the start of the 20th century the government provided only about $10,000 annually for research in nutrition, today the National Institutes of Health (NIH) spends a reported $28 billion for medical research. An estimated twenty billion dollars of that money goes for animal research.[3] And while the NIH is the major donor for animal research, several other government agencies also fund animal testing. These include the Consumer Product Safety Commission, the Department of Defense, the Department of Energy, The Department of Transportation, the Environmental Protection Agency, the Food and Drug Administration, the National Aeronautics and Space Administration (NASA), the National Institute of Environmental Health Sciences, the National Institute for Occupational Safety and Health, the National Toxicology Program, and the Occupational Health and Safety Administration.[4]

At first, the new focus in animal research was for medicines, drugs, and treatments in the cure for disease such as trying to discover a vaccine to treat polio. But as more and more money became available, animals started being used for non-medical purposes. Today, government supported and corporate sponsored animal research is used to test for almost anything related to human interests, including space travel. Research involves testing on consumer products like household cleansers and cosmetics such as lipsticks and eye makeup (this research includes rubbing corrosive substances on animals' skin and dripping caustic chemicals into their eyes); weapons and military research (this research includes shooting and blowing up animals and exposing them to toxins, gasses, chemical bacteria, severe burns, and deadly viruses); surgical experiments (trying out high risk surgical procedures on animals such as for heart and brain surgery); psychology (causing animals to suffer depression, despair, hopelessness, and fear); cognition studies (manipulating the brains of animals to determine the effects on sensory systems, cognitive ability, and behavior);

104

brain damage research (this research includes using electric shocks and food deprivation); maternity research (this research involves maternal deprivation studies separating babies from their mothers); addiction testing (addicting animals through forced inhalation, forced feeding, forced infusion, and forcing animals to eat food that contains alcohol); and space travel research (subjecting animals to antigravity and microgravity conditions through various procedures which has included cutting off the tails of monkeys and putting them in straight-jackets with restraining rings screwed into their skulls and various electrodes implanted throughout their bodies before sending them into space, and suspending newborn rats upside down from their legs for periods of up to 45 days to explore the affects of anti-gravity on muscle atrophy).[5] Many other kinds of experiments have been done and are being done.

It takes a multitude of animals and animal researchers to use up more than 20 billion dollars supplied by the government, so animal researchers are free to invent research projects to try to answer questions about nearly anything no matter how unorthodox or bizarre it may be. Drawing from an enormous pool of available animals, millions of whom are genetically engineered, specific animal research projects in the 21st century vary widely. Favorites consist of confinement experiments (San Diego State University, Colorado State University, the University of Arizona College of Medicine, and many others) in which researchers stuff animals into tubes so small that the animals cannot move a muscle. These are done, purportedly to test for stress, though it takes little imagination to design tests for stress without using animals. Other tests have been done such as trying to find out how the brain instructs the eyes to control the center of gaze.[6] In that particular experiment, conducted at the University of Connecticut, the researcher drilled holes into the skulls of monkeys and then attached tiny steel coils directly into the monkeys' eyes. Two monkeys died as a result. At least this researcher was reprimanded and forced to abandon the project, though there are seldom any consequences to pay for experiments gone wrong.

Researchers copy each other in order to find projects to do. For example, a researcher at the University of California San

Francisco also likes to implant coils into primates eyes. Like the researcher at the University of Connecticut, this researcher claims he is studying the neurological activity of monkeys in Alzheimer's research, though his work has been soundly discredited by a highly reputable neuroscientist.[7]

Anything goes today, including sexual stimulation of the genitalia of female animals (Columbia University, Dartmouth College, and the University of Virginia) to test whether this produces pleasure for the animals.[8] The National Institute of Mental Health likes to do castration experiments on monkeys in aggression tests. Other favorites include forced heart attacks on monkeys and dogs (University of Connecticut Health Center and Ohio University). Other researchers damage animals' brains in order to put the animals into spin chairs to test spin reactions to brain damage (Johns Hopkins University). Rotating chairs is also a favorite at Emory University where a researcher subjects animals to rotation in high decibel sound experiments.

Addiction testing is especially lucrative for many animal research laboratories. Claiming they are performing a service for humanity by doing nicotine addiction testing for infants, researchers conduct experiments that involve implanting nicotine pumps in the backs of female primates, impregnating them, and then after the mothers give birth, taking away their babies for testing. (Oregon Health and Science University) This drives the mothers nearly insane with grief, and the separation from their mothers terrorizes the infants.[9,10] Addicting monkeys to cocaine and heroin and then subjecting the animals to forced withdrawal is another experiment researchers like to do. (Harvard University and the University of Minnesota).[11] Addiction researchers and their sponsoring universities seem oblivious to the simple fact that by any standard of justice it is unfair to require animals to pay for the addiction problems human beings have created for themselves. This subject will be more fully explored in chapter 16.

In spite of the estimates previously provided, exactly how many millions of animals are experimented upon every year cannot be calculated with a degree of accuracy that satisfies anyone. This is mostly because 85% of experiments are done upon mice, rats, and birds for which no registration is required with the United States Department of Agriculture. These animals are not protected under the provisions of the Animal Welfare Act and therefore no accounting for them is required. Credit for their exclusion goes to the National Association for Biomedical Research and its founder, lobbyist Frankie Trull, who convinced the late ultra conservative Senator from the State of North Carolina, Jessie Helms, to sponsor an amendment to a farm subsidy act that excluded mice, rats, and birds under the definition of animals. The amendment removed these animals from the provisions of the Animal Welfare Act, which was passed by the U.S. Congress in 2002 without a vote. As it presently stands, because of this amendment, the Animal Welfare Act has consigned millions of animals to unsupervised experiments costing them suffering beyond all imagination. Animal researchers are free to do whatever they want with these animals with no legal restraints.

With so much money floating about as an enticement for animal research, hundreds of universities, biomedical research institutions, private medical facilities, and other institutions have opened animal research laboratories to go after their share of those very big government tax dollars. These institutions get hundreds of millions of dollars every year from the NIH to conduct animal research as typified by the following list. University of California, Los Angeles, $194,110,000. University of California, San Francisco, $203,196,000. Harvard University, $441,273,869. Johns Hopkins University, $256,886,000. Yale University, $199,066,000. Stanford University, $164,374,000. Vanderbilt University, $170,982,000. Emory University, $239,303,364. Duke University, $162,309,000. Baylor University, $173,047,000. University of Pennsylvania, $256,060,000. University of Wisconsin, Madison, $141,655,452. University of Washington, Seattle, $418,889,748. University of Michigan, $216,825,000.[12]

With the growing awareness of how the animal research industry operates, American universities are increasingly being accused of moral corruption and being blinded by dollars for participating in and encouraging institutionalized animal cruelty.

The animal research industry may be accurately described as a huge money dispensing machine fueled by the abuse and suffering of innocent animals that pays huge dividends for those who are plugged into it but provides far too little to justify its existence when examined objectively. Public relations intended to conceal the true nature of animal research are a part of the animal research enterprise and keep the industry feeling good about itself and the world feeling good about it. Closer inspection, however, soon uncovers just how few benefits animal research really has provided for humankind after experimenting upon billions of animals for over a century. In many instances this research has caused enormous harm to the people of America and the citizens of the world. This is the topic for discussion in the next chapter.

Chapter 10

The British Booklet:
Dissecting The Big Lie Piece by Piece

What is alleged in defence of those hateful practices, everyone knows; but the truth is, that by knives, fire, and poison, knowledge is not always sought and is very seldom attained. The experiments that have been tried, are tried again; he that burned an animal with irons yesterday, will be willing to amuse himself with burning another tomorrow. I know not, that by living dissections any discovery has been made by which a single malady is more easily cured. And if the knowledge of physiology has been somewhat increased, he surely buys knowledge dear, who learns the use of lacteals at the expense of his humanity. It is time that universal resentment should arise against these horrid operations, which tend to harden the heart, extinguish those sensations which give man confidence in man, and make the physician more dreadful than the gout or stone."

Samuel Johnson: Idler #17 (August 5, 1758)[1]

From around 1975 forward critics of animal research began assembling evidence and building the necessary momentum to challenge the necessity for animal research. Many animal rights organizations formed rising rapidly in prominence through undercover investigations and whistle-blower reports which put the systemic abuse of animals in animal research laboratories squarely in the public's eye. Shocking instances of animal cruelty were exposed such as vivisectors at the University of Wisconsin who were videotaped mocking and laughing at primates upon whom they were performing head trauma experiments. A vivisector at the

University of North Carolina was caught on film beheading an unanesthetized mouse with a pair of scissors while saying "Say Bye-Bye." Countless examples of extreme cruelty taking place at university animal research laboratories continued to be brought to light with each passing year.[2] Some of the more infamous reports included the cocaine tests done at New York University in which chimpanzees were locked inside cocaine smoke-filled refrigerators. Another researcher at this university subjected primates to a continuous three hour-long studio-generated sound that was10 decibels louder than a shotgun blast. At Columbia University, researchers removed one eye from baboons in experiments attempting to induce strokes before abandoning them in cages without care or painkillers. These researchers also implanted metal pipes in monkeys' craniums in useless menstrual stress studies. At Rockefeller University in New York City, researchers locked cats in stereotaxic frames and severed their brains from their spinal cords after which they discontinued anesthesia in senseless so-called "fictive" (feigned) vomit experiments in which they also forced cats to vomit 97 times in the space of three and one-half minutes.

The suffering the animals in the above described experiments endured ended only when they died from the effects of the experiments or when the researchers killed them. The experiments themselves contributed nothing to science or medical knowledge though they did furnish well-paid employment for the researchers and a safe environment where they could give free reign to their curiosity and publish self-congratulatory papers and books implying they had made useful contributions to science.

Increased protests and antivivisection activities forced vivisectors into a corner from which they could no longer evade answering public concerns that they were abusing animals without moral, intellectual, or spiritual justification and that their conduct toward animals was all too often little more than thinly veiled cruelty-for-pay. Animal researchers suddenly found that they could no longer mold the public into a compliant receptor of their views as more and more people disagreed that animals were unconscious, unfeeling things. People keep dogs, cats, hamsters, rabbits, goats, sheep, pigs, monkeys, snakes, parrots, mice, rats, guinea pigs, lizards, donkeys, horses, and all kinds of nonhuman animals as companion animals in their homes or on their property where they grow to care and love them and are loved by them in return. These nonhuman animals teach people what animal researchers deny: that animals are conscious, intelligent, sentient beings who possess inherent rights that deserve to be acknowledged and respected just as human beings acknowledge and respect their own self-established rights.

The change in public attitudes has made an impact on the way science and academia view animal research. Renowned animal research advocate Professor Peter Carruthers described the change as follows:

> The dominant position in both philosophy and psychology throughout much of the Twentieth Century was that animals aren't capable of genuine thought.... Animal behavior was believed to be the product of conditioning.... But the adequacy of the account has been crumbling rapidly since at least the nineteen eighties.[3]

(Professor Carruthers will be profiled in later chapters of this book for his work on theories of animal consciousness.)

In spite of the citizen-led effort to end vivisection and animal research, the animal research industry continued to expand. As described briefly before, it is now a multibillion-dollar, government-funded, closed-door industry involving government, corporate, and university laboratories serviced by and in conjunction with private subsidiary companies such as cage and animal food manufacturers, lab equipment manufacturers, animal breeders, animal dealers, animal transporters, chemical companies, pharmaceutical companies, and many others. This is the empire fueled by public funding which animal researchers and their university, medical center, and other institutional sponsors are anxious to sustain. It is a way of life in which the effort aimed at eradicating disease is only a minor component. The primary purpose is to provide high paying careers for those members of the educated class willing to sign on to a philosophical belief system founded on killing animals. Its continuance is assured through the steady stream of money from the public treasury provided to the government agencies, universities, and corporate institutions which support it backed by various rationales that it contributes to human welfare.

One of the primary methods animal researchers employ for maintaining their status is by extolling the accomplishments of animal research. Animal research lobbying groups such as Americans for Medical Progress trumpet medical advances purportedly made by experimenting upon animals such as the discovery of anesthesia and insulin and the development of the polio vaccine.[4] But claims such as these are often disputable, habitually exaggerated, and frequently prove to be false upon closer examination. It is well documented, for example, that anesthesia was discovered from observations of the effects of pain-killing drugs on human beings, not through animal research. It started when Crawford Williamson Long (1815-1878) observed a man take a heavy fall which caused him no pain after inhaling ether at an ether party. Long translated his observations of the party drug into surgical anesthesia in 1842 when he removed a tumor from the neck of a young man to whom he gave ether to stifle the pain. The young physician got the results he anticipated. His patient experienced no pain during the operation.

Insulin was discovered by a more indirect route but also required no animal research, though animals did play an unwitting and unnecessary role. It began in 1788 when Thomas Crawley discovered the relationship between pancreatic damage and diabetes through autopsies on diabetic patients. His work was eventually followed by that of Dr. Moses Barron who in 1920, while observing the human pancreas, noticed that diabetes resulted from damage to the islets of Langerhans ("islands" of cells in the pancreas which regulate blood sugar levels to maintain normal functioning). This was a very different observation from the one wrongly made by the famous French animal researcher Dr. Bernard (see chapter 8) who mistakenly attributed diabetes to liver damage. Baron wrote a paper on what he had discovered titled "The relation of the islets of Langerhans to diabetes with special reference to cases of pancreatic lithiasis." Based on Barron's observations, Frederick Banting (1891-1941), working with Charles Best (1899-1978), created an extract that contained insulin and in 1922 injected it into a diabetic patient, a young boy aged 14, which resulted in a remarkable turnaround of the disease.[5]

In discovering insulin, Banting first experimented on live dogs and was able to produce a crude form of insulin. But the only reason he experimented on dogs was that he felt obligated to use them because the University of Toronto had donated them for his use along with a laboratory for the purpose of testing his theories. Banting was a complete unknown and grateful for the opportunity. But Banting loved dogs and hated experimenting on them. He was soon relieved of the loathsome practice when he realized that he could extract pure insulin tissue from the pancreases of embryonic calves without experimenting on dogs.[6] Thus his experiments upon live dogs were never necessary and no research on live animals was ever required to produce insulin. Banting also would never have discovered insulin if he had not come across Baron's paper based on observations of the islets of Langerhans, which Baron also discovered with no reliance on animals. It was only after reading and rereading Baron's paper that Banting was inspired to start his own work searching for a cure for diabetes.[7]

Contrary to claims made by Americans for Medical Progress, the discovery of anesthesia and insulin should not be credited to animal research. In fact, the discovery of insulin represents a perfect example of how animal research on live animals is often used to try to discover something for which animals are never required to begin with. Concerning the case Americans for Medical Progress and other animal research advocates like to make about the importance of animal research in the development of the polio vaccine, the devastating effects this research has had on humanity will be discussed in the next section.

As a model for the kinds of exaggerations and fabrications animal researchers make in order to promote the benefits of vivisection, a good example for reference is a sleek British publication put out in 2007 by an alliance of some of the top medical organizations in the United Kingdom such as the Academy of Medical Sciences, the Association of the British Pharmaceutical Industry, GlaxoSmithKline, Laboratory Animal Science Association, Lilly, the Physiological Society, the Royal College of Physicians, the Society for Endocrinology, and many others. The booklet is titled *Medical Advances and Animal Research: The contribution of animal science to the medical revolution: some case histories.*[8]

The purpose of this impressively titled, handsome looking British publication is to try to prove that the longer life and better health which people can look forward to in today's world can be directly attributed to animal research. The claims made in this publication, however, are based on exaggeration, misstatements of fact, blurring of the truth, false statements, misrepresentations, and a disregard for evidence that points to far different conclusions.

The obfuscation in the British Booklet begins immediately when it states that among ten medical advances that have changed the world "Blood transfusion has saved the lives of countless people and animals. The technique was developed when citrated blood was shown to be safe for transfusion in dogs in 1914." From this brief description the reader is expected to conclude that the success of blood transfusion is directly accounted for by animal research. But this tells only one small part of the story. What gets omitted is the part about the repulsive blood transfusion experiments animal researchers performed over several centuries as they groped their way through a sea of wild guesses in attempting to figure out how to transfuse blood. This also included experimenting on intellectually disabled children in the year 1660. Less than a decade later in the late 1660s, blood transfusion experiments turned out to be so dangerous that they were suspended for 150 years in France after Dr. Jean-Baptiste Denis, a royal physician to King Louis XIV, transfused the blood from a sheep into a human and then the blood of a calf into another human.. Both patients died as a consequence. Even during the 19th century after blood transfusions had begun to be performed with greater success, many people still died from the procedure because the discovery and need for blood group compatibility had yet to be understood. While the toxicity of sodium citrate, which was used to prevent clotting of preserved

114

blood, was tested on dogs in 1914, like the British Booklet states, the main features of blood transfusion that have made it safe and effective did not require the use of animals.[9] These included the discovery of blood types, cross checking of blood between patients and donors, and the breaking down of plasma into different components and products, a chemical process. As for using dogs to test sodium citrate, it is difficult to believe that scientists could not have devised tests for toxicity that did not require the use of animals if they had been willing to address the challenge instead of taking the most obvious and easiest way out, which was to rely upon animals to test for toxicity.

The exaggerations in the British Booklet continue without pause. In the "Introduction," a quote from a Royal Society position paper on animal research dating from September 2006 states that "From antibiotics and insulin to blood transfusions and treatments for cancer or HIV, virtually every medical achievement in the past century has depended directly or indirectly on research on animals." Once again the reader is expected to swallow the hyperbole without question. Of course, if the statement were true, how could even the most radical opponents of animal research make a case against animal research based on the success or failure of the actual research itself that anyone would accept as credible? When this statement is taken apart and tested for accuracy, however, it turns out to be 100% false and an intentional misrepresentation of the truth.

The first thing that meets the eye is that the statement is presented without citations or evidence to support the claim. Upon investigation, it turns out that the primary clause in this statement, "virtually every medical achievement in the past century has depended directly or indirectly on research on animals," is also contained in an earlier position paper put out by the Royal Society in January of 2002, which also offered no proof or citations to back the statement. Robert A.J. Matthews, a reader at the Aston University of Information Engineering in Birmingham, England, has pointed out that the statement appears to have originated as nothing more than an unsupported contention made in a one page statement put out by the Public Health Service of the United States Department of Health and Human Services in 1994. It was published in the *Physiologist* and was titled "The Importance of Animals in Biomedical and Behavioral Research."[10], [11] There, stated in its entirety, the article opens with the sentence that reads "Virtually every medical achievement of the last century has depended directly or indirectly on research with animals." Except for a change in a preposition or two, this is the exact same quote cited above in the British Booklet and also in the Royal Society position paper, both, like the original source, presented with no references to support the claim.[12] The Royal Society simply copied it in order to create its own declaration in support of animal research and the British Booklet did the same, though from what source these organizations obtained their copies cannot be determined here since they are not cited.

This unfounded statement has circulated widely. After the Royal Society picked it up, it was then copied by The House of Lords in a July 16, 2002 report titled "Select Committee on Animals in Scientific Procedures."[13] Following this report, the now defunct Research Defense Society copied the declaration which it published in a 2005 paper titled "Declaration on Animals in Research." The declaration was cosigned by three Nobel Prize winners (Sir Paul Nurse, Dr. Tim Hunt, and Sir John Sulston); 500 British and 200 non-British scientists, among whom were 190 Fellows of the Royal Society and the Medical Royal Colleges; and 250 professors.[14] The declaration contained the same phrase word for word claiming that "virtually every medical achievement of the last century has depended directly or indirectly on research with animals." As this brief investigation proves, this statement turns out to be nothing but an unreferenced declaration that a fourth grader could have made up. Yet these prestigious medical experts, including the three Nobel Prize Winners, signed this unsupportable declaration. It was once more a case of that class referred to before known as "The Great Assumers" assuming that what they wanted to be true was true. All of the signatories signed this declaration without ever checking its veracity in the hopes of trying to get the public to assume the same thing that they assumed, that "virtually every medical achievement of the last century has depended directly or indirectly on research with animals." This must be called what it was and still is today: a pipe dream and a lie.

A search of the internet reveals that this fictitious statement continues to be used today by pro-animal research advocates such as *Animal Research for Life,* a website sponsored by the European Federation of Pharmaceutical Industries and Associations.[15] Institutions as diverse as the Center for Veterinary Health Services at Oklahoma State University also cite the quote. This university found a novel and equally disingenuous way of using it by citing it as though it is a quote from an authoritative source—the Public Health Service. Printing the phrase in a caption above a pastoral photo of cows and attributing the quote to the Public Health Service, the university then assures the public directly below the photo that Oklahoma State University "provides a humane and compliant environment for all animals involved in research, teaching, and testing activities."[16] As we have just seen, however, the Public Health Service supplied no references to support their fictitious claim that "Virtually every medical achievement of the last century has depended directly or indirectly on research with animals."

That this statement is fictitious should be apparent to any-one who considers the many medical achievements made without animal research some of which are described in this chapter, and should also have been apparent to all signatories of the statement including the three Nobel Prize winners, the 250 professors, and the 190 signers of the declaration from the Fellows of the Royal Society and the Medical Royal Colleges.

The British Booklet makes many other unsubstantiated claims that turn out to be false. It heralds, for example, the discov-ery of penicillin and implies that it was developed because of animal research. This is what is says in its entirety about penicillin. "Florey and Chain [Howard Walter Florey (1998-1968) and Sir Ernst Boris Chain (1906-1979)] first tested the effects of penicillin in mice in 1940. By 1941, penicillin was being used to treat dying soldiers. This research won the Nobel Prize in 1945." The blurb is short and sweet with an air of authority that would associate the discovery of penicillin with animal research leading to the Nobel Prize. We are led to believe that if animal researchers had not experimented on mice, the wonderful drug penicillin, which has saved many lives, would never have been discovered. The award of the Nobel Prize seals the case and no further debate is required. But this paints a false portrait by ignoring what really happened in the discovery of penicillin.

Penicillin was discovered by accident by Sir Alexander Flemming (1881-1955) in 1929. He almost did not publicize his discovery because he found it to be ineffective after trying it out on rabbits. As a consequence, Flemming believed that his new antibiotic was a failure. He didn't know at the time that this was because rabbits excrete penicillin in their urine before it has an opportunity to take effect. Thus Flemming's animal tests on rabbits almost caused one of the greatest antibiotics ever to be discovered never to find its way into common use. In subsequent tests, however, Flemming tried out his new product on human beings which, under certain conditions, seemed to produce good results. He did no follow-ups, nevertheless, though he did publish a paper about his research. Nine years later Howard Florey stumbled onto the paper and was impressed enough to investigate further. Like Flemming, Florey also tested penicillin on humans and found it to be effective.[17] Florey, Ernst Chain, and also Flemming himself ended up working together to refine the antibiotic so that it could be mass produced for human use. In their work, Florey and Chain tested the antibiotic on mice because by then these tests were mandated by law.

It is clear that penicillin would have made its way into mainstream medicine without ever being tested on animals had animal testing not been required. In fact, if Flemming had chosen guinea pigs for his first tests he might have thrown out penicillin entirely because penicillin kills guinea pigs. It was only the tests on humans that encouraged and gave the necessary impetus forward to turn penicillin into the important antibiotic it became. These are facts acknowledged by Flemming himself who said: "How fortunate we didn't have these [legally mandated] animal tests in the 1940's, for penicillin would probably never have been granted a license, and possibly the whole field of antibiotics might never have been realized."

Florey said virtually the same thing:

Mice were used in the initial toxicity tests because of their small size, but what a lucky chance it was, for in this respect man is like the mouse and not the guinea-pig. If we had used guinea-pigs exclusively we should have said that penicillin was toxic, and we probably should not have proceeded to try and overcome the difficulties of producing the substance for trial in man.[18]

The only role animals played in the discovery of penicillin was confined strictly to being used as test objects as mandated by law. The *discovery* itself was made by Flemming without the use of animals.

The British Booklet claims that it was "Nobel Prize-winning research on guinea pigs in the 1940s [that] led to the antibiotic streptomycin," used to treat tuberculosis. But this is as misleading as the statement that implied penicillin was developed through animal research. The facts are that guinea pigs had nothing to do with the development of the streptomycin antibiotic. On the contrary, this drug was developed without and prior to any re-search on animals by Selman Abraham Waksman (1888-1973), who won the Nobel Prize in medicine in 1952 for having developed it, not for using guinea pigs in his "Nobel Prize-winning research," as the British booklet would have the reader believe.

It should be noted that Streptomycin can cause fatal reac-tions in animals such as gerbils, hamsters, rats, and mice.[19] Fortunately, when the researchers working on this project chose guinea pigs for their mandated tests they chose the right animal. Had they chosen gerbils or hamsters, or mice, or rats for their initial tests, the story of streptomycin may not have had such a favorable conclusion.

Waksman tested his new antibiotic drug in vitro (test tube) which showed its efficacy against the bacillus that caused tuberculosis. Only then was the antibiotic tested in vivo (in animals) using guinea pigs and only because these tests were obligatory.[20] So guinea pigs had nothing to do with the creation of streptomycin, and would not have been tested on animals without previous in vitro testing. As was the case with penicillin, streptomycin was tested on animals because it was required by law. Animal research was not necessary for the creation and use of this drug to treat tuberculosis.

If animal research had been rejected centuries earlier and if scientists had pursued the treatment for disease without using animals, the likelihood is high that they would have discovered the cures for the diseases that today animal researchers claim were only discovered because of animal research. In today's world, DNA comparisons, computer modeling, stem-cell research, and many other techniques have already replaced the need for using animals in testing for many drugs and suggest that animal research has never been necessary in finding cures for human disease.[21]

The editors of the British Booklet called on Professor Robert Winston to write the forward. Winston is a medical doctor, scientist, television presenter, and a politician who sits with the Labour Party in the House of Lords in London. He is also an enthusiastic animal research advocate. In his forward Winston wrote that "Polio would still claim hundreds of lives annually in Britain without the animal research of the Nobel laureate Albert Sabin."[22] This is another of those statements which exaggerate the positive while ignoring the negative. Sabin himself stated that many false leads and dangerous vaccines were produced along the way to inventing his vaccine for polio.[23] As for animals, it seems quite apparent that they were never really needed in the production of a polio vaccine.

In 1949, Dr. John Enders, Dr. Thomas H. Weller, and Dr. Frederick C. Robbins learned how to grow the polio virus in laboratory cultures of human tissue.[24] (Weller and Robbins were students of Enders at the time.) The tissue used was the discarded foreskins from circumcised baby boys.[25] The scientists also used

120

other discarded human tissue from operations on children and adults. For their efforts, these three scientists were awarded the Nobel Prize in medicine in 1954.

The discovery of how to grow the polio virus was the key to the creation of the polio vaccine that both Jonas Salk and Albert Sabin manufactured. It enabled Salk to develop a killed virus vaccine into a fully functional state by 1952 and to introduce it in a large nationwide field trial by 1954, while capturing the nation's attention and gratitude.[26] Sabin was also testing his oral polio vaccine on humans in a correctional facility in Ohio by 1954. Then in 1956, the Soviet Union picked up on it in a mass immunization program. Czechoslovakia and Mexico also embarked on large filed trials using the Sabine vaccine, though it was not approved for use in the United States until 1960.[27]

"Salk and Sabin were standing on the shoulders of Enders," noted Walt Schalick, a medical historian who is also a resident in pediatrics at Harvard-affiliated Children's Hospital and in physical medicine and rehabilitation at the Spaulding Rehabilitation Center.[28] The in vitro discoveries made by John Enders also paved the way for vaccines against "measles, German measles and mumps" and it contributed to "major advances in the fight against cancer and in genetics."[29]

In order verify that he had indeed isolated the polio vaccine, Enders reportedly injected his cell culture into mice and monkeys to see if it would produce polio's paralytic effects, which it did. It should be easy enough to see, however, that what Enders really required in order to test his discovery was not animals for verification purposes, but nonanimal, diagnostic tools for detecting viuses contained in the human tissue cultures he developed for testing. Since he did not have those tools, he relied upon animals. Today, while both human culture and monkey culture cell lines are used in culture virus detection, new viral diagnostic techniques are leaving these traditional culture diagnoses behind.[30] Any virus can now be potentially isolated through sensitive detection of specific viral nucleic acids (DNA), suggesting that "during the next decade, applications of nucleic acid detection techniques will drastically reshape the field of diagnostic virology."[31] Today, oral samples are

121

widely used for detecting viral nucleic acids. Gone are any days for injecting a deadly virus into an animal to test whether or not a researcher has been able to successfully isolate a specific virus as was the case with Enders.

The above example illustrates how the so-called requirement for using animals to test for human disease is greatly exaggerated. What is really needed is a more concentrated intellectual and creative focus on the problem under investigation. If animal researchers had spent the amount of time necessary honing in on the development of techniques for virus development and detection instead of just throwing millions of animals at the polio problem, animal testing would never have been required for developing a polio vaccine.

It has been estimated that Salk and Sabin used between one million and five million monkeys in developing their vaccines.[32] The facts now reveal, unfortunately, that it may have been the use of primates in polio research that is responsible for the creation of AIDS and the subsequent AIDS epidemic causing millions of deaths. Evidence also strongly suggests that the Salk vaccine may be responsible for causing millions of deaths from cancer with millions more yet to come. Without the reliance on animals for testing, a polio vaccine could have been developed much faster and the deadly side effects from the polio vaccine that have now come to light could have been avoided.

I

Was Animal Research the Cause of AIDS?

To fully investigate the polio story, it is necessary to look at the story of AIDS in relation to polio because AIDS serves as a prime example of the possible side-effects of animal research gone terribly wrong.

In general, the science community has accepted the theory that AIDS had its origin in a species of chimpanzees. This means that AIDS had to have been transferred to humans from chimpanzees at some point in time. The question to be examined is how the transference took place and when.

122

Other scientists besides Salk and Sabin were working to develop a polio vaccine in the 1950s and 1960s. One of these was Hilary Koprowski (b. 1916). Though the name of Koprowski is not as well known as Salk and Sabin, the trio of Salk, Sabin, and Koprowski were the big three working on the polio vaccine during this period and were the principle polio vaccination pioneers.

In 1999 the British journalist Edward Hooper suggested in his book *The River* that a batch of Koprowski's vaccine may have contained chimpanzee tissue contaminated with the AIDS virus. And, according to this theory, the transfer of the virus that causes AIDS may have occurred when Koprowski sprayed his oral polio vaccine into the mouths of 325,000 people living in the Congo in Africa between 1957 and 1960. All in all, over one million people were vaccinated with Koprowski's vaccine. What really gives Hooper's theory life, is that the first cases of AIDS occurred in the Congo in 1959 during the same period in which Koprowski was vaccinating people with his oral vaccine spray.

Koprowski denies that he ever used chimpanzee tissue in his vaccine and responded to criticisms in a letter to the editor printed in Science in 1992. [It might be noted that Koprowski never sued Hooper for making this claim, though he did sue Rolling Stones Magazine for reasons related to it.] In the same year the Wistar Institute, which handled some of Koprowski's vaccines, established an independent panel to investigate the claim and concluded that the probability of the Congo trials as being the source of AIDS was "extremely low."[33] But the Wistar Institute was the laboratory that prepared some of the vaccine for Koprowski to administer. Obviously, there was a conflict of interest. How much faith should be placed in the independence of this report when the investigation was conducted by an organization that was possibly involved? In addition, Wistar is a biomedical research institute that has its own animal facility that "provides services in laboratory animal medicine and husbandry, as well as routine animal procurement, inventory, and care, for all Wistar scientists using animals in their research." This is not an organization eager to admit any wrong doing related to animal research.

Criticized in 1999 for its failure for self-examination, Wistar agreed to allow three independent laboratories test stored samples of its polio vaccines that were used in the 1950s. The results were reported in 2000 at a meeting of the Royal Society and found no traces of SIV, HIV-1, or DNA to indicate that chimpanzee cells were used to prepare the vaccines. Wistar hailed the results and declared that:

> Taken together, the findings provide strong evidence to refute the theory that an oral polio vaccine prepared at The Wistar Institute and administered to people in the then Belgian Congo in the late 1950s provided the route of transmission for HIV or HIV-related viruses from chimpanzees to humans, as has been proposed by Mr. Edward Hooper in his book *The River* (Little, Brown and Co., 1999). [34]

However, only some of the vaccines stored by Wistar were tested and none were shown to be the vaccines that were administered to the people in the Congo. The investigation was also coordinated by Wistar which chose the laboratories that conducted the tests and provided $20,000 out of a total of $100,000 to help fund the study. This is not to question the autonomy of the laboratories, but surely, a far more thorough and independent investigation was called for.

More pertinent to the discussion, however, was that subsequent information emerged which showed that Koprowski had prepared some of his own vaccines in Africa none of which existed for testing in the year 1999 and none of which appears to have been sent to the Wistar laboratories at the time they were created. These could have contained chimpanzee tissue as seems possible from a 2004 documentary produced by the Canadian Broadcasting Corporation. The film confirmed Hooper's findings. Particularly damaging was an interview conducted with several members of Koprowski's original research team in the Congo. They repeatedly said that kidney tissue was taken from living chimpanzees and was used in producing the live polio vaccines. Further they described removing the organs from the tranquilized chimpanzees for that purpose.

The thesis that contaminated vaccines led to the AIDS epidemic is called the OPV (Oral Polio Vaccine) theory. In order to try to refute this theory, some scientists developed another theory holding that AIDS developed from bushmeat hunting in which hunters could incur bites or cuts while hunting and preparing killed chimpanzees for eating. (Bushmeat refers to meat taken from animals in the tropics of the Americas, Asia, and Africa.) These scientists theorized that this bushmeat was the means for AIDS transmission. But as Hooper noted immediately, if that was the case why had bush hunters not developed AIDS decades ago and not just during the period in which Koprowski administered his vaccine? The bushmeat theory continues, nevertheless, and scientists and scientific publications have disproportionately favored this side using their authority to slant the debate in favor of the bushmeat theory while doing their best to minimize the influence of the OPV argument. This becomes apparent in that bushmeat proponents blocked publications in scientific journals, failed to perform relevant scientific tests (in the 1990s), and tried to limit the screenings of an award-winning French/Canadian film, *The Origins of AIDS*, that showed both sides of the debate but leaned in favor of the OPV side.[35]

Brian Martin is a Professor of social sciences at the University of Wollongong, Australia, the author of 12 books and hundreds of articles on nonviolence, whistle blowing, and scientific controversies. He is also the vice president of Whistleblowers Australia and the author of a large website on the suppression of dissent. In regard to the scientific validity of the bushman theory, Martin had this to say:

> ...the bushmeat theory is so undeveloped that it is difficult to point to evidence supporting it. It is based on the assumption that SIV entered humans from chimpanzees via an unknown interaction, perhaps in the early 1900s in southern Cameroon, and that it then became transmissible in humans. It gives no expla-

nation for why this occurred so recently, given millions of years of human-chimp interaction, other than to assume AIDS remained localized and undetected until increased commerce and urbanization promoted spread of the disease. (However, commerce and mass movements of people in Africa go back centuries, including the slave trade.) It gives no explanation for the dates and locations of early HIV-positive blood samples and early AIDS cases and their apparent correlation with the dates and locations of Koprowski's African OPV trials.

Clearly, the OPV vs. bushmeat controversy is a debate that needs far greater public airing. In the meantime, many people continue to believe that Koprowski's spray of his polio vaccine into 325,000 human mouths and the 675,000 other people who took it may have been the mechanism responsible for the transference of the virus into humans and it is likely that this was the cause of the AIDS epidemic.

The British Booklet completely ignores the OPV/AIDS controversy but praises the "spectacular" success of science in finding new medicines leading to normal life expectancy for 40 million people living with HIV. Statements like these also ignore the fact that no cure for AIDS has yet been found, and the attempts to find a cure through animal research have proved to be a dismal failure. Dr. John J. Pippin, director of academic affairs for the Physicians Committee for Responsible Medicine, formerly of the Harvard Medical School and a speaker and panelist for the NIH National Human Subjects Protection Workshop, the American College of Cardiology, and the Society of Nuclear Medicine, points to the "abject failure of a quarter-century of primate research on AIDS to provide any useful insights...." He further notes that this animal research has failed "...to produce even a single case of human AIDS in any primate studied" and has failed "to identify even one useful AIDS drug from primate studies." Pippin also contends that "...genetic and physiological imperatives dictate that no animal model, even higher primates, gives information applicable to humans."[36]

The AIDS epidemic has led to an estimated 33 million people being currently infected with AIDS and the deaths of approximately 25 million people from the time AIDS first started.

II
Is the Salk Vaccine Responsible for
Causing Millions of Deaths by Cancer?

The suspicion that the AIDS virus was transferred to humans through animal research cannot be eliminated and should not be swept under the rug by the animal research industry and its supporters especially considering that it is accepted scientific fact that vaccines prepared from primate tissue can be carriers of primate viruses. This story emerged in the early 1960s when scientists discovered that SV 40 (simian virus No. 40) had survived the formalin in the Salk vaccine. As a result, the virus was unwittingly injected as part of the Salk vaccine into 100 million Americans between 1954 and 1961 and millions more people worldwide.[37],[38],[39]

Some scientists suspected almost immediately that the SV 40 was a cause of cancer in humans. But for decades the government — notably the National Cancer Institute (NCI) — maintained there was no connection between SV 40 and human cancer. However, critics charged that government studies to back the NCI case were flawed. An "intense" disagreement between the two sides ensued that lasted for years. Finally, in 2001 a conference of 60 leading scientists from China to New Zealand met in Chicago with SV 40 as the central topic on the agenda. Dr. Michele Carbone of the Loyola University Medical Center in Maywood, Illinois, who opened the conference and who believes that SV40 is carcinogenic in humans, said: "Sixty-two papers from 30 laboratories from around the world have reported SV 40 in human tissues and tumors. It is very difficult to believe that all of these papers, all of the techniques used and all of the people around the world are wrong."[40] The consensus that emerged from the conference, which included leading scientists in the field, was that the presence of SV 40 in human tumors was no longer questionable. Sweden's renowned tumor biologist George Klein, a former chairman of the Nobel Assembly, said of the work of Michele Carbone and Dr. David Schrump (an investigator at the NCI), that it "strongly suggests that the virus plays a role (in causing tumors)."[41] At that time SV 40 had been linked to several cancers including brain cancers, bone cancers, pituitary and thyroid tumors, lymphomas, and mesothelioma (a fatal tumor of the membrane surrounding the lungs).

Many scientists today believe SV 40 can be spread from human to human without vaccination, and that the Salk vaccine is responsible for having cost the lives of tens of millions of Americans. Moreover, they believe that the diseases connected with SV 40 continue to spread, though the means of transmission remains a topic of investigation. As William Carlsen, staff writer for the San Francisco Chronicle observed at the time of the 2001 Chicago conference, "The recent SV 40 discoveries come at a time of growing concern over the dangers posed by a range of animal viruses that have crossed the species barrier to humans, including HIV, which scientists now believe came from chimpanzees and ultimately caused the AIDS epidemic."[42]

The British Booklet, of course, makes no mention of the SV40 virus or AIDS in relation to the polio vaccine. The issue to date has also not become a matter of public concern. Certainly the polio vaccines developed by Koprowski and Salk deserve a big question mark and should be sufficient reason for people to reflect on the issue of safety when it comes to experimenting upon animals to solve human medical problems.

The general impression held by the public is that the polio vaccine is an excellent example of how animal research can lead to the cure of a catastrophic disease. The belief is fostered by publications like the British Booklet which claims that "this advance [the polio vaccine] alone has saved millions of lives" because "forty years of research using monkeys and mice led to the introduction of the vaccine." These same sources are not willing to present the public with the evidence surrounding the controversies over the

OPV theory of AIDS transmission or the SV 40 link to several deadly cancers. Their silence, in fact, helps keep the story hidden.

III
Did Polio Really Pose a Threat so Enormous that it Required Killing Millions of Monkeys?

Advocates for animal research are not eager for the public to know that investigators have exposed that the once so-called polio epidemic may have resulted from mistakes in the presentation of the statistical data.

In retrospect, polio as a threat for paralysis and to human life may have been hugely overestimated so that the taking of the lives of millions of monkeys to find a cure for the disease may have been done because of a threat that did not exist in even near approximation to the extent perceived. This is because the data used in the statistical analysis of polio incidence in the 1950s made it appear that the number of people afflicted with polio was of epidemic proportions so vast that it easily invited hysteria when in reality it was not. This mistakes occurred when healthcare officials lumped together cases of non-paralytic symptoms of polio, cases of paralytic symptoms of polio, and cases of other nonspecified symptoms of polio into one category. This increased the overall statistical number of polio cases. That happened because the name polio in any form was equated with paralysis. As a consequence, when people thought polio, they thought of a disease causing paralysis that afflicted large numbers of people.

Frightened to the point of hysteria, people worried that the threat of contracting polio was so great that even normal social intercourse between friends and family members could lead to paralysis and death. Looking back, however, it turns out that two-thirds of polio cases were "non-paralytic" and amounted to nothing more than "a mild expression of symptoms no more serious than a bad cold."[43] This means that polio in general was far less dangerous than supposed and should have been divided into separate categories that isolated the dangerous form of polio from the non-dangerous. When a reclassification of the data was eventually done, the incidence of polio declined suddenly and dramatically. And though this decline was attributed to polio vaccines, a more important factor may have been involved which was the reclassification of the data, not the polio vaccine. For example, the cases of non-paralytic polio symptoms discussed above that were statistically combined with paralytic symptoms and other non-specific symptoms, were not confirmed by laboratory diagnosis at the time they were diagnosed because the culture technique for analyzing them was not developed until the mid-1950s. After 1960, however, these cases of "non-paralytic polio" were diagnosed using the new technology which caused them to be reclassified as cases of "aseptic meningitis." This happened in the following way.

From 1951 to 1960, 70,083 cases of non-paralytic polio cases were reported compared to 0 cases of aseptic meningitis. From 1961 to 1982, 589 cases of non-paralytic polio cases were reported compared to 102,999 cases of aseptic meningitis, and finally, from 1983 to 1992, 0 cases of non-paralytic polio were reported compared to 117,366 cases of aseptic meningitis.[44] The cases of non-paralytic polio disappeared as if by magic. Reclassification of statistical data is one way in which a disease can vanish overnight.

In addition, several diseases of the period had polio-like symptoms such as spinal meningitis, inhibitory palsy, epidemic cholera, cholera morbus, ergotism, famine fever, bilious remittent fever, spinal apoplexy, scurvy, berri-berri, pellagra, acidosis, etc. Many of these diseases were likely misdiagnosed as polio.[45]

More bad news for those heralding the triumph of the Salk vaccine was that the facts seem to indicate that the vaccine actually increased the incidence of polio, not reduced it. Of the five geographical locations in which the Salk vaccine was made compulsory by law, polio cases rose by 300% to 400% as follows:

North Carolina: 78 polio cases in 1958 before compulsory shots. 313 cases in 1959 after the shots were administered.

Connecticut: 45 polio cases in 1958 before compulsory shots. 123 cases in 1959 after the shots were administered.

Tennessee: 119 polio cases in 1958 before compulsory shots. 386 cases in 1959 after the shots were administered.

Ohio: 17 polio cases in 1958 before compulsory shots. 52 cases in 1959 after the shots were administered.

Los Angeles: 89 polio cases in 1958 before compulsory shots. 190 cases in 1959 after the shots were administered.[46]

Considering the foregoing discussion in regard to the rose-tinted claim made by the British Booklet, or for that matter, any other publication on animal research that proclaims that the polio vaccine saved millions of lives, such organizations are failing their scientific responsibility to report how disastrous the animal research that produced the polio vaccines may really have been and what the real facts are. Even if they disagree, if they are scientists, scientific integrity requires the presentation of both sides, not favoring one side because they would rather assume what is not true is true.

IV
The Half-Truths that Animal Researchers Tell to the World

Exaggeration and the refusal to acknowledge problems associated with animal research is the norm when animal researchers step up to the podium, and the booklet put out by the British medical establishment succinctly illustrates this point. Beside the misrepresentations, distortions, and lies already noted, the British Booklet also praises heart disease and cancer research while ignoring the fact that both heart disease and many forms of cancer (as well as Alzheimer's) can be vastly reduced by eliminating animal protein from the diet thus eliminating the need for much of the research that is done to find cures for these diseases.[47]

As a more specific example, while praising the development of drugs through animal research that reduce estrogen blood levels, thus providing a treatment for breast cancer (in which estrogen is a tumor promoter), the British Booklet ignores the fact that the body itself can do a much better job in lowering its own estrogen blood levels and the risk of getting breast cancer by eliminating the consumption of animal products. The booklet also conveniently ignores facts such as that drugs like Tamoxifen, which are used to lower estrogen levels, can cause serious side effects such as uterine cancer, stroke, blood clots, and cataracts. Lowering estrogen levels through nutrition causes no side effects.

The British Booklet raves about insulin for having saved many people with diabetes from "wasting away to premature death." But we have seen that no animal research was required in the discovery or development of insulin. The British Booklet also fails to inform the public that the elimination of animal products from the diet can eliminate Type 2 diabetes so that it frequently is not necessary to get this form of diabetes in the first place. The same diet can also make it possible for people with Type 1 diabetes to live a normal life. It is difficult to understand why scientists, who, by the nature of their profession, are supposed to be dedicated to truth would not want to present such life-saving messages to the world.

Continuing in the endeavor to take credit where none is due, the British Booklet claims that "research carried out on ex-perimental animals, including primates, has led to an electrical implant (similar to a heart pacemaker) for the treatment of Parkinson's Disease." This treatment, called deep brain stimulation (DPS), which involves the electrical stimulation of certain areas of the brain, was invented in 1987 and in the late 1980s became established as an important treatment for Parkinson's Disease and other movement disorders.[48] While today, animals are being used to test various hypotheses in regard to DPS, the treatment for Parkinson's Disease clearly did not start from nor did it result from an initial investigation in which animals were used in a partnership arrangement in finding a cure for the disease. On the contrary, DPS rose out of and was preceded by treatments involving chronic stimulation of subcortical structures in the brain in the early 1950s in treating psychiatric patients.[49] The present claims made by the British Booklet for DPS in relation to Parkinson's is just another example of the animal research industry trying to take far greater credit than it deserves.

Animal researchers tell the world that animal testing and vivisection are compassionate endeavors. Professor Winston, in his introduction in the British Booklet, goes so far as to say that "The work we do is performed with compassion, care, humanity and humility. All my rabbits, when I worked with them years ago, were stroked and petted every day." Winston seems oblivious to how out of touch with reality this kind of statement appears to people who have real compassion in their hearts and minds for animals, the kind that would never lift a finger to harm one of them. He apparently does not see that for many people stroking and petting an innocent animal and then subjecting it to experimentation can only be defined as deceptive and cruel and much, much more. If an animal is conscious enough to enjoy being petted — which Winston acknowledges by the fact that he takes credit for having compassion, care and humanity based on petting his rabbits — which is also an acknowledgement that the rabbits were consciously aware enough to understand that they were being treated with compassion, care and humanity by being petted — were they also not conscious enough to want not to be experimented upon? It startles the imagination that animal researchers do not grasp simple concepts like this.

The facts about animal research — the exaggerations of the animal research industry and animal researchers notwithstanding — indicate that whenever animal research is done, problems and failures arise, many of which are deadly for humans. The thin veneer that covers scientific pretentions proclaiming the wonders of animal research and its necessity for finding a cure for the killer diseases becomes readily transparent upon investigating these claims more closely

V
The Failure of Animal Research
and Its Deadly Consequences

One of the most important factors to grasp in the study of animal research is that animals are not a part of the creative process that discovers cures and treatments for disease. The role they play has been and continues to be to function as slave objects to be used to test the wild conjectures animal researchers make in their curiosity experiments. The use of animals to test the hypotheses animal researchers make, however, has not provided the significant benefits they claim. In fact, animal research frequently leads to misleading results and often ends in disaster because of the simple and obvious fact that humans and all animals being individually biologically unique, quite naturally metabolize substances differently.

One of the most spectacular failures of drugs successfully tested on animals that failed when tried on humans was the drug Thalidomide which in the 1950s and 1960s caused babies to be born with webbed feet or arms and other physical deformities. Animal research publications like the British Booklet ignore image-damaging facts like these when they promote the so-called benefits of animal research.

Many failures in animal research have occurred. They include the failure of tests on primates to lower the risks for birth defects and premature births. They also include the failure of monkey tests in identifying nonsteroidal anti-inflammatory drugs to reduce cardiovascular risk. And they include the failure of forced-smoking experiments on animals that resulted in decades of continued acceptance of cigarette smoking as being a non-lethal habit just because these tests did not cause animals to develop cancer and heart disease like human beings do.[50] This misperception was responsible for many unnecessary deaths and much suffering for many people.

The physiological differences between human and nonhuman animals assure failure in the vast majority of animal tests. The medication Chloramphenicol, an antibiotic, was found to cause a fatal blood disease in humans, but not in animals. Tylenol kills cats. Digitalis causes high blood pressure in dogs. As we have seen, penicillin is ineffective in rabbits and kills guinea pigs. Streptomycin can kill gerbils, hamster, mice, and rats.

There is no shortage of failures in animal research available to consult. Others include the inability of animal researchers to develop vaccines for many diseases such as HIV (as stated), hepatitis C, or malaria, in spite of decades of experimenting on chimpanzees, the closest nonhuman relative who shares 98% of our DNA.[51]

The FDA has also been required to pull Rezulin from the shelves in the year 2002 when it was linked to liver damage, though the drug manufacturer fought for 27 months to keep it on the market, earning 1.8 billion dollars during that period. The consequences for users of Rezulin, used to treat Type II diabetes, have been deadly for some 400 users with anticipated cases of liver damage expected to rise to 14,000.[52] Animal research never detected the danger.

A more recent failure of major proportions is Vioxx, the drug used to treat osteoarthritis and rheumatoid arthritis. This drug has been taken off the market because it is believed to have caused thousands of heart attacks. This danger was also not identified in tests done on animals.

The identifiable damage and negative consequences to human health resulting from animal testing dates back to at least the early 20th century during the period when animal research was first starting to be used to try to find the cause and cure for human disease. In 1914, for example, Lafayette Mendel and Thomas Osborne conducted studies on the protein and amino acid requirements of rats which showed that rats grew better on animal protein than on vegetable protein.[53] This led to the suspicion that vegetable foods could not meet normal growth requirements because they contained insufficient amounts of amino acids. The result was a growing fear in the general public about failing to consume enough animal protein daily so that people consumed far more protein than was needed. It took nearly 40 years before the research of Dr. William Rose at the University of Illinois overturned this mistaken hypothesis by showing that the amino acid requirements for rats was far different than for humans because baby rats require ten times more protein than human babies.[54] This means that for 40 years millions of people consumed an excess of animal products that have now been shown to be linked to many forms of cancer, heart disease, stroke, diabetes, Alzheimer's Disease, multiple sclerosis and other diseases all because people feared not meeting their amino acid requirements based on tests done by animal researchers. As a result, millions of people ended up with nutrition-related diseases that could have been avoided by the consumption of less animal protein.

Unfortunately, these false beliefs about the necessity of a diet high in animal protein have still not been dispelled to any significant degree so that even today millions of people continue to get sick and die as a result of consuming too much animal protein. Living according to wrong information can, quite simply put, be deadly. Animal research is responsible for this state of affairs.

It is not difficult to observe along the continuum of animal research starting from the very beginning, that if human beings had stopped and decided to end any further tests on animals, they either would have found another means of testing their hypotheses to avoid killing themselves, or they would have arrived at a point in their research where there was no need to test their varying hypotheses because the truth or falseness of their hypotheses would have became self-evident. All that would have been required to end all animal testing was a circumspect and patient approach that could be applied to hypotheses in a scientific way. Rather than using a creative, patient approach to understanding very difficult medical enigmas, as the history shows, animal researchers adopted a policy of throwing as many animals as they could acquire at various medical problems and theories to see if any might stick. Salk and Sabin threw millions of monkeys at polio and Dr. Koprowski developed his vaccine using chimpanzee tissue without sufficient knowledge to understand the possible danger. In the end the results of the polio vaccines have turned out to be highly questionable and possibly deadly for millions of people.

The "throw and stick" method was laid out by Dr. Bernard in France when he said: "Why think when you can experiment.

Exhaust experiment and then think." It was, as has been noted, Dr. Bernard whose throw and stick method taught him wrongly that diabetes was caused by damage to the liver. Today, the animal research industry has made millions of animals available to be thrown at any conceivable experiment animal researchers devise. Animal researchers live in throw and stick heaven.

In today's world, after mandatory animal testing is done to validate or invalidate a medical hypothesis, the hypothesis must then be tested on human beings in experiments called clinical trials. Ninety-two percent of new drugs that have tested positive on animals in medical research have had to be discarded because they failed in the follow-up clinical trials.[55] According to Safer Medicine, a British organization of scientists and doctors concerned about the safety of animal research which has hosted international conferences at the Royal Society and the House of Lords, "Scores of treatments for stroke have tested safe and effective in animals in recent years but not a single one has emerged as safe and effective for patients."[56] They further note that "Shockingly, adverse reactions to prescription medicines (all tested for safety on animals) are now the fourth leading cause of death in the western world."[57] The message can hardly be denied by any unbiased, rational observer that almost all animal tests for drugs are failures which cost the lives of many humans and millions of animals who are sacrificed in the name of humankind's mistaken hypotheses. It should be clear that this is a haphazard, time-consuming process and that testing on animals has proven to be particularly unreliable and dangerous, the truth of which many animal researchers will acknowledge in private. In fact, according to a survey commissioned by Europeans for Medical Progress in 2004, 82% of 500 General Practitioners surveyed were "concerned that animal data can be misleading when applied to humans" and 83% would also "support an independent scientific evaluation of the clinical relevance of animal experimentation."[58]

The new message about animal research is simple and it is succinct. Animals belong to the community of life where they must be allowed to live out the lives that they were born to live. They do not belong under the vivisectors scalpel. And they do not belong in the vivisector's laboratory as subjects in a sea of grandiose theories the huge majority of which will never fulfill any function other than to make money for those associated with the animal research industry including, of course, the animal researchers themselves and their supporting universities, biomedical research institutions, private medical facilities, and other institutions.

Chapter 11

The Shifting Tide in the Debate
on Animal Consciousness

For 2300 years philosophers against animals, animal research scientists, and advocates backing animal research have based
their beliefs on various versions of Aristotle's hierarchical view of
nature. This theory, stated in its most transparent terms, holds that
because humans are rational beings capable of thought whereas, by
human standards, animals are not, humans stand at the apex of a
hierarchical system created by nature in which those at the top are
free to exploit those at the bottom. Fortified by the Medieval
church's backing of Aristotelian philosophy, the mechanistic
theories of Descartes and his followers in the 17th century, the
growing disregard for animals in the 18th century, and justifications
for vivisection raised by animal researchers like Francois Magendie
and Claude Bernard in the 19th century, animal researchers in the
20th and 21st centuries have managed to convince the public that
animal research is absolutely necessary for the betterment of
humankind, particularly in regard to solving human health problems.

The general acceptance of animal research has resulted in an
erosion of the natural affinity human beings have shown for other
life forms that have shared their world from the beginning of time.
Archaeological evidence of mutually productive relationships
between humans and animals is available going back at least 1.5
million years and supplies sufficient grounds for opposition to
animal research by critics determined to retain a sense of community and kinship with nature and respect for the other species that
live with them on planet earth.[1] They point out that the Aristotelian
rationale animal researchers have used to justify their experiments
represents an abandonment of the same capacity the Aristotelians

claim divides humans from nonhumans the most, the ability to think rationally. David Hume (1711-1776), the Scottish philosopher, historian, economist, essayist and recognized precursor of cognitive science, made a similar criticism when he wrote the following:

> Next to the ridicule of denying an evident truth, is that of taking much pains to defend it; and no truth appears to me more evident than that beasts are endowed with thought and reason as well as man....We are conscious that we ourselves...are guided by reason and design, and that we perform those actions, which tend to self-preservation, to the obtaining pleasure and avoiding pain. When therefore we see other creatures, in millions of instances, perform like actions, and direct them to like ends, all our principles of reason and probability carry us with an invincible force to believe the existence of a like cause.... The resemblance betwixt the actions of animals and those of men is so entire in this respect, that the very first action of the first animal we shall please to pitch on, will afford us an incontestable argument for the present doctrine.[2]

Observations like this made by Hume and, for that matter, by most people who spend the time to research the subject, are enough to resolve any doubts that animals are far more than non-thinking things bereft of emotion and feeling. Anyone who has ever watched a dog frolic in a bank of fresh snow knows that dogs experience joy. And though, as Hume says, "Tis needless in rny opinion to illustrate this argument by the enumeration of particulars," countless thousands of particulars do exist which show that animals possess consciousness and think no matter how much animal researchers and philosopher/theorists dedicated to animal research attempt to deny it.

Are animals conscious beings? Animal researchers insist that they are not but have never conducted a scientific investigation using the scientific method to determine the truth of the matter ever since animal research began 2300 years ago. That animals do possess consciousness is self-evident to most people who keep companion animals in their homes. The author likes to use the following illustration to demonstrate the consciousness of one of his four cats, Goldie Boy.

> One morning at about 6:30 a.m., Goldie Boy decided he didn't want to wait any longer for breakfast. He had had enough of lying on the bed beside his close friend and companion watching him sleeping away. It was morning and that was signal enough for everyone to be up and awake, at least by his count. Besides, he was hungry. Being a clever little boy, Goldie Boy therefore extended one of his claws and very slowly began to embed the point of it ever deeper into the soft flesh of one of his companion's eyelids until his sleeping friend woke with a jolt. The little cat was careful to draw not a speck of blood or leave even a mark. And his face expressed a look of supreme satisfaction for having accomplished his mission.

Goldie Boy knew exactly what he was doing and precisely how deeply he could embed his claw into the flesh of his friend's eyelid without hurting him in order to wake him up. It is the exact same consciousness a human being possesses in knowing how hard not to squeeze someone in a loving embrace so as not to hurt them but yet to express their love and affection.

In spite of a super abundance of anecdotal evidence like the foregoing, animal researchers insist that such examples are mean-ingless while demanding that the entire world accept their thor-oughly unproved and unsupportable hypothesis that animals are not rational beings, the theory which they inherited from Aristotle and the animal researchers who followed. They have gotten away with this by turning their backs on the rational observations that most people make about animals and by a collective insistence that being scientists, they must be right and everyone else is wrong.

Anecdotal evidence supported by scientific research and common sense is gradually becoming the new standard to which society is beginning to turn in establishing its values pertaining to animal consciousness and the rights of animals. Many factors are responsible including a new genus of scientists and philosophers who, dissatisfied with the scientific and philosophical superficiality that historically has been used to justify animal research, began stepping forward in the last quarter of the 20th century to present the results of their research. Though small in number, they were soon making their own determinations as to whether the rationalist view that animals lacked consciousness was true or false.

On the philosopher side, Peter Singer exposed many of the fallacies used in support of animal research in his epic 1975 study *Animal Liberation*. Eight years later, Tom Regan, another philosopher, argued that animals, like human beings, had inherent rights in his landmark book *The Case for Animal Rights*. On the scientific side, reporting on her work in Africa, anthropologist Jane Goodall overturned scientific prejudices by presenting compelling evidence that chimpanzees were capable of rational thought, sophisticated emotions, and complex social interactions.

Many other scientists and philosophers have also weighed in to challenge the rationales behind animal research with their own work in support of animal rights. For example, animal cognition scientists have tested animal consciousness in living primates and many other animal species. Using anecdotal, experimental, and observational methods, they investigate animals in relation to subjects like anthropomorphism, learning, memory, thinking, consciousness, planning, play, aggression, dominance, assessment of self, social knowledge, empathy, conflict resolution, joy, fear, jealousy, anger, impatience, friendship, love, and many others. They also devise various means by which they can measure animal consciousness such as MSR (mirror self recognition) tests. This is a test developed by psychologist Gordon Gallup which has shown that chimpanzees, gorillas, and orangutans can recognize themselves in a mirror and have a concept of themselves.[3] Other studies, such as those which show that birds store food suggest that they plan ahead. Planning of this nature is an indication of consciousness of the same kind that humans employ in their daily work and activities.

Professor David DeGrazia, who specializes in biomedical ethics at the George Washington University in Washington, D.C., points out that "the cumulative force of various empirical findings on intentional behavior, episodic memory, imitation, mirror self-recognition, mind reading, and metacognition in animals shows that bodily self-awareness is quite widespread in the animal kingdom, and that social self-awareness and (even) introspective self-awareness are likely present in various higher species (e.g., monkeys, apes, and cetaceans)."[45]

Research in animal cognition does not hesitate to examine anecdotal evidence in a scientific way to show that animals do think. This has helped to dispel claims by animal researchers that any view favorable to animals had to be derived from anthropomorphic sympathies wherein people attribute nonexistent human characteristics to animals.

A good example of a "thinking" animal was reported from Sweden's Furuvik Zoo where a male chimpanzee liked to assemble a collection of rocks in the morning before the zoo opened. There he waited silently nursing a private fit of rage eager to throw his stash of rocks at arriving zoo visitors. Mathias Osvath wrote up the incident in a paper for the journal *Current Biology* and concluded that the incident showed convincingly "that our fellow apes do consider the future in a very complex way. It implies that they have a highly developed consciousness, including lifelike mental simulations of potential events."[6]

The work of animal cognition scientists and ethologists has shown a few cynical colleagues what should have been apparent from the very start when Aristotle began his experiments. Animals do have emotions and they are sentient beings capable of conscious thought. Results obtained in animal cognition and ethology studies has forced mainstream scientists who practice vivisection and their supporters to back off the naive justifications for vivisection upon which their predecessors relied. Many mainstream scientists who practice vivisection, if asked privately, will acknowledge that animals do possess consciousness.

Fortunately, a few advocates for animal research have been willing to debate their differences with animal rights proponents publicly, a step in the right direction that offers some hope that a few animal research supporters are becoming more willing to cross the divide to hear what their opponents have to say. Most animal researchers, however, are not anxious to talk about matters that could threaten their livelihood which could become a reality if the world were suddenly to wake up to the realization that animals are conscious, intelligent, emotional beings that deserve as much respect as human beings give to themselves. Should that happen, animal research would end and so would the high salaries paid to animal researchers footed in large part by the American public through the National Institutes of Health and other government agencies to the tune of over twenty billion dollars annually. Generally, the animal research industry wants the world to continue to think that animals are mindless creatures incapable of thought and feeling who experience only inconsequential pain and suffering because this provides the rationalization that justifies their profession. Meanwhile, the new vision that animals are conscious beings is gradually being absorbed by the general public.

Chapter 12

The Philosopher/Theorists of Animal Research and Their Shiny New Theories:

The work of animal cognition scientists and ethologists are persuasive in showing that animals are conscious, feeling, thinking beings which experience suffering and joy in their lives just like human beings. Yet even as the arguments supporting the nonrationality of animals begin to give way because they cannot be logically or scientifically supported, a new breed of philosopher/theorists and professional animal research advocates has emerged to buttress the same ancient theories which justify animal experiments based on the same ancient claims that animals lack consciousness, do not experience pain to any significant degree, and therefore have no inherent rights.

I
Using Language to try to Defeat the Animal Rights Movement

Grasping that they might be losing the debate, this new group of animal research supporters has become adept at inventing erudite highly sophisticated sounding arguments which they present in peer journals and books aimed at a professional audience as a means of promoting animal research. To read their work often requires a familiarity with subjects like philosophy, psychology, biology, and/or linguistics. Writings like these impress policy makers and help maintain institutional policy toward animal research in government agencies like the NIH and the university and biomedical research system which supports and relies on animal research. Consider, for example, the following two paragraphs taken from the beginning of an article written by Professor

Peter Carruthers, a professor of Philosophy at the University of Maryland. (Professor Carruthers' work will be discussed in greater detail in subsequent chapters.)

2. Against First-Order Representationalism

One major difficulty with first-order-representation-alist accounts in general, is that they cannot distinguish between what the *world* is like for an organism, and what the organism's *experience of the world* is like for the organism. This distinction is very frequently overlooked in discussions of phenomenal conscious-ness. People will move (sometimes in the space of a single sentence) from saying that an account explains what *colour* is like for an organism with colour-vision, to saying that it explains what *experiences of colour* are like for that organism. But the first is a property of the world (or of a world-perceiver pair, perhaps), whereas the latter is a property of the organism's experience of the world (or of an experience-experiencer pair). These are plainly distinct.

We therefore need to distinguish between two different sorts of subjectivity - between worldly-subjectivity and mental-state-subjectivity. In fact we need to distinguish between phenomenal properties of the world, on the one hand, and phenomenal properties of the subject's experience of the world, on the other. First-order representationalism may be adequate to account for the former; but not to explain the latter, where some kind of higher-order theory is surely needed. Which of these two deserves to be called "phenomenal consciousness"? There is nothing (or nothing much) in a name; and I am happy whichever reply is given. But it is the subjectivity of experience which seems to be especially problematic - if there is a "hard problem" of consciousness, it surely lies here. And a first-order theory can plainly make no progress with it.[1]

The paragraphs above have not been taken out of context from a random source in order to show how dense and esoteric this author's writings can be or to find an example that sounds like gobbledygook. These are the opening two paragraphs of an article titled "Animal Subjectivity" which follow a short introduction so that the author obviously presupposes an understanding by the audience of the material he presents. The article was written for the purpose of discussing what the author refers to as the "phenomenal consciousness of animals." Professor Carruthers has also written a book titled *Phenomenal Consciousness*.

Language like the above intended for a specialized audience evokes comparisons with the use of Latin in the Medieval church as a useful tool for distancing the clergy from the parishioners and the public thus preventing them from participating in the kinds of policy making the clerical decision-makers were undertaking to manage their affairs. Being abstract is one of the tools writers in support of animal research rely upon in writing for both peer journals and for the general public. It serves as a method for manipulating the information flow about animal research in an attempt to control the future destiny of animals. These writings influence the decision makers who set priorities in regard to animal research including its promotion, funding, and policy setting and also serve to keep the public in the dark and from storming the brigades. An examination of the subject matter in the writing above, however, consciousness in animals (which will be undertaken in chapter 13), reveals that it simply dresses up the same old theories with fancy new names, surrounding them with complex arguments that obfuscate and make them difficult to understand.

II
The Language of Animals

One popular theory that has been in circulation for centuries that present-day philosopher/theorists continue to try to prop up, states that animals lack consciousness because consciousness requires language. In 1998 Euan MacPhail, a British psychologist, wrote *The Evolution of Consciousness*, a book that hones in on the subject. The media eagerly awaits books like this and jumps on board as soon as they are published as though the authors have latched onto some new and exciting theory never heard before. When MacPhail's book came out, reviewers described it as an intellectual tour de force and a book that proves that animals lack consciousness. But MacPhail's book, based entirely on speculation, proved no such thing. He contended that there is no proof that any nonhumans possess consciousness and that it is the use of language itself by the infant growing up that creates a sense of self that is the necessary condition for consciousness. An examination of the historical record comparing the human animal to the nonhuman animal, however, reveals the insufficiency of this theory.[2]

Anthropologists and archaeologists tell us that our human ancestors did not have the anatomical capability for uttering language prior to 150,000 or so years ago. If this is true, the only logical inference that can be drawn is that if language is a requirement for consciousness then prehistoric humans who did not speak language could not have been conscious beings and further that consciousness is a construct that without language does not exist.

It follows from this kind of argument that consciousness only began once human beings started speaking words and that before language existed humans were just one of countless other species of living creatures mindlessly running around the jungle, all possessing not a shred of awareness of what they were, who they were, where they were, or what they were doing. Simple observation, such as taking note of the artifacts left behind by prehistoric human beings, shows that this could hardly be true. Further, when an event or an action occurs in an environment—say a threat from another species—human beings, who possess language, might cry out with words like "watch out!" or "help!" A dog, being unable to speak words, might respond with barks or growls. A lion with a roar. A little monkey with a chittering, fearful sound. A bird with a squack or a cheep. But all of these species along with humans would be having a similar experience which could only register in the mind "consciously."

While philosopher/theorists for animal research continue to paraphrase and rearrange the wording of their definitions for consciousness and invent new and criteria for trying to prove that animal consciousness does not exist, such as that language is a requirement for consciousness, human consciousness surely existed for millions of years before the advent of language. It is only logical that human consciousness prior to language must have been similar to how other species consciously experienced their environments, taking into account the many variations that exist between species. This makes common sense. And "common sense," the author submits, is made not through language, but in a place in the mind where words do not exist but for which many words do exist to describe it, including intuition, perception, awareness, spontaneous realization, insight, sixth sense, mental acuity, instinct, hunch, and many more.

The archaeological and anthropological evidence shows that way before the invention of language human beings were communicating with each other in a sophisticated manner such as through making tools and weapons, building shelters, cooking, and using pigments, possibly for body adornment or for the purpose of creating rock art.

It is clear that no matter how factual and scientific the evidence offered in opposition to their theories may be, animal researchers and their supporters will continue to ignore all evidence that disproves their theories while they recycle the same ancient ideas about animal consciousness, polishing them up to make them appear new. This is the manner in which they keep theories alive such as that animals lack consciousness or that language is a requirement for consciousness.

Animal researchers from the days of Aristotle to the present have made the mistake of assuming that the human word-reliant process called language is what thought consists of with little reference to the different levels of perception which words attempt to convey. Because only human beings are capable of using language to describe different levels of perception, animal researchers have wrongly assumed that animals do not perceive the exterior and interior world around and within them. In assuming that animals do not possess consciousness because they do not possess language, these researchers have overlooked the function of language, which is to communicate these inner and outer perceptions, the interactions of which produce consciousness..

Animals perceive the world around them just like human beings do, taking into account their species-specific variations. The major difference is that animals do not have the anatomic capability to funnel their perceptions into articulated, representational sounds in order to organize and express them in the succinct manner that language permits. Even so, animals are able to use and combine their individual perceptions of both their outer and inner worlds in ways that have meaning for them. These perceptions become a part of their consciousness in the same way as happens with human beings such as when a dog knows what is about to happen when the dog's companion keeper picks up a stick from the ground in preparation for throwing it for the dog to fetch. The dog's knowledge in such an event is an expression of the dog's consciousness of exterior events. When the author's cats come to him to communicate that they want him to pick them up and hold them because they want his affection and love, this is an expression of their consciousness of interior events. Memory is involved, obviously, just as it is with human beings.

Pre-20th century philosophers and physiologists like Aristotle and Immanuel Kant did not have the archaeological evidence available today that would have told them the story of how sixteen or so earlier species of humans occupied the earth for about seven million years without the ability to speak words. As for how the latest species to appear on the planet, Homo sapiens, fits into the puzzle, it was only after wandering around Africa for 50 to 100 thousand years or so after their arrival some 250,000 years ago that they began articulating words and fashioning them into language after, it is theorized, an anatomical change (the dropping of the larynx) permitted them to do so.[3]

Clearly, humans did not just suddenly become "rational" beings capable of thinking once they acquired the use of language.

Like every other species of animal, thinking for the human animal consisted of the interaction of nonverbal perceptions contained in the mind prior to acquiring language skills. Depending upon their anatomic structure and whether they were land, sea, or air animals, animals (including humans) communicated through a variety of techniques that included a diversity of vocalizations, calls, noises, gestures, changes in the pitch of vocally produced sounds, facial expressions, eye contact, head posture, body language, scents and smells, and, far from least, intuition and sensitivity toward intention. Whoever thinks that animals do not have a sensitivity toward intention only has to approach a dog in a manner the dog might perceive as threatening. The author suggests caution should the dog being approached be on the large side with a strong protective sense toward his/her companion keeper.

Armed with today's archaeological and anthropologic information, it should be self-evident, just as Hume observed, that animals have always been conscious creatures able to think just like human beings have always been able to think before they acquired the ability to utter sounds in the coherent and systematic way called language. Consciousness and its expression is consistent with all species of animals, including humans, in that it occurs but differs according to the individual characteristics of species and what and how they communicate. This can be partially understood in the case of nonhuman animals by observing their reactions to events in their environments.

The major difficulty in measuring consciousness between nonhuman animals and human animals is that human animals possess language which makes it easier to measure consciousness through the medium of words. The absence of some kind of verbal language presents an obstacle in understanding nonhuman consciousness, comparatively speaking, because nonhuman animals (with the exception of parrots, hummingbirds, songbirds, bats, and cetaceans—a subject that will not be addressed here) cannot express themselves through words. Some animals, of course, whales and dolphins, communicate with each other through other kinds of complex vocal sounds.

III
What is Animal Consciousness?

A general idea of what animal consciousness might be like can be obtained comparatively speaking by examining human consciousness minus language. This can be achieved easily enough by silently observing a given situation without verbalizing (with thoughts) what is happening in the visual field being observed. It quickly becomes apparent that everything in this visual field has meaning that is instantly understood according to past experience. If a bird flies across the sky, the observer understands that he/she has just seen a bird flying across the sky. Or, if we could go back in time to walk the forest floor 175,000 years ago before the advent of language and observe a fellow member of our Homo sapiens species using a rock as a hammer in constructing a roof for a dwelling, we would understand the exact meaning of what we were observing, though we might do no more than utter some kind of nonverbal sound to express the experience. The same applies to animals. When the author's three cats observe him preparing their dinner, they know exactly what he is doing and watch with the keenest interest sometimes uttering a chorus of cat meows. They understand everything they see all day long with a similar sense of perception. When a bird flies across the sky animals observe it in the same way as Homo sapiens except that what they see is experienced according to species-specific characteristics. A cat watching the bird might instantly be absorbed in the desire to "catch it." A human might observe the beauty of the bird in flight.

Is it possible that a cat might also marvel at the beauty of a bird's flight in its own way? Questions like this cannot currently be answered without speculation because the evidence does not exist to answer these kinds of questions accurately. The study of animal aesthetics, however, contributes to an understanding of what may go on inside the minds of animals in regard to aesthetic appreciation of their environment. It has been observed, for example, that Bowerbirds "arrange objects of selected shapes and colors on their bower as a means of attracting a partner."[4] Human beings do the same in a variety of ways including the clothing they select to wear when they go courting. On such occasions, humans are careful to dress in a manner that pleases them aesthetically based in part on color. The prospect that Bowerbirds have an aesthetic appreciation of the objects and their colors they arrange on their bowers as they search for a mate is a distinct possibility. Similarly, the idea that a cat can appreciate the beauty of a bird in flight should not be ruled out.

Homo sapiens were fortunate to develop the ability to create different sounds to communicate the wide varieties of experience that occurred within their fields of interior and exterior perception. They were able to use these articulated sounds and to systematically organize and develop them into language. Thus when humans saw a neighboring human building a roof, as in our prehistoric example, they would have fashioned the word "roof" as a partial means for describing the experience. The word "bird" would have sufficed to describe living creatures with flapping protuberances that glided across the blue expanse above that they learned to call "sky." Such words as "roof," "bird," and "sky" were descriptive of events that occurred in their exterior field of perception. To describe their interior field of perception, they would have fashioned a different set of words such as "love" to describe amorous emotions toward other Homo sapiens. But words like roof, bird, sky, and love are only simple symbols used in an attempt to describe deeper levels of exterior and interior perception. Assigning individual vocalizations to perceptions and then combining them with other vocalizations describing various perceptions drawn from a large repertoire of exterior and interior perceptions and then organizing them in a coherent way produces language. This is an obvious oversimplification, but it illustrates how words are used to describe the interior and exterior worlds of perception that reside in the mind. It is the combining of these perceptions verbally that animals are incapable of doing because they are anatomically capable of articulating only a few individual sounds into coherent expressions of their perceptions. Nevertheless, their minds are far from empty and animals have their own language for communicating their perceptions to each other. If we listen and pay close attention, we are certain to learn a little more about what they are saying.

Chapter 13

A Philosopher/Theorist Under the Microscope

University of Maryland Professor of Philosophy Peter Carruthers is a leading philosophy theorist who specializes in philosophy of mind, philosophy of psychology, and cognitive science. Though he has been called a modern-day Cartesian [Cartesian = Descartes.], in regard to animal issues, he only modestly notes that he has "also published on the mentality of animals." However, he has often been invited to participate in symposia, conferences, discussions, and workshops across the country and internationally as a speaker or to give papers addressing various philosophical issues including the subject of animal minds and animal thought. In July of 2012 he was an invited plenary speaker for the Fifth British Wittgenstein Society conference on *Enactivism, Animal Minds, and Wittgenstein*, held at the University of Hertfordshire in England. His work on animal mentality also includes several articles in peer journals, and he has written a book on the subject titled *The Animals Issue: Moral Theory in Practice*.[1]

An uncompromising proponent of the "animals lack consciousness" school of thought in contemporary philosophy of mind, Professor Carruthers' philosophy about animals offers valuable insight into some of the concepts animal researchers and their supporters rely upon as a rationale for advocating animal research.

I
Nonconscious Animals in the World
of Professor Peter Carruthers

A good point of entry into Professor Carruthers' world and how he regards nonhuman species is his statement that he is "…one

154

of those who maintain that language mastery is at least contingently connected with the capacity for conscious thought..."[2] (The inadequacy of the theory of language as a necessity for consciousness is discussed in chapters 11 and 12.)

Because Professor Carruthers is a recognized scholar and expert in philosophy of mind who has written articles on animal consciousness throughout his career, it should prove instructive to examine if he has made any changes in his thinking about the consciousness of animals in recent years in response to the changing perspectives on animals that have emerged as the result of animal cognition studies. In the past, for example, Professor Carruthers used the term "nonconscious" to describe the state of mind of animals. He promoted the idea that all animals lived in this state of "nonconsciousness" and that rights accrued only to "conscious" creatures which animals were not. Only human beings, therefore, had rights while animals had none. The question that cannot be avoided, naturally, is whether ideas like this are scientifically sound and whether they have any scientific basis.

On the back cover of his book *The Animal Issue: Moral theory in practice*, Professor Carruthers comments that at various times he has been "the owner of numerous cats and a dog, to all of whom he was devoted." Like Robert Winston, who wrote the forward for the British Booklet discussed in chapter 10 and who informed his audience that he petted his rabbits before experimenting upon them, Professor Carruthers wants his readers to think kindly of him. But an examination of his work reveals that Professor Carruthers' views are extreme. In fact, some of his statements have been so excessive that they can hardly be viewed as other than a betrayal of animals. For example, in a 1989 article titled "Brute Experience," Carruthers said "that there is no moral criticism to be leveled at the majority of people who are indifferent to the pains of factory-farmed animals." In other words, all the documented brutalization of animals on factory farms is perfectly acceptable. Further, he wrote that:

> Much time and money is presently spent on alleviating the pains of bruteswhich ought properly to be

directed toward human beings, and many are now campaigning to reduce the efficiency of modern farming methods because of the pain caused to the animals involved. If the arguments presented here have been sound, such activities are not only morally unsupportable but morally objectionable."[3]

Though Professor Carruthers would revise his words in regard to pain experienced by animals nearly a decade later (without apologizing for any harm they may have caused), what did not change was his general belief that animals lack consciousness.[4] Whether or not in essence he still believes that animals do not feel pain remains a question mark, at least for this reader. In any event, judging from comments he makes today, as we shall see, he has, at least, recognized that the arguments he once used to promote and defend his positions were far from reliable.

In his article "Brute Experience" Professor Carruthers paints a portrait of himself in which he is swept along as he listens to the finale of Franz Schubert's Arpeggione Sonata. [The Arpeggione, a bowed guitar-like instrument, was invented in Schubert's day (1797-1828) and quickly fell out of fashion. Today, parts written for the Arpeggione are played by other instruments, most notably the cello or viola.] Captivated by the strains of the Arpeggione, Mr. Carruthers' absently dries some dishes unconscious of what he is doing. Because he is performing an action of which in retrospect he realizes he was unconscious—drying the dishes—he labels this action "nonconscious."[5] Professor Carruthers then hypothesizes that it is this state of "nonconsciousness" that is the permanent state of mind of all animals all of the time. With absolutely no proof, he wants people to believe that animals go through life completely unaware of what is going on around, outside, or inside them except in a similar manner in which Professor Carruthers "nonconsciously" dried the dishes while listening to the Schubert Arpeggione Sonata. Though he portrays this state of mind as one that "feels like nothing," he nevertheless describes it by telling his readers that if consciousness may be equated with light, then the lives of the brutes may be nothing but "darkness."

[The word "brute," as a name for animals, was often favored in describing animals prior to the mid-20th century. It conjures up stereotypic images of animals as fearsome, ferocious, loathsome, and dumb animals. Images like these assist in the endeavor to maintain that animal consciousness is distinctly separate from human consciousness, though any circumspect observer will have little difficulty in locating abundant images of humankind recorded throughout history that are far more ferocious than any exhibited by any animal when confronted with threatening circumstances.]

The state of "nonconsciousness," according to Carruthers at the time he wrote "Brute Experience," accounted for why humans need not be concerned about any pain animals might experience at the hands of humans. Animals, because they do not possess con-sciousness, can only experience pain nonconsciously so that they do not feel it. Consequently, they do not deserve human sympathy. Only humans can experience pain both nonconsciously and con-sciously. Carruthers put it this way:

> Since the disappointments caused to a dog through possession of a broken leg are themselves noncon-scious in their turn, they, too, are not appropriate objects of our sympathy. Hence, neither the pain of the broken leg itself, nor its further effects upon the life of the dog, have any rational claim upon our sympathy.[6]

Possibly no follower of Descartes ever said it better. If Carruthers was right, of course, and the dog felt no pain, conceiva-bly there might be no reason to sympathize with the dog, at least on account of pain. But is Carruther's right? If so, should we not revise our opinion of Dr. Magendie, who nailed a dog to a table with big spikes and cut open its face without anesthesia, to one in which we believe that really he was just doing a little harmless excision since the dog felt no pain? (See chapter 7.) And for those physicians back in Descartes' day who beat dogs and poked fun at those who pitied them claiming that the animals were just clocks whose cries of pain when struck were only the noise of a little spring that had been touched—should we no longer vilify them since, after all, the dogs were just experiencing something of a nonconscious nature that did not rise to the level of conscious pain? Or, have not all such theories from Descartes to Carruthers been nothing more than assumptions and conjectures, intellectual exercises based on intellectual fantasies for which no evidence has ever been produced?

This is a question that deserves to be answered. Theories like those Professor Carruthers helps promote, feed into and assist in keeping alive the mindset that animals are just non-feeling things to be used and abused however humans see fit. This is the mindset that is responsible for much of the cruelty toward animals taking place in the world today in animal research laboratories; on factory farms and fur farms; through blood sports (cock fights); in circuses, rodeos, and zoos; in hunting and trapping activities; and wherever animals are abused and mistreated.

Marc Bekoff, Professor of Environmental, Population, and Organismic Biology at the University of Colorado, and Dale Jamieson, Professor of Philosophy at the same University, took on Carruthers' "fallacious reasoning" and "false premises," as they referred to them, which Carruthers laid out in his article "Brute Experience." In their article, titled "Carruthers on nonconscious experience," Bekoff and Jamieson pointed out that the examples Carruthers used to establish "nonconsciousness" were not necessarily even "nonconscious" but could as easily have been ascribed to selective attention [focusing more on one activity than another], and that a failure to remember something is also not "a reliable criterion" for a nonconscious experience [if such a thing exists].[7] The authors also pointed out that actions like drying dishes can become automatized by repetition so that this so-called nonconscious mental state could have originated as a conscious one that by means of repetition became available to be repeated unconsciously. They also noted that Carruthers' nonconscious state of mind was never supposed to be available to the conscious state of mind (since animals supposedly *always* lived in a state of nonconsciousness), but that if some interruption occurred, such as a dropped dish that broke, the so-called nonconscious state of mind in which dishes were being dried would immediately have been interrupted and consciousness would have been instantly restored. So drying dishes in this example could not possibly have been nonconscious in the way Carruthers defined it since it could easily change to a conscious state. The nonconscious state of mind Carruthers tried to invent was a state of mind that could never know what a conscious state of mind was like so that it would be impossible to return to consciousness if a dish suddenly was dropped and broken. Further, Bekoff and Jamieson took note that experiments had shown that rats monitor [keep track of] their activities so that they had to be conscious, not nonconscious. [This applies to many other species also.] Moreover, while Carruthers described the state of nonconsciousness as something that did "not feel like anything" where phenomena are experienced, in contrast to consciousness, he provided no proof to back up the claim. He simply stated it. Carruthers, then, at least in this instance, turns out to have been just another one of the "Great Assumers" who assume that what they think is factual just because they think it but have no facts with which to back up their thoroughly untested, unscientific assumptions.

II
Does the Ability of Humans to Think About Their Own Thoughts Combined with the Presumption that Animals Do Not Offer a Legitimate Justification for Animal Research?

Undaunted, Carruthers continued his campaign to convince people that animals are not conscious beings. Perhaps it was because his theory of "nonconsciousness" was so soundly discredited by Professors Bekoff and Jamieson that he began to use a new line of argument based on so-called "high-order theory" vs. "first-order theory" as the means for trying to define animal consciousness. He had adopted these terms by at least 1998 and was still using this line of argument as late as 2011 as is apparent in his 2011 article "Animal Mentality: Its Character, Extent, and Moral Significance." (See below.)

For purpose of clarity in the discussion that follows, and in order to avoid any ambiguity, when necessary, the argument stated here will replace the term "higher-order theory" with the terms "human consciousness" or "human" and will replace the term "first-order theory" with the term "animal consciousness." Strictly speaking, "higher-order theory" refers to a state of mind in which a creature is able to consciously think about his/her thoughts and experiences and to be consciously aware that he or she is engaged in this kind of thinking. This "higher-order theory" classification, as Carruthers sees it, can be applied only to human beings, with the possible but not likely exception of great apes such as chimpanzees and gorillas who might also be capable of higher-order thought. In contrast, the classification of "first-order theory" is used to describe a supposed state of mind of animals that can perceive, experience, respond to, and relate to all phenomena in their environments. However, they are incapable of higher-order (human) thinking such as thinking about their own thoughts or speculating on the mental processes of other animals or humans. So goes the theory.

Carruthers divides humans from animals by relying upon this high-order/first-order classification as the basis for the division. While he accepts, as stated, that it is possible, though not likely, that some higher primates such as chimpanzees might be capable of human consciousness, for all other animals, he assumes that "no one would seriously maintain that dogs, cats, sheep, cattle, pigs, or chickens consciously think things to themselves (let alone that fish or reptiles do)."[8] Yet what does a dog do who brings a stick to his/her companion to throw so that he/she can fetch it, if the dog has not thought beforehand that he/she would like his/her companion to throw the stick so that he/she can fetch it while thinking of the pleasure he/she would derive from running to fetch the stick and returning it to his/her companion to throw again? Memory, of course, would be involved in the dog's experience, but so would desire and the belief the dog would surely have that if he/she brought the stick to his/her companion to throw, the companion would throw it. This constitutes having beliefs and thinking about events and their outcome. Carruthers, however, apparently thinks that anecdotal evidence like this purporting to show, to whatever degree, an ability for animals to perceive events compared to the way humans perceive events would seriously underestimate "the representational complexity of human consciousness experiences."[9]

But just how complex does thought have to be before it qualifies as consciousness by Professor Carruthers' criteria? Recent dog cognition research has shown that dogs are capable of remembering and identifying hundreds of objects and that, unlike primates, they do it easily. It also appears that dogs are able to "infer what novel utterances mean." For example, given the name verbally of a completely new toy of which they have no previous knowledge, a dog can locate the new toy after it has been concealed among hundreds of other toys, the names for which the dog is individually familiar. Animal psychologists say that this is the exact same way children learn at a very early age. [10] If children can be said to be conscious at this stage of their development based on criteria like this, it suggests that the same criteria should apply to dogs. And since humans do not perform invasive vivisection experiments upon children because they are conscious beings, should animal researchers not be required to stop performing experiments upon dogs for the same reason—that is, if humans are to think of themselves as rational, logical, human beings who practice fairness and justice in their lives?

Ideas, theories, presumptions, and guesses about what constitutes animal consciousness get batted back and forth like ping pong balls among philosopher/theorists and their supporters who believe in animals research. These ping pong balls find their way into peer journals and books that form the basis for a modern philosophy of animal consciousness which denies that animals are conscious beings with rights of their own. For example, Kenan Malik, the Indian-born British author of *Man, Beast and Zombie*, has trained in neurobiology and argues, like Kant, that animals are to be treated as a means to an end. He speaks in defense of animal experimentation and takes the position that animals have no rights. Another British philosopher, Roger Scruton, a leading conservative figure of the New Right in England, believes that rights belong only to human beings and should not be expanded to include other species. In America, Judge Richard Posner of the United States Court of Appeals of the 7th Circuit at least understands that animals actually experience pain, but believes that this should not be a factor in any research that advances societal needs, a concept upon which animal researchers have relied for centuries. At the University of Michigan, Professor Carl Cohen, a professor of philosophy, upholds the traditional view that animals have no rights and has proposed that "the holders of rights must have the capacity to comprehend rules of duty governing all, including themselves."[11] While this may sound good superficially speaking, this is, in any case, a human-manufactured concept lacking any real depth against which animals have no voice to protest. Fortunately, as we have seen, other scientists and philosophers are engaged in exposing and defeating theories and ideas like these that turn out to be nothing but a recycling of ancient assumptions that have never had any scientific or factual basis from the very beginning.

In Professor Carruthers' world, humans live in an exalted state of classical music, literature, art, philosophy, and sophisticated conversation where the content of conscious experience is available to be consciously thought about. According to him, this capacity is what constitutes human consciousness, or what he calls high-order theory, as distinct from first-order theory (the world of nonhuman animals). But by what authority does Professor Carruthers maintain that the ability to think about one's conscious experience defines consciousness? Whether or not a living creature thinks or does not think about his/her own experiences is only one factor among many in trying to define consciousness and, as a consequence, has limited value.

Proceeding down the evolutionary ladder, Professor Carruthers tells us that on the next lower rung higher level mammals like chimpanzees may be capable of human-like consciousness but probably are not because they are not evolved enough to have the need to express or think in human ways—that is the capacity to think about their thoughts and to be aware that they are doing it. Again, this is an extremely limited way of attempting to define consciousness and does not even take into account similarities in thinking that are common to all species which revolve around the basic instincts of all animals including the human animal. Like, "What's for supper, Mom?"

162

Professor Carruthers maintains a distinction between the mental states of humans and animals because he postulates that the process of evolution is what gave humans a mind capable of thinking about their own thoughts. Accordingly, because animals are not as evolved as humans, they have no need to think about their own thoughts and, as a consequence, their mental states exist on a lower level that is nonconscious.[12] This is a fanciful supposition for which no proof exists, though on first hearing it may sounds impressive. But theories like these are superficial in their content and usually turn out to have far less depth than appears on the surface when seriously examined. It cannot be assumed that human evolution is more sophisticated than animal evolution just for the sake of convenience. Animal psychologists, for example, believe that the mentality of dogs evolved from wolves through social contact with humans where they learned that in order to survive and live with humans they were required to abandon the violent and aggressive social behavior that characterized their lives as wolves and adopt the kind of social behavior that was favorable to and makes them beloved of humans.[13] The minds of animals are just far more complex than the surface observations animal philosophers have used over the centuries in their attempts to define the status of animals in the human world.

Leaving the simians behind and descending further down the evolutionary ladder, Professor Carruthers brings us into the domain of the lower animals which he assumes (with no scientific basis for the assumption) do not "think things to themselves" (cats, dogs, pigs, etc.).[14] Next come the lower vertebrates such as fish, amphibians, and reptiles, the mental status of which Carruthers explains he is agnostic.[15] At the very bottom of the ladder we reach the insect kingdom. Carruthers tell us that insects are insentient.

III
Thoughts of a Caterpillar

Turning to insects for a moment, Professor Carruthers borrows a term from Descartes to inform us that some animals are "*automata*, despite their apparent sentience." [Emphasis by author.]

Carruthers, at this point (1992), reserves the term "automata" for invertebrates like caterpillars and says that the behavior of caterpillars that "wriggle vigorously when impaled on the end of a pin" is mere *tropism*, "a mechanical feedback process of a very simple sort." [His use of the term "mechanical" fits in well with Cartesian (Descartian) philosophy.] By Carruthers account at that time (1992), "insects feel no pain."[16]

When Carruthers wrote these statements he must have been unaware of the scientific research that had been done and was ongoing about the consciousness of invertebrates. In fact, some studies on the brain and behavior of cephalopods (marine mollusks, like squid and octopuses) had already been done by M.J. Wells in 1962.[17] By 1980, V.P. Wigglesworth was suggesting that insects feel pain and should be "narcotized in procedures that have the potential to cause pain." Then in 1991, Jane Smith, a lecturer in the Department of Biomedical Science and Biomedical Ethics at the University of Birmingham Medical School in Birmingham, England published a paper titled "A Question of Pain in Invertebrates." Writing about the analysis of some researchers who found no evidence of insect consciousness (Gould and Gould, 1982), Smith wrote:

> Perhaps such a view simply reflects a paucity of (human) imagination. Griffin (1984) surely would urge us to maintain an open mind on the issue, having provided behavioral evidence which, he argues, should challenge "the widespread belief' that an insect, for example, is too small and its central nervous system too differently organized from ours to be capable of conscious thinking and planning or subjective feelings."[18]

Smith summarized various invertebrate research projects and noted that "the Canadian Council on Animal Care's list of 'Categories of Invasiveness in Animal Experiments' recognizes that 'cephalopods and some other higher invertebrates have nervous systems as well developed as some vertebrates' and so might be included in categories in which pain and distress (including "severe pain") is caused."[19]

By 2005, several years after his earlier statements that insects did not feel pain, Carruthers seems to have caught up with invertebrate research. In his 2005 book *Consciousness: Essays from a Higher-Order* [human] *Perspective*, he writes:

> Indeed, there is a case for thinking that beliefs and desires are very widely distributed throughout the animal kingdom being possessed even by ants, bees and other navigating insects.

And while Carruthers continues to insist that animals are not conscious, by at least 2004 he allowed that animals suffer pain, stuck, though they were, by his account, in the lower mental state of animal consciousness (first order theory).

> And so if an animal finds its own pains awful we can allow that it must believe its pains are awful....So there seems nothing to prevent animals from finding their pains awful, even if their pain experiences aren't phenomenally conscious ones.[20]

Carruthers seems to be hedging his bets by admitting that animals experience pain, though they are still not "phenomenally conscious." By 2011 he seems to have undergone a complete transformation in regard to animal consciousness when he writes in an article titled "Against the Moral Standing of Animals:"

> I shall assume that most animals have minds much like our own. They have beliefs and desires, and engage in practical reasoning in the light of their beliefs and desires. (This is true even of some invertebrates, including bees and jumping spiders, I believe.) Many animals feel pain and fear, and (in some cases) an emotion much like grief. (For discussion of the evidence supporting these claims, see Carruthers, 2006,

165

ch.2) In short: most animals can *suffer*. Stronger still, I shall assume for these purposes that most animals undergo experiences and feelings that are *conscious*, having the same kind of rich phenomenology and inner "feel" as do our own conscious mental states.[21]

In his 2011 article titled "Animal Mentality," Carruthers also writes that "Many animals experience pain, of course, including invertebrates such as hermit-crabs."[22] Statements like these appear to be the opposite of what Carruthers maintained in previous years. But before the reader gets too excited and begins to feel that Professor Carruthers may have at last seen the light, it is necessary to explore a little further where it soon becomes apparent that the identical Professor Carruthers who has been present from the very beginning is still hard at work. Even as he acknowledges that animals experience pain, this comes with the qualification that though "Many animals experience pain....if a higher-order theory is correct then they [animals, vertebrates and invertebrates] aren't *aware* that they are experiencing pain, and their pains aren't phenomenally conscious."[23] [The emphasis is by Carruthers.]

Carruthers uses the Kantian term "phenomenally conscious" in place of the term "nonconscious" to reaffirm his opinion that animals lack consciousness. ("Nonconscious" was Carruthers' preferred term in his article "Brute Experience" (1989)) He employs the term in the negative, i.e., animals *are not phenomenally conscious* because they do not experience consciousness in the way humans do. They cannot, therefore, be aware of phenomena including the experience of pain. This is just a continuation of Carruthers theory of "nonconsciosness" to which he subscribed at the time he wrote "Brute Experience."

Moreover, Carruthers confirms just how anti-animal he continues to be when, in making the argument that only humans deserve moral standing, he defines his position with what he terms a slogan consisting of these words: "Humans in, animals out."[24]

It is apparent that Professor Carruthers has been forced by emerging scientific evidence to change the terms he originally used to clothe his ideas in a manner that conformed to the latest facts and scientific research. But clearly, beneath the suit lies the same kind of thinking: animals are things because of the differences that exist between humans and nonhumans. Humans are up here. Animals are down there. The division between the two cannot be bridged. The recognition of the common qualities that unite all life forms has no meaning. Animals are not rational according to a hierarchical perspective. They are, therefore, inferior. This is the bottom line. It is the same old

Aristotle/Galen/St.Augustine/Aquinas/Descartes/Kant paradigm. Even though Professor Carruthers acknowledges that "…animals possess many remarkable cognitive capacities…" and that "…apes seem to possess at least some of the ingredients of human moral psychology, such as sympathy for others and engagement in reciprocal social interactions," still he refuses to grant that animals are "rational agents" (an entity capable of choosing between right and wrong) or that animals have moral standing, theorizing that they do not from the perspective of "contractualism." Contractualism is a philosophical concept loosely defined here as a theory of an agreement between two parties for the ultimate benefit of both where all factors are equal and nothing is concealed. The catch is that for both parties to enter into a contract they have to be "rational agents" (capable of choosing between right and wrong) which, Carruthers believes, animals are not.

The above account describes the basis upon which Carruthers tries to maintain that animals do not have moral standing. It is his way of trotting out the same old theories dressed in different attire. But while these philosophical concepts Professor Carruthers employs are suitable for university classes and conferences where these kinds of issues are mulled over, they have no scientific basis. They do not represent the reality of what animals intrinsically are in regard to consciousness for which much scientific evidence has already been assembled, some of which has been presented in this book.

Professor Carruthers has set before his audience arguments that are based on subjective assumptions that cannot be proved. He admits, for example, that "we don't know how to imagine a pain that isn't phenomenally conscious."[25] For the sake of argument, allowing, for a moment, Carruthers' premise that animals experience pain but aren't aware of it because they are not phenomenally conscious, how can this premise be conjectured if we cannot "imagine a pain that isn't phenomenally conscious?" The theory that animals are not phenomenally conscious is nothing but a wild guess with nothing to support the conjecture.

Subjective assumptions do not represent reality or truth and quickly fall apart. Added to Carruther's difficulties in supporting his claims with evidence, he is opposed by other philosopher/theorists who take a broader view in the debate about the conscious mental states of animals. Rocco J. Gennaro, Professor of Philosophy at the University of Southern Indiana, has challenged Carruthers and has noted that "… most of us believe that many animals have conscious mental states…"[26],[27] And for the general public, almost everyone who has ever lived with an animal in their home can describe examples of consciousness related to their animal friends such as the one described earlier by the author in relation to his cat Goldie Boy. To think of the action Goldie Boy took as a nonconscious experience as he sought to awaken his companion on the grounds that Goldie Boy is a "lower" animal incapable of thinking about his own thoughts in the manner in which human beings ostensibly do, lacks the objectivity to be taken seriously, nor does it come close to accurately describing what happened. All Goldie Boy had to think to define himself as a conscious being was that he wanted to wake his companion up and to communicate that fact to him. That quite suffices as consciousness no matter how Professor Carruthers or other animal research advocates might demand that cats and dogs possess the same sophisticated kind of mind owned by human beings that supposedly has nothing more to do than think things about itself all the time.

It is one thing to say that the mind of one animal is more sophisticated than another and quite another to say that the mind of a nonhuman animal is nonconscious (or, if the reader prefers, "not phenomenally conscious") because it is less sophisticated than that of a human animal, which is what Professor Carruthers has essentially postulated.

IV

A Stab in the Shamanistic Dark

Professor Carruthers appears almost shamanistic when he repeats the mantra that "if animals aren't phenomenally conscious, then their mental lives are all 'dark on the inside.'"[28] He first stated this mysterious theory in "Brute Experience." There he said that "if consciousness is like the turning on of a light, then it may be that their lives [animals] are nothing but darkness." If, as Professor Carruthers has admitted, we don't know how to imagine "a pain that isn't phenomenally conscious," how is that we can imagine what the inner state of an animal's mind is like, whether light, dark, intangible, or a mystery to be solved? From a hierarchical perspective, if an animal's mind is all dark on the inside, it would naturally follow that the mind of a human is all light on the inside, or, as Professor Carruthers describes human consciousness, like "turning on a light." It seems rather obvious, however, that the human mind holds a vast variety of multifarious images, qualities, perceptions, memories, desires, reflections, emotions, thoughts, states of mind, introspections and much, much more including on occasion, perhaps, darkness and light. It also seems rather apparent that while the human mind may be complex, there is still much in common between the human mind and that of nonhuman animals which are also complex.

Just as in "Brute Experience," Professor Carruthers leaves the premises in his article "Animal Mentality" hanging with no resolution even though this article was written in 2011, twenty-two years later. Now he tells the reader that "the prospect of widespread phenomenal consciousness among animals appears quite bleak, from a higher-order [human] perspective."[29] Further, he relates that "on the other hand, there are theories of phenomenal consciousness that probably imply that few if any animals besides humans are phenomenally conscious."[30] While these two statements may adequately present assumptions about animal consciousness, they have not overcome the same inadequacies of the arguments Professor Carruthers presented in "Brute Experience." The theories he relied upon yesterday and still relies upon today are unscientific and are not supported by evidence or fact. This is the same method that philosophers who deny the rights of animals have always relied upon right from the start, beginning with Aristotle.

As to what the mind of a nonhuman animal is really like, it seems far more logical to suspect that the quality of animals' minds might well be described as that which enables them to fulfill the functions of what their objectives in life consist, doing gorilla things, or cat things, or pig things, or dog things, or caterpillar things. In this respect their minds are exactly like human minds which are designed to do human things simply because that is what the human mind does, though the neural pathways that relate to the functioning of different species may differ such as for dogs who remember easily, chimpanzees who remember only with difficulty, or human beings who are able to think about their own thoughts and how right they may be even when they are substantially wrong. Like Alexander Pope wisely said: "Man has reason enough only to know what is necessary for him to know, and dogs have just that too."

From the time of Aristotle to the present, animal researchers have traditionally measured consciousness from a hierarchical perspective that demands that animal intelligence match human intelligence if it is to be accepted as rational or "conscious." This is a narrow "might makes right" approach, illustrated also in Professor Carruthers' deeply rooted beliefs as expressed most concisely through his comparison of humans to animals through "high-order" vs. "first-order" theory and in his logo "Humans in, animals out." Unfortunately, in the world today, any animal who is "out" is a suitable candidate for slaughter on a factory farm; to be sliced into by a researcher's scalpel in a university animal research laboratory; to be skinned alive or anally electrocuted on a fur farm; to be tormented and tortured in blood sports, rodeos, or circuses; to be imprisoned in zoos; to be drowned or starved to death caught in the jaws of a hunter's trap isolated from all that gives life meaning; or to be killed or wounded by a hunter's high-powered bullet and, unable to defend itself, either be set upon by predator animals or die alone bleeding to death from the bullet wound without relief for pain in the underbrush where it has fled, thinking about, if it is a female who has just given birth, of her babies left alone in her lair where they will now starve to death or be devoured by other predators.

As this examination of Professor Carruthers' theories have shown, no matter how hard animal researchers and their supporters try, they cannot prove the kinds of hypotheses they propound, either intellectually, philosophically, scientifically, or spiritually. Their only recourse is to declare that they are right no matter what and proceed accordingly like Professor Bernard did when he brought the terrified dogs up from his basement prisons to his laboratory to undergo vivisection in late 19th century France. Might makes right. This is the approach animal researchers have taken since the inauguration of animal research 2300 years ago when Aristotle emaciated dogs and then strangled them to death so that he could dissect them. If animal researchers have their way, they will continue the same process for the next 2300 years.

Chapter 14

The Flat Earth of Immanuel Kant

The wild guesses, assumptions, presumptions, and suppositions made by animal researchers and their advocates have brought considerable suffering to the world. None have been more damaging than the philosophical speculation that animals are nonrational, mindless creatures.

Immanuel Kant said the following:

> Beings whose existence depends not on our will but on nature have, nevertheless, if they are not rational beings, only a relative value as means and are therefore called things. On the other hand, rational beings are called persons inasmuch as their nature already marks them out as ends in themselves.[1]

This line of thought corresponds with the same Immanuel Kant introduced in chapter 7 who said: "animals are not self-conscious, and are there merely as a means to an end. That end is man." Like Aristotle, Kant did not think it was important to challenge the conventions and biases of his day in relation to animals. Kant had grown up in a society that was increasingly accepting vivisection. The Reverend Stephen Hales was already bleeding animals to death in his blood pressure experiments when Kant was just three years of age. (See chapter 7.)

The fallacies in Kant's unapologetic speciesism is laid out by the philosopher himself:

> The fact that the human being can have the representation "I" raises him infinitely above all the other

beings on earth. By this he is a person....that is, a being altogether different in rank and dignity from things, such as irrational animals, with which one may deal and dispose at one's discretion.[2]

In order to represent themselves with the pronoun "I," of course, humans had to have acquired language, and, referring once again to this major point of contention between reality and supposition pointed out in this book, humans did not acquire language until around 150,000 years ago. According to Kant, then—applying this point—the nearly seven million years of human existence that preceded the human ability to speak language and refer to themselves as "I" means that humans were irrational animals during that entire seven million year period with whom, according to Kant, it would have been proper to deal with and "dispose" of at one's discretion which, apparently, quite a few larger wild predator animals did when it came time for dinner.

Granted, Kant was at a disadvantage. Without the archaeological evidence available in today's world from which to derive information, Kant's world was a flat earth. The same applies to Descartes and, for that matter, to Aristotle. These three philosophers and all who followed prior to the mid-20th century who championed the Aristotelian rational/nonrational hypothesis about animals were also unaware that human existence could be traced back more than seven million years and that for most of that period human beings functioned without language. Science in the day of these philosophers also had yet to consider that thought can be unconscious and does not require language as, for example, happens with chess players when they are contemplating moves on the chess board.

It can only be a matter of speculation as to whether current archaeological and anthropological research and scholarship might have caused Aristotle, Kant, or Descartes to revise their outlook on animal rationality if they were they alive today, or whether, like Professor Carruthers and others, they would have just devised new terms for expressing a speciesist world outlook. The fact that people like Theophrastus, Margaret Cavendish, David Hume, David

Hartley, Jeremy Bentham, John Tweedle, Percy Bysshe Shelley, Arthur Schopenhauer, Richard Wagner, Francis Power Cobbe and many others had no problem going beyond the norms of their times to overcome stereotypic thinking in relation to the treatment of animals offers the philosophers who supported animal research few excuses for their failure to do the same. Theophrastus, Cavendish, Hume, Bentham, Shelley, Hartley, Tweedle, Cobbe and all the others who opposed vivisection and animal cruelty lived on the same flat earth.

Like Kant, most humans generally assume that their species has the right to divide and apportion the rights of other species according to human desires and wishes based on a philosophy of being which holds that humans are superior to animals and that this superiority gives them the right to exploit other species. Humans slaughter billions of animals every year to meet their perceived needs, including for food, clothing, industrial uses, and entertainment. The animal research industry itself slaughters billions of animals every few years. Yet the medical and ecological evidence shows convincingly that humans are paying serious consequences for using and abusing other species against their will in terms of their personal health and damage to the earth and its life forms. It is not difficult to foresee that the abuses of animals lead in the direction of a cataclysmic ending for humankind if these trends continue.

Were he able to survey the world today, Immanuel Kant might well take back those words spoken some two hundred years ago with such rash abandon when he said that animals, because they were irrational, were suitable to be disposed of "at one's discretion."[3] He might even join with other concerned people who are putting their ears to the earth to learn how to get along with nature while rejecting the reliance on ideas and ideals that still emanate from ancient societies dependent upon the blood of sacrificed animals for their intellectual and spiritual nourishment.

Chapter 15

Are Animals More Moral Than Humans?
Who Gets to Decide?

Immanuel Kant indicated in his *Lectures* that humans do have direct duties to animals but only insofar as they affect their duties to people. John Calvin said the same in the 16th century. (See chapter 5) In the 13th century Thomas Aquinas wrote:

> Now it is evident that if a man practice a pitiable affection for animals, he is all the more disposed to take pity on his fellow-men.[1]

Carrying on the tradition, Professor Carruthers asserted the following basis for being concerned about the way animals are treated:

> To meet this challenge we should claim that while we do have duties towards animals, they are *indirect*, in the sense that the duties are owed to someone other than the animal, and that they fail to have any corresponding rights in the animal. According to one suggestion, they derive from a direct duty not to cause unnecessary offence to the feelings of animal-lovers or animal owners, and it is to them that we have the duty. [2]

Any concern for animals needs to be held in check, however, even *indirect* concern, because, as Professor Carruthers warned:

> ...increased feelings of sympathy for animals can only serve to undermine our judgments of relative

importance, having the same moral effect as de-creased concern for humans.[3]

This kind of thinking is in line with a continuum extending from the work of predecessor philosophers like Kant and theologists like Calvin which, in turn, was grounded in the writings of earlier philosophers and theologians like Thomas Aquinas. While there is always much to be gained from studying the ways in which the world's leaders in their spheres of influence have met the challenges of their day, latching onto their words and deeds without ample questioning and deep enough reflection as to their rightness and significance can lead to a loss of independence of mind and a blurring of the capacity to recognize what is moral and what is not.

As previously shown, Professor Carruthers theorizes that animals have no consciousness in any manner meaningful enough that would give them rights, such as the right not to be exploited and abused by human beings. Because he does not believe animals have rights, quite naturally he sees no reason for humans to try to protect animals from abuse and exploitation. To make his point Carruthers relies on the concept of rational agency, as previously referred to, which has been handed down by philosophers like Kant. A rational agent is an agent (a living creature) which does the right thing based on its beliefs. Because animals, according to the theory, do not have the capacity to choose right from wrong in regard to beliefs they may hold, they do not qualify as "rational agents." Applying the concept, Professor Carruthers informs us that "there seems no reason why rights should be assigned to nonrational agents. Animals will, therefore, have no moral standing..."[4]

There is, however, no scientific basis for the assumption that animals do not make moral decisions. Though in their infancy, studies are being done which focus on the capacity of animals for choosing right from wrong which should help determine whether human assumptions such as the denial of rational agency for animals held by humans for centuries have any basis in fact or if they are just the normal guesswork applied to animals.

According to Harvard psychologist Marc Hauser, widely known for his work in animal cognition, scientists are learning that animals possess the same "building blocks that make moral judgments possible in humans." In an interview for American Scientist, he reports that Tamarin monkeys and chimpanzees show evidence "that individuals distinguish between intentional and accidental actions." Furthermore, "animals seem to distinguish between animate and inanimate objects…[which are] critically involved in moral judgments."[5] Scientists have also been studying a related topic in animals for decades: biological altruism. Some scientists just attribute biological altruism to genetics where altruism can be traced to survival mechanisms in individual species, though no consensus has emerged on the subject. In this connections, it should also be apparent that various survival mechanisms often account for human altruism which might be attributed to genetics so that genetics should not be used to minimize altruism in animals unless the same criteria is applied to human altruism.

If animals possess a moral sense then it can hardly be denied that they are not only rational agents, but conscious beings and far more than "things," as Kant called them, or any other term that attempts to define animals as being incapable of rational thought. The exact knowledge of how approximate animals may be to humans in possessing a moral sense may yet lie in the future insofar as establishing definitive evidence goes, but it is worthwhile to note that some forward-thinking scientists have already made their positions known that some animals quite convincingly make moral decisions. In *Shadows of Forgotten Ancestors*, the late Carl Sagan and his wife and colleague, Ann Druyan, who survives him, described a horrendous animal experiment that showed convincingly that macaque monkeys possess an ethical sense that far outshines that of most humans.

> In the annals of primate ethics, there are some accounts that have the ring of parable. In a laboratory setting, macaques were fed if they were willing to pull a chain and electrically shock an unrelated macaque whose agony was in plain view through a one-way mirror.

Otherwise, they starved. After learning the ropes, the monkeys frequently refused to pull the chain; in one experiment only 13% would do so - 87% preferred to go hungry. One macaque went without food for nearly two weeks rather than hurt its fellow. Macaques who had themselves been shocked in previous experiments were even less willing to pull the chain. The relative social status or gender of the macaques had little bearing on their reluctance to hurt others.

If asked to choose between the human experimenters offering the macaques this Faustian bargain and the macaques themselves—suffering from real hunger rather than causing pain to others—our own moral sympathies do not lie with the scientists. But their experiments permit us to glimpse in nonhumans a saintly willingness to make sacrifices in order to save others—even those who are not close kin. By conventional human standards, these macaques—who have never gone to Sunday school, never heard of the Ten Commandments, never squirmed through a single junior high school civics lesson—seem exemplary in their moral grounding and their courageous resistance to evil. Among these macaques, at least in this case, heroism is the norm.[6]

In concluding this passage, Sagan and Druyan appropriately ask if we humans would do as well. Certainly the question deserves to be put to the animal researchers who designed this cruel experiment and to animal philosopher/theorists who deny the capacity for morality in animals in spite of evidence to the contrary. Generally, it can be stated that the basis for the judgments philosopher/theorist advocates for animal research make relative to the lives of animals such as that they have no moral standing consists of little more than conjecture arising out of human self-assumed superiority over all nonhuman species. .

Chapter 16

Indifference to Suffering:
Animal Slavery and Humanitarian Research

In her book *Experimenting With Humans and Animals: From Galen to Animal Rights*, Anita Guerrini describes the vivisection technique of one of the early animal vivisectors, William Harvey (1578-1657). (See also chapter 6.)

> He walked over to a stack of cages and opened the topmost one, gently pulling out a large rabbit. Its nose twitched as the doctor carefully tied it to a board with holes drilled in it through which he passed the thin cord that bound the animal's limbs. The rabbit lay on its back, blinking and quivering, its limbs splayed, its chest rising and falling quickly. The doctor took a sharp, thin-bladed knife and with practiced skill laid open the rabbit's chest. The animal struggled and panted, but the bonds held fast. The doctor sliced through the breast-bone and spread open the ribcage with his strong fingers, exposing the rapidly beating heart. He cut a strong thread of silk and tied it around the rabbit's aorta, watching with satisfaction as the animal's heart grew engorged with blood while the vessel beyond the ligature became white. He delicately sliced the aorta and saw the blood spurt out in regular pulses. As the rabbit slowly expired, the doctor seized a notebook and began to write, looking up to observe the rabbits' heart as it slowed.[1]

Indifferent to the suffering he caused the animals upon whom he experimented without anesthesia or mercy, Harvey repeated this experiment hundreds of times on many kinds of animals to prove that the blood circulated through the body.

People who gasp in horror at this vision yet still say "but if he hadn't done this we wouldn't know about blood circulation," are missing the point. Such arguments are similar to a plantation owner in 19th century America saying, "if the slaves hadn't picked cotton last summer we would have been poor this winter without heat." Stealing the rights of another person against his or her will constitutes the theft of that persons rights with all the accompanying suffering that attends the crime. To take away the rights of an animal is not only bullying and cruel, it is an expression of extreme cynicism in that is shows a lack of confidence in the human potential to solve the mysteries of existence without resorting to unconscionable practices such as enslaving animals.

As is the case with human slavery, animal researchers do their best to claim that animal slaves have no inherent rights. But they have yet to present either a scientifically sound or an ethically believable case that they have the right to enslave and conduct experiments on animals against their will. No animal research, no matter how pure the motives underlying it claim to be, can overcome the objections that subjecting weaker species to human domination cannot be morally, philosophically, spiritually, or intellectually justified without resorting to excuses and rationalizations.

Given the history of how technology has developed, it is more than apparent that humans would have eventually devised another method for discovering blood circulation without vivisecting animals had they totally rejected vivisection in Harvey's day. This is not a baseless assumption. The theory of blood circulation was known by the ancient Chinese as far back as 2560 BC. By 600 BC physicians in India were pumping blood through cadavers. Leonardo Da Vinci also made very accurate drawings of the heart and blood vessels before Harvey was born without vivisecting animals and recognized that the arteries providing blood flow were equipped with valves to prevent the blood from changing course.[2] Both Galen and Harvey, on the other hand, reportedly made several mistakes in their blood circulation studies based on vivisection.

With the natural abilities and talents human beings possess and considering the knowledge about blood circulation that already existed prior to both Galen and Harvey's time, the mysteries of blood circulation would surely have been uncovered in the Western world without the need for vivisecting animals just as many medical mysteries are being solved today without resorting to the practice.[3]

Few would dispute the assertion that animal research as it is practiced in the 21st century might be summarized as a system in which animal researchers and their supporters believe that their work is absolutely essential for human progress and that it is for the benefit of humankind no matter how unrelated to human disease it may be. Animal researchers feel assured that they are leading lives of accomplishment by conducting tests upon enslaved animals. In the process, they plug into the support system set up by fellow animal researchers past and present in collaboration with the US government in which various government agencies award them huge grants of public money in research funds. After a life of comfortable living supported by animal slaverey, they bestow honors and prestige upon themselves for their work and go off into the sunset to live out their golden years. This mutual support system for animal researchers and government employees keeps government funding for animal experiments in operation and surrounds animal researchers with a wall of protection from outside criticism.

It is only fair and right to acknowledge that some animal researchers really do believe that their work is for humanitarian purposes. However, this group, like all other animal researchers, are reluctant to admit that any problems exist within the animal research industry and will not acknowledge that animal research that has nothing to do with serious medical research is morally wrong even when it is clear that it is just part of a "one hand washes the other" system that builds personal and institutional wealth for animal researchers and their supporting institutions at the expense of the lives of enslaved animals innocent of any wrongdoing.

All animal researchers, including these "humanitarian" researchers who perceive themselves to be highly ethical in their use of animals, deserve the sharpest criticism for not taking a stand against drug, alcohol, and tobacco addiction testing. It cannot be difficult to comprehend that it is not ethical under any circumstances to subject animals to experiments that cause them suffering and the forfeiture of their lives in order to attend to the addiction problems human beings have created for themselves. Even the most fundamental code of ethics dictates that human beings should acknowledge responsibility for their own problems including their addictions. It can hardly be more unjust than to require innocent animals to pay for human mistakes. In the case of fetus addiction, the excuse that the research is for the protection of babies during pregnancy also does not succeed because alternative treatment options are available including therapies for addicted, pregnant mothers-to-be. Any research in that direction is unethical anyway and should only be done without the use of animals which could never be ethical even if human fetuses are involved. Two wrongs cannot a right make.

An examination of their writings reveals that animals have no more meaning for animal researchers in the 21st centuries than they did for William Harvey when he was slicing open the chests of rabbits in the 17th century. This is true whether the research is for humanitarian purposes or for repetition, curiosity, and addiction testing. For vivisectors, including those who would excuse their work on humanitarian grounds, an animal may as well be a piece of cardboard, a plastic bottle, or a random piece of junk. Consider, for example, the writings of Alexander Leaf, MD (d. 2013), in relation to the use of animals to examine diet and the prevention of heart disease.

Dr. Leaf was the Jackson Professor of Clinical Medicine Emeritus at Harvard University after whom the Alexander Leaf Distinguished Scientist Award for Lifetime Achievement was established. He was elected to membership in the American Academy of Arts and Sciences and was one of the first physicians elected to the National Academy of Sciences. But, for Dr. Leaf, the living of life meant much more than a list of credentials to boast about. He also distinguished himself by his travels to the Caucasus Mountains, the Hunza Valley of Pakistan, and the foothills of the Andes where he learned by his study of the people of these regions that a diet high in vegetables and low in animal fat led to long and healthy life free from heart disease.

Dr. Arnold S. Relman, a professor emeritus at Harvard Medical School and former editor in chief of The New England Journal, described Dr. Leaf as a man who "had a moral sense that science was not just for answering basic questions about the human body, but for dealing with the broader questions of human suffering and human welfare." That this appraisal was on target is evident in that Dr. Leaf was a founding member of Physicians for Social Responsibility, an organization that concerned itself with social and environmental issues which was formed to oppose nuclear proliferation.[4]

[The paragraphs that follow were written before the death of Dr. Leaf.]

Unfortunately, as with many brilliant individuals, when some of Dr. Leaf's articles involving animal research are examined, an ethical side emerges that from a scientific as well as an ethical perspective is far from fully formed. For example, an article written by Dr. Leaf and his associates titled "Omega-3 Fatty Acids and Ventricular Arrhythmias" stated the following:

> The first investigators to demonstrate the anti-arrhythmias effect of w-3 fish oil fatty acids were two Australians, Peter McLennan and John Charnock. In the late 1980s they were publishing their simple and clear experiments. They subjected young rats to a diet in which they could control the major fat component for a period of 3 or 4 months. Then they simply ligated the coronary arteries of the rats and counted the number of rats, which died of irreversible ventricular fibrillation...[5] [Fibrillation: very rapid irregular contraction of the muscle fibers of the heart resulting in a lack of synchronism between heartbeat and pulse.]

The kind of dispassionate language that Dr. Leaf employs in expressing his esteem for work that killed enslaved rats does not come from someone who spent much time reflecting on whether or not animals are living, breathing creatures with their own lives to live who have an enormous interest in avoiding suffering and staying alive. It may reasonably be inferred by the above passage that Dr. Leaf, like Aristotle and Immanuel Kant, was also conditioned by his times to believe that animal research was an acceptable practice without considering in any great depth the morality of the issue.

With Dr. Leaf's model of research, we encounter once again the grand enigma of how some of the most intelligent people in the world are so capable of participating in cruelty to innocent animals without questioning their own actions. An obvious disconnect exists between intelligence and morality. It is almost as if these researchers were viewing life through a tunnel without knowing how to emerge to view the vista that spreads before them as far as the eye can see.

Ironically, in spite of his work on diet in his exotic travels, Dr. Leaf seems never to have grasped that it is the consumption of animals that produces the heart disease for which he and his colleagues sought a cure by experimenting upon animals. The same work continues today with many other animal researchers though the threat of heart disease and stroke can be virtually eliminated in most instances by eliminating the consumption of animal products.[6] This is no secret, so it is apparent that animal researchers doing animal testing for trying to find a cure for heart disease and stroke want to keep their cake and eat it at the same time. They want to find a cure for heart disease and stroke that still allows people to consume animals. How ethical can it be to experiment upon animals to try to find a cure for a disease when one already exists just because the cure requires humans to do something they are reluctant to do—stop eating animals?

When they are examined, the writings of animal researchers reveal a lack of sympathy and concern for the enslaved animals upon whom they experiment, subjecting them to unwanted surgery, unnecessary suffering, and unwarranted death. At the same

184

time, an inordinate sensitivity and empathy for the research itself can be anticipated. This becomes more than apparent in the same article by Dr. Leaf, et al., where the following observation is recorded:

> To return to our interest in seeing if we could confirm the findings of Charnock and McLennan, we turned to Prof. George E. Billman at the Ohio State University Department of Psychology since he had a highly reliable dog model of sudden cardiac death. Dr. Billman operates on a dog tying off the left main arterior descending coronary artery to create a large anterior ventricular infarct. At the same operation, he leaves a hydraulic cuff around the left circumflex coronary artery and exteriorizes this so that he can occlude the artery later at will. During the month he allows the dog to recover from the MI and surgery he trains it to run on a treadmill.[7]

The above is a description of Ohio University Professor George E. Billman's work which Leaf describes with obvious admiration. In this work, Billman causes a dog to have a heart attack which he revives just before it is ready to die. After permitting the dog to recover, he then forces it to run on a treadmill whereupon he causes it to have a fatal heart attack by constricting an artery by means of a sleeve he has inserted around the dog's coronary artery.

This example describes how easily so-called "humanitarian" research to solve human medical problems can be far from humanitarian in its execution. While it cannot be accurately concluded that all so-called humanitarian animal research is as callous and cruel as the above example, it is not difficult to infer that it very often is. In any event, any experiment that takes away the rights of an individual animal without its permission, which is enslavement, must be considered cruel.

In another article, this one pertaining to fatty acids in the Mediterranean diet, Dr. Leaf refers to his own research using dogs:

In addition, studies have reported potent anti-arrhythmic effects of long-chain PUFAs, especially of the n-3 class, manifested by prevention of ischemia-induced fatal ventricular arrhythmias in rats, marmosets, and dogs, and there is suggestive evidence that these n-3 fatty acids may prevent sudden cardiac death in humans. This has been the focus of research by my laboratory group, who have found that a concentrate of free fatty acids of fish oils, but also the pure individual n-3 PUFAs eicosapentaenoic acid (EPA), docosahexaenoic acid (DHA), and α-linolenic acid (LNA), all prevent fatal ventricular arrhythmias in a reliable dog model of sudden cardiac death with a very high probability.[8]

As always, the language directed toward animals is robotic and dispassionate. Clearly, in these experiments a dog is little more than a thing just as has been observed in the other research projects examined in this book. No consideration has been given to the contributions dogs have made in non-invasive animal cognition projects that might raise their status so that they could be treated more humanely and exempted from cruel experiments like the sudden cardiac death experiments conducted by Dr. Leaf and Prof. Billman. The previous description of the remarkable memory of dogs and their ability to infer things from the objects in their environment come instantly to mind—studies that are assisting animal psychologists in discovering new things about human behavior. In fact, from such studies it should be apparent that whoever should deny that a dog has an intelligent mind is very uninformed and that vivisectors who vivisect dogs are vivisecting animals who possess highly intelligent minds. It is reasonable to hope that such facts would give a compassionate and reflective person pause before subjecting a dog to heart attack experiments.

Animal research that shows the potential for human benefit often proves to have been unnecessary erasing the entire purpose for the research right from the beginning. In Dr. Leaf's studies on fatty acids, for example, which centered around the prevention of heart disease, it turns out that the consumption of fish to obtain those fatty acids (the findings for which was the motivation for Dr. Leaf's project) is far more dangerous than any health benefits that might accrue from eating them. Consuming fish is extremely hazardous, though the healthcare establishment has been slow to communicate the extent of the risk to the public. The danger results from the toxic chemicals and high levels of methylmercury found in fish at concentrations as high as nine million times those found in the water in which they swim. Methylmercury is associated with rises in blood pressure, impaired neurological function in infants, and reduced fertility in adults. Chemicals and pesticides in fish are also suspected as being possible agents in promoting non-Hodgkin's lymphoma and other cancers. The American Cancer Society cautions that besides the fear of mercury contaminants, tuna, salmon, and larger fish may also contain dioxins and PCBs (polychlorinated biphenyls). Dioxins are toxic chemicals associated with cancer risk, which, according to the FDA, find their way into the human body through the ingestion of animal fats. PCBs are probable causes of cancer including deadly liver cancer. Farm-raised fish may contain even more toxins than fish caught in the wilds because they are fed fish that have ingested contaminants like PCBs.

Would it be too impertinent to ask if anyone has had a tuna sandwich or "thrown a shrimp on the Barbie" lately?[9]

Of course, people can continue consuming fish if they wish and if they enjoy playing Russian Roulette. It should be apparent, in any event, that studies done on animals that were experimented upon and killed by animal researchers in order to show that consuming fish might prevent heart disease, such as those conducted by Dr. Leaf and his associates, were experimented upon and killed for benefits that cannot be scientifically justified considering the dangers of consuming fish.

The healthcare establishment which supports the consumption of seafood is not anxious to admit facts like these nor are universities, biomedical research institutions, private medical facilities, and other institutions which support heart research using animals in studies that encourage eating fish. It is far better to enslave innocent dogs and kill them than to admit the truth about the many flaws and ethical concerns which surround this kind of research, and, anyway, dogs are an expendable commodity even if they do have better memories than chimpanzees—not that dogs have anything to teach humans about memory. Do they?

Unfortunately, mainstream scientists do not take the kind of research seriously which shows that heart disease, stroke, diabetes, and many forms of cancer can be prevented and vastly reduced by eliminating animal products from the diet. They also disregard facts such as that people who want to consume omega 3 fatty acids but avoid the risk of getting them from diseased fish can get them from a variety of non-animal food sources that include beans, nuts, soybeans, walnuts, black currant seed oil, flaxseed oil, soybean oil, pumpkin seed oil, walnut oil, Purslane (an exotic weed (a vegetable)), and seeds like flax seeds, hemp seeds, and pumpkin seeds.[10]

Once animal researchers decide on a project and set a goal, they forge ahead without consideration of whether there is really any necessity for the work in which they are engaged. Besides, since it is a research projects most likely being funded by the NIH or another government agency, it is always lucrative for everyone involved, excluding the animals, naturally.

Thousands upon thousands of dispassionate descriptions of enslaved animals experimented upon and killed against their will in so-called humanitarian research projects such as those conducted by Dr. Leaf and Professor Billman are filed away in university and medical facility archives around the world. Most of these experiments have never benefitted anyone, but they have cost the taxpayers billions of dollars and have resulted in the deaths of billions of innocent animals.

Chapter 17

Why Animal Research is a Pseudo Science

The terms "scientist" and "science" when attached to animal research lend it the legitimacy required for broad public acceptance. But many critics of animal research claim that it is an illegitimate science which the science community should reject because animal research does not meet the standards of true science. Can animal research claim to be a science according to the requisites of science? If it cannot, should the science community reject it just as it rejects a field like astrology which it regards as a pseudo science? What do the facts say?

Before 1833 when the British philosopher, theologian, historian, and Renaissance man William Whewell (1794–1866) coined the term "scientist," the word science had been associated mostly with natural philosophy as a designation for the study of nature (the nonhuman world). Back then a scientist was referred to as a "man of science" or a "natural philosopher."[1] From the 16th to 18th centuries forward, men like Bacon, Galileo, Kepler, and Sir Isaac Newton were developing a type of reliable knowledge constructed from strong, fact-based, premises that were provable and upon which people could depend, known today as the "scientific method." This became the norm associated with the group of people who call themselves scientists, even though the term was not commonly used until after 1870.

The positive reputation of science as a profession continued to evolve in a progressive upward spiral which helped give the word science the favorable connotations associated with the word today. By the mid-20th century, the term scientist represented a distinct kind of highly trained, technically skilled researcher who obtained a specialized kind of knowledge derived from the practice of the scientific method, often in conjunction with the latest technological advances for whatever was being studied.

To meet the criteria of science and the scientific method, a hypothesis, or problem, needs to be stated with an expected outcome which is then tested objectively and experimentally in an unbiased way to determine if it should be accepted or rejected. In the process, previous information regarding the hypothesis and the results of experiments made to evaluate it need to be collected and added to the appraisal in attempting to prove or disprove the hypothesis being tested. The experiment itself must also be repeatable and all data must be shareable so that it can be reproduced by any other investigator who wishes to corroborate or challenge the data produced. This is what is called science.

Does animal research meet the criteria of science and the scientific method? For the following reasons the answer must be an unqualified "no."

From a scientific standpoint, the problem for every animal researcher who has ever subscribed to or presently subscribes to the rationale separating the human animal from the nonhuman animal based on the hypothesis of hierarchy is that there has never been a scientific validation of the hypothesis either before or after Aristotle. Yet this hierarchical hypothesis is the foundation upon which animal research stands. Excluding the work of animal cognition scientists, or scientists and individuals doing related work, there has never been any systematic effort to determine whether the hypothesis that animals cannot reason and do not feel pain is true or false, which is a major premise upon which the legitimacy of animal research depends. Animal researchers have always simply assumed and declared that animals were suitable subjects for research and vivisection simply because animals were nonrational "things," as Kant called them, and further, that animals did not experience pain. Or, for those animals who did seem to experience pain, it was assumed that it could not compare to human pain and was therefore irrelevant. This is not science. It is conjecture and the imposition of assumption and belief upon a premise.

Real science conducted by animal cognition scientists in today's world has shown conclusively that different animals reason and think and that they suffer pain. As discussed, these animal cognition scientists test and debate animal consciousness in many different ways.[2] In the process they are proving what most people know instinctively, that animals are conscious, intelligent beings who experience pain and pleasure and a wide range of emotions which reveal striking correlations between human and nonhuman consciousness. For example, the brains of rats release large amounts of dopamine when they play.[3] This also happens with humans. Dopamine is associated with pleasure so that rats, rather obviously, experience pleasure. Studies also show how the amygdale, an almond-shaped structure in the brains, is activated in both humans and rats when they are angry.[4] Just as obviously, rats, like humans, also experience anger. For their part, as we have seen, food storing animals reveal "that some animals have conscious forethought."[5] Crows have also been observed hiding their food from other crows. This shows conscious awareness and complex interspecies interactions.

In order to claim scientific legitimacy, animal researchers must be required to acknowledge what the research shows which is that their science is founded on experimenting on conscious, thinking, emotional beings who experience pain and suffering caused by their research. To date, however, animal researchers have been unwilling to acknowledge this evidence and make it a part of the description of their work available for public inspection and comment. They fear an admission like this would get in the way of their grant applications to the NIH and other funding organizations. They also worry that acknowledging to the public that animals are conscious, intelligent, emotional beings would be a major impetus to giving animals rights similar to those human beings have assigned to themselves such as the right not to have their freedom and their lives taken from them without their permission and the right not to be physically abused and have their lives disrespected. An admission like this would be a huge blow to the animal testing industry and the pretensions held by animal researchers that they are legitimate scientists. As a consequence, they hide the truth from the public.

For 2300 years animal researchers have accepted without question and without any testing the premise that animals are not rational and do not suffer pain in any meaningful way. This represents an enormous abdication of scientific responsibility. Even today, as discussed, no one in the animal research industry is willing to apply the scientific method to the hierarchical concepts upon which the industry and animal researchers rely for justifying animal research. Fortunately, animal cognition scientists are doing it for them whether they like it or not.

The scientific method requires full disclosure of all research and experiments so that their reproducibility is testable. Research on animals, however, has always been characterized by secrecy. The animal researchers quite simply do not want the outside world to see what they are doing. They perform their experiments behind locked doors while deceiving the public as to the true nature of their "science." This has been true right from the beginning when Aristotle strangled dogs to death in order to be able to dissect them.

The cruelty of the animal research being conducted behind these locked doors gets brought to public attention by whistle blowers or undercover investigators who manage to get inside animal research laboratories to observe what goes on there. Animal researchers who conduct experiments upon enslaved animals behind closed doors are not scientists from the standpoint of the definition of science in the scientific community where one of the primary rules is that the research must be sharable to all. Full disclosure is required for scientific legitimacy. Until animal researchers are willing to unlock their doors so that suspicions of fakery in how they write up the results of their experiments can be satisfied, no faith can be put in the truthfulness of the reports they make of their research.

For the animal researchers, full disclosure of their experiments would, of course, in many cases expose the cruelty to which many animal researchers subject the animals upon whom they experiment. This they want to conceal from the public at all costs.

No other field in science is based on cruelty except animal research. It rightly deserves the designation: "The cruel science."

Animal researchers derive their theory that animals are non-rational creatures as the rationale for the legitimacy of animal research by comparing animals to human beings using the criteria for reasoning, thinking, feeling, and consciousness that applies to human beings. The rather obvious possibility that animals might think and reason in different ways or that they might function with different abilities, talents, and priorities that are equally as profound as those possessed by human beings has never been a matter animal researchers have been willing to consider, debate, or put through rigorous testing employing the scientific method. At the same time, the researchers deny that the foundation for animal research is unscientific. And though they reject this charge, they will not open their doors to let the public see what they are doing. They persist in conducting their work protected by a wall of secrecy.

The insistence of animal researchers on concealing their work disqualifies them as scientists according to the standards set for the scientific method. True science must be shareable to everyone so that it can be reproduced by any other person, qualified or unqualified, who wishes to corroborate or challenge the data experiments produce. When experiments are done in secret, it is not possible to rely on the reports that the data ostensibly produces as being true.

Animal researchers have insisted from the very beginning that comparing animals to humans is the way to measure the value of nonhuman species. Because they cannot meet human standards, such as being able to walk on two feet (excepting birds and one or two other species) or to talk and express what goes on inside their minds and hearts with words, animal researchers have judged animals to be inferior. This is equivalent to judging the differences between human and nonhuman species to be differences of kind rather than differences of degree which is a profound distortion of reality. A mistake like this turns into tyranny when it imposes severe penalties on animals by condemning them to suffering and death for their failure to meet human standards without providing

193

any method by which animals might defend themselves against the charges brought against them, including the opportunity for humans to speak in their defense. In fact, whenever humans do attempt to speak on behalf of animals, animal researchers do everything in their power to discredit them. Quite simply put, animal researchers have never willingly permitted a defense of animals to take place and have done everything possible to prevent it from happening, including, with minor exceptions, the refusal to publicly debate the controversies that surround animal research and vivisection.

Animals researchers have sentenced animals to torture and death without a trial. They have condemned animals based on their "assumed" inability to reason and feel pain with no scientific evidence and no tests or experiments ever having been done to support the premises upon which animals are condemned. If anything in the debate lacks reason, it does not occur on the side of the animals. It is the dishonest and unscientific method used to conclude that nonhuman animals lack the ability to think (reason) and that animals do not experience pain to any significant degree. This is the foundation upon which animal research has been constructed from the beginning and for which no evidence has ever been presented in support of the hypothesis.

We stand at the dawn of a new century. It is the animal researchers who now must be required to prove their justifications for their work. They are the ones who must prove to the world that animals do not think, are nonrational, are without emotions, and do not feel pain in any meaningful way. If they cannot back up the rationale upon which their science is based using the scientific method, and if they are unwilling to open their doors in order to prove the reliability of their reports so that anyone who wishes can examine their research, they deserve to be designated a pseudo science unable to meet the requirements of true science.

Chapter 18

The Path to Greatness

Who has not yearned for the fulfillment of that dream handed down since ancient days where nations no longer lift sword against nation, nor do they learn war any more.[1] But as the scriptures describing this dream point out, that requires establishing a covenant with the creator who includes the wild animals of the fields, the birds of the air, and the creeping things of the ground in "his" domain. When human beings abandon their mistreatment of other species, cruelty as a hallmark of civilization will become a relic of the past. Only then will nations possess the capacity to beat their swords into plowshares and learn war no more.

Today, because of the close connection to the major problems of the world with the human mistreatment of animals, of which animal research is a major element, the need for an agreement to protect the nonhuman animal population of the world from human cruelty has become imperative. The justification for animal research developed from hierarchical concepts that regarded animals as having been put on the earth by nature and God for humans to use however they desired. The message, however, did not come from nature and it did not come from God. It came from the prejudices of pagan people conditioned by centuries of sacrificing animals that had become a part of everyday living. The message these messengers from God and nature managed to convey to the animal researchers who followed in their footsteps was that cruelty toward animals was the acceptable and natural state of mind for human beings except that, being sanctioned by God, cruelty was the wrong word to use. Words like anatomist, physiologist, vivisectionist, and animal research scientist sounded much better and fell into favor for these abusers of animals who convinced the world that not only were animals put on earth just to serve humans, but that they lacked consciousness and either felt no pain or that their pain was inconsequential compared to the way human beings experienced pain. It was proper to cut open animals without anesthesia in the days before it was invented, or nail animals to boards and slice open their bodies while they were still living because, being animals, they felt no pain. None of these animal researchers ever stopped to investigate whether theories like these were truthful or whether they were just lies which kept repeating in an endless cycle from which there seemed no escape. Today we have still not shaken loose from the same lies which continue over two thousand years later, but now the associated problems have multiplied significantly with the creation of the huge animal research industry which survives by experimenting upon and killing enslaved animals.

Animal research today has become an indispensable part of the system human beings have devised that defines animals as "things." In this system humans may freely use these "things" however they desire as a matter of convenience At birth, animals become the exclusive property of human beings even if they are born in the wilds where ownership would be next to impossible to enforce. It makes no difference. If you are born an animal, you belong to any human being who wishes to claim you.

Some positive consequences do result for a few members of the nonhuman animal population which have some contact with humans—as in the case where they are well cared for and loved by humans who keep companion animals in their homes. All too frequently, however, only the worst possible outcome can be expected for animals unfortunate enough to stumble onto the path of a human being. Communities commonly pass ordinances mandating the roundup of cats and dogs for the purpose of exterminating them to reduce their population size. Animal shelters in many states sell cats and dogs to animal research laboratories, a procedure which in Minnesota and Oklahoma is required by law upon the request of any animal research facility. Animal research facilities also obtain animals for research from Class B dealers who comb communities looking for stray animals that may be lost or abandoned to sell to research laboratories. Countless reports of animal cruelty make the news all too frequently, and laws that apply to the public intended for protecting animals are weak and mostly unenforced. An enraged man in Kentucky recently took revenge for being rejected by his would-be girl friend by stabbing her two companion cats to death. In this case the criminal's actions at least landed him in prison, though the sentence resulted more for breaking and entering the woman's apartment than for murdering the defenseless cats. When a Maryland lawyer was convicted of killing the cat of a client's wife when he was intoxicated by putting the cat in a microwave oven and turning it on, he received only a 15 month suspended sentence, a few hours of community service, a $1500 fine, and an order to undergo alcoholism treatment. For the most part, no matter how badly they may torture and mistreat animals, animal abusers are seldom sentenced to prison, and crimes against animals usually lead to little more than a slap on the wrist and a wagging finger warning the offender not to do it again. If one were suddenly granted the privilege of speaking to the entire world of animals in a language they understood, could anyone offer better advice than to recommend that they run like hell whenever they encounter that abusive and cruel species known as Homo sapiens?

The proclamation made by human beings that only their race has rights and deserves respect among all species that occupy the earth is the guidepost which humans have followed extending far into the distant past, and the world is paying heavily for pursuing that path. Its effects are found today in the inhumane treatment of animals on factory farms mercilessly slaughtered for food; the horrors of anal electrocutions and skinning of animals alive on fur farms for the pleasure of the wealthy; the brutal hunting and trapping practices of hunters armed with high powered weapons, steel-toothed traps, and drowning cages; the enslavement of animals in circuses; the forced confinement of animals in zoos; the brutalization of animals for entertainment at rodeos and blood sports events; and in the torture and killing of animals against their will in animal research laboratories. The attitudes of the world toward animals are visible everywhere, in the marketing of disease-producing meat and dairy products, in the pollution of our rivers and streams and the air we breathe, in the fraudulent procurement and waste of billions of tax dollars every year by our universities to conduct senseless animal research when that money should be going to support positive societal agendas, in the development of societies addicted to prescription and nonprescription drugs to cure the diseases caused by animal-based diets, in the creation of poverty in the developing world that results from raising grain to feed livestock for human consumption that should be going to raise crops for feeding the poor, in the plaguing of our children and adults with a diet of obesity-producing animal foods, and by the loss of our own personal health and the premature death of our loved ones resulting from eating animals. The human conspiracy against the animal kingdom also finds vivid expression through the aggressive ways in which humans interact with their families, friends, loved ones, and neighbors and in the violent manner in which nations interact with each other.

Fortunately, the action necessary to undo all the damage is easily within reach. When human beings begin to respect the other life forms that live on this planet, they will release their grip on violence as the preferred method for settling their differences and turn to good will for realizing their potentials. Rather than exploiting other species just because they possess the power to do it, humans will begin to recognize the benefits of relating to each species individually and by considering the unique character and value of each species in ever greater depth, including the functioning and purpose of their existence and what each species has to offer and teach in relation to the world and the universe.

If we are to survive the major challenges the world faces today, the negative relationships we have with animals and the abusive ways in which we treat and exploit animals need to change. The loss of biodiversity; the destruction of the rain forests; the ruination of the world's health; the contamination of the earth's rivers, oceans, and atmosphere; and the upheavals arising from increasing world poverty are already overwhelming human capacity to deal with the predicament we humans have created for ourselves, much of which can be traced directly to the hierarchical world view humans have toward animals which so readily approves of the exploitation and abuse of animals. At the philosophical heart of all these problems lies the speciesist world view that" might makes right" in a world in which only humans have rights. A way must be found to change the human belief system dependent upon the cruel exploitation of other species.

Animal research is one of the most important parts of the solution for when we discard animal research, we will have taken down one of the main pillars supporting the edifice of cruelty and exploitation of animals upon which humans depend. Steps like these need to be taken if our rivers and streams are ever to flow as pure as crystal once again, if the air we breathe is to become fresh and clean, if our obese children are to lose their excess weight and laugh and sing and dance once more, if we are to restore our health and eliminate the diseases of cancer, heart disease, stroke, diabetes, Alzheimer's disease, and many of the other chronic conditions that plague us. When we do these things there will be enough food to feed all the people of the world. In this kind of atmosphere, we will look forward to a far more secure future as we build a much better world than one dominated and controlled by cruelty and killing. This is the vision of a future world of which already millions of people are consciously aware and living out in their daily lives. It quite simply recognizes the human connection with all species and of the necessity to support and assist the other living creatures who cohabit our planet when it is possible even if that assistance means no more than a hands-off policy that allows biodiversity to follow its nature-intended course. In this way even the smallest creatures like little bees can contribute unimpeded to nature's ways by pollinating the fruits and vegetables that we eat, and we in turn can assist them by respecting their lives while not using them in ways that threatens and disadvantages their existence—such as inter-rupting their natural life cycles by gathering their honey to satisfy our tastes for sweets. If we still desire sweets anyway, it then becomes our duty to find nonviolent, nonaggressive ways for finding and developing them without destroying other life forms..

It takes only a little imagination to recognize that the won-der that equals a human being applies also to any other living creature like a buzzing fly, or a centipede, a great plumed lyre bird, a tiny mouse, or a roaring lion. Such a recognition leads to a greater understanding of the human connection to all forms of life and this extends outward to the universe. At this juncture humans can abandon their "might makes right" approach to other species that takes their rights from them and exploits them to meet human demands. It is essential to grasp simple concepts like these and make them a part of our lives if we are to hold our world together and prevent it from coming apart. This is the path to the future that the world is presently engaged in taking. It represents a new consciousness signaling a new beginning and way of life unlike any that the world has ever conceived before. It marks an end to the reliance on weaker species that have no means to protect themselves from human arrogance. The new world begins when we change disrespect to respect in our treatment of all species as we set new standards and new goals for our interactions with the other living creatures of the earth. This is the next giant stride forward for human beings to take along their evolutionary path toward greatness.

Appendix

Some Notes of Interest on the Apostle Paul and St. Augustine

St. Paul

The Apostle Paul's life work represented a remarkable transformation from his early years in which he persecuted Christians with a vengeance, dragging men and women from their homes to prison, voting for death for Christians at trials, and standing guard over the clothes of murderers while they set upon and killed Stephen, the first Christian martyr. The turnaround for Paul occurred when he was about 25 or 26 years of age as he traveled the road to Damascus where he hoped to capture Christians and bring them back to Jerusalem for trial. As he described it, a light from heaven suddenly fell around him from which the voice of Jesus called out: "Saul, Saul, why do you persecute me?" Jesus then commanded Paul to go to the Gentiles "to open their eyes so that they may turn from darkness to light and from the power of Satan to God, so that they may receive forgiveness of sins and a place among those who are sanctified by faith in me."[1] For three days Paul lay blinded by the light, but once he could see again, he embarked upon a lifelong journey to communicate Jesus' message of love, compassion, and salvation to the world. It was Paul who famously wrote: "When I was a child, I spoke like a child, I thought like a child, I reasoned like child; when I became an adult, I put an end to childish ways." To this he added: "And now faith, hope, and love abide, these three; and the greatest of these is love."[2]

For the remaining 30 or more years of his life, Paul traveled around the Mediterranean Basin and parts of Europe where he preached the gospel that Jesus was the Son of God and the Messiah and that there was to be a new covenant between all humankind and God based on the crucifixion and resurrection of Jesus. With great courage, Paul dedicated himself to founding churches, establishing Christian communities, and teaching and writing about the life of Jesus and his works.

Often imprisoned and beaten by antiChristian adversaries for the radical message he sought to impart, Paul is believed to have been beheaded in Rome around 67 or 66 AD. After his martyrdom, the letters Paul had written to the Christian communities he visited were collected and eventually incorporated into the Bible as part of the New Testament canon. They comprise nearly half of the books of the New Testament.

St. Augustine

In his youth Augustine reveled in pleasure for a while, a period he described in his humorous prayer: "Grant me chastity and continence, but not yet." Augustine had two affairs with women, the first a long term relationship. He was poised to marry a much younger woman in a proposed marriage his mother had arranged when he converted to Christianity. He was 34 at the time.

After his conversion, Augustine's writings about the pleasures of the flesh, which he shunned, would exert a major influence on the church that is still felt today. He believed that human sexuality had been wounded and needed redemption through Jesus Christ. He contrasted love as enjoyment through God against lust which was not through God.

When it came to the scriptures, Augustine did not think they needed to be taken literally if they contradicted proved scientific fact and God-given common sense in which case they should be seen metaphorically. In this connection, he urged Christians not to be "doggedly literal minded."[3] Augustine also helped shape the doctrine that the Bishops and Priests are successors to the Apostles and that their authority in the church comes from God.[4] Another belief attributed to the austere philosopher is that some people are predestined by God to be saved, yet that anyone can be saved.

Augustine reasoned that either truth and wisdom are God or God is something about truth and wisdom. For Augustine, the " intelligible realm," with God as its source, promises the only lasting relief from the anxiety prompted by the transitory nature of the sensible realm [which contains the world of the senses].[5]

Bibliography

About.com. "Lefkandi," See Toumba,
http://archaeology.about.com/gi/o.htm?zi=1/XJ&zTi=1&sdn=archae
ology&cdn=education&tm=115&gps=263_101_796_367&f=10&tt=8&
bt=0&bts=0&zu=http%3A//faculty.vassar.edu/jolott/old_courses/cro
sscurrents2001/Lefkandi/

Albert the Great. *Questions Concerning Aristotle's on Animals*,
translated by Irven M. Resnick and Kenneth F. Kitchell Jr. in *The
Fathers of the Church, Medieaval Continuation* . (The Catholic
University of America Press, 1984).
http://books.google.com/books?id=vCFFpzofHqIC&pg=PA38&sour
ce=gbs_toc_r&cad=3#v=onepage&q&f=true

Akerlof, George, and Robert Shiller. *Animal Spirits: How human
psychology drives the economy and why it matters for global capitalism*.
Princeton University Press, 2009.

American Chemical Society. "The trials of streptomycin."
http://acswebcontent.acs.org/landmarks/antibiotics/trials.html

American Vegetarian Convention New York City 1850. From the
Vegetarian Advocate (London), July 1, 1850.
http://www.ivu.org/congress/1850/convention.html

Andre, Claire, and Manuel Velasquez. "Who Counts?" Mark Kula
Center for Applied Ethics, University of Santa Clara.
http://www.scu.edu/ethics/publications/iie/v4n1/counts.html

Andrews, Kristin. "Animal Cognition." *Stanford Encyclopedia of
Science*. May 6, 2011. http://plato.stanford.edu/entries/cognition-
animal/

Animal Research for Life. "Past Research." EPFIA. 2011.
http://www.animalresearchforlife.eu/index.php/en/past-research

Animal Welfare Information Center Newsletter, Vol. 5, no. 2. "The
Importance of Animals in Biomedical and Behavioral Research."
Summer 1994.
http://www.nal.usda.gov/awic/newsletters/v5n2/5n2phs.htm

Atkinson, Melissa S. "Aristotle and Aquinas: Intrinsic Morality
versus God's Morality." Melissa Atkinson's blog Rebirth of Reason.
http://rebirthofreason.com/Articles/atkinson/Aristotle_and_Aquina
s_Intrinsic_Morality_versus_Gods_Morality.shtml

Bailey, Candice. "Muti killings is a way of life in rural areas," *IOL
News*, January 16, 2010. http://www.iol.co.za/news/south-
africa/muti-killings-is-a-way-of-life-in-rural-areas-1.470603

Ballantyne, Coco. "Planning of the Apes: Zoo Chimp Plots Rock
Attacks on Visitors." *Scientific American*. March 9, 2009.
http://www.scientificamerican.com/article.cfm?id=chimpanzee-
plans-throws-stones-zoo

Bekoff, Marc, et al.. *The Cognitive Animal: Empirical and Theoretical
Perspectives on Animal Cognition.* Cambridge, MA: MIT Press, 2002.
http://books.google.com/books?id=TztyW8eTnIC&pg=PA105&lpg=
PA105&dq=Marc+Bekoff+et+al.,+The+Cognitive+Animal:+Empirical
+and+Theoretical+Perspectives+on+Animal+Cognition&source=bl&
ots=uHmbTAnmCk&sig=r8KsoLR5fNJi4ut1jyvUQermZxk&hl=en&
ei=gL4xSrvΛGYSGtgſuyIyCQ&sa=X&oi=book_result&ct=result&res
num=2

Bernard, Claude. *An introduction to the study of experimental
medicine.*

Bodnar, Istvan. "Aristotle's Natural Philosophy," *Stanford
Encyclopedia of Philosophy*, Dec. 31, 2009.
http://plato.stanford.edu/entries/aristotle-natphil/

Boon, B. "Leonarda da Vinci on artherosclerosis and the function of the sinuses of Valsalva." *Netherlands Heart Journal*, 496-499. December 17, 2009. http://www.ncbi.nlm.nih.gov/pmc/articles/PMC2804084/

Boyle, Matthew Brendan. *Kant and the Significance of Self-Consciousness* 2005. Doctor of Philosophy Dissertation, University of Pittsburgh. http://d-scholarship.pitt.edu/9302/1/boylemb_etd2005.pdf

Breger, Louis. *Dostoievsky: The Author As Psychoanalyst*. New York: New York University, 1989. 2, http://books.google.com/books/about/Dostoevsky.html?id=jJqMm3f h9tIC

Bynum, W.F. *Science and the Practice of Medicine in the Nineteenth Century*. Cambridge, Melbourne: Cambridge University Press, 1994. http://books.google.com/books?id=tv65dPNmdsgC&pg=PA286&lp g=PA286&dq=Bynum,+Science+and+the+Practice+of+Medicine+in+t he+Nineteenth+Century&source=bl&ots=CjApW9n7-2&sig=gclYmZrCCQhE2TOYFuSdDeIpt3M&hl=en&ei=DiDBTr-FHebL0QHe6emrBA&sa=X&oi=book_result&ct=result&resnum=5& ved=0CEUQ6AEwBA#v=onepage&q&f=true

Calvin, John. *The First Epistle of Paul the Apostle to the Corinthians*, trans. By John W. Fraser, ed. by David Wishart Torrance and Thomas Forsyth Torrance. Wm. B. Eerdmans Publishing, 1996. http://books.google.com/books?id=---9jl1EjJtkC&dq=Therefore+that+humane+treatment+of+oxen+ought+ to+be+an+incentive,+moving+us+to+treat+each+other+with+conside ration+and+fairness&source=gbs_navlinks_s

Cantrell, Dan. "Dostoievsky and Psychology." http://www.fyodordostoevsky.com/essays/m-cantrell.html

Carlsen, William. "Rogue virus in the vaccine Early polio vaccine harbored virus now feared to cause cancer in humans." *San Francisco Chronicle*, 2002.
http://www.laleva.cc/choice/vaccines/vaccines_whyNOT.html

Carruthers, Peter. "Against the Moral Standing of Animals."
http://www.philosophy.umd.edu/Faculty/pcarruthers/The%20Animals%20Issue.pdf

Carruthers, Peter. "Animal Mentality: Its Character, Extent, and Moral Significance." In *The Oxford Handbook of Animal Ethics*, Part IV, Ch. 13, edited by Tom L. Beauchamp and R.G. Frey. Oxford University Press: 2011.
http://www.philosophy.umd.edu/Faculty/pcarruthers/Animal%20mentality%20and%20value.pdf

Carruthers, Peter. "Animal Subjectivity." *PSYCHE*, 4(3). April, 1998. http://www.theassc.org/files/assc/2377.pdf

Carruthers, Peter. "Brute Experience." *The Journal of Philosophy*, Vol. 86, No. 5, 258. May, 1989. http://www-personal.umich.edu/~lormand/phil/teach/mind/readings/Carruthers%20-%20Brute%20Experience.pdf

Carruthers, Peter. "Suffering without subjectivity."
http://drum.lib.umd.edu/bitstream/1903/4357/1/Suffering-without-subjectivity.pdf

Carruthers, Peter. *The Animals Issue*: Moral Theory in Practice. Cambridge: Cambridge University Press, 1992.

Carvalho André Luis de Lima and Ricardo Waizbort. Pain beyond the confines of man: a preliminary introduction to the debate between Frances Power Cobbe and the darwinists with respect to vivisection in Victorian England (1863-1904)." Hist. cienc. saude-Manguinhos, vol.17 no.3. Rio de Janeiro (2010).

http://www.scielo.br/scielo.php?pid=S0104-
59702010000300002&script=sci_arttext&tlng=en

Christianity in View. *Timeline of Paul's Ministry*.
http://christianityinview.com/paulstimeline.html

Cisneros, Martin V. "Hosea 2:18: God's New Covenant Between
Man and Animal." *all-creatures.org*, http://www.all-
creatures.org/discuss/hosea2.18-mvc.html

Cohen, Carl. "The Case for the Use of Animals in Biomedical
Research." In *Ethical issues in biotechnology*, edited by Richard
Sherlock and John D. Morrey. Lanham, Maryland: Rowman &
Littlefield, 2002.
http://books.google.com/books?id=mlVh3ysN4ZwC&pg=PA231&lp
g=PA231&dq=Richard+Sherlock+and+John+D.+Morrey,&source=bl
&ots=3N0FvizTeN&sig=HpMfuuYWjlFuPZga846iGNFxz5U&hl=en
&ei=UcbHTrarK6H50gHD4rEL&sa=X&oi=book_result&ct=result&r
esnum=6&sqi=2&ved=0CFEQ6AEwBQ#v=onepage&q=Richard%20
Sherlock%20and%20John%20D.%20Morrey%2C&f=false

Cohen, S. Marc., Patricia Curd, and C.D.C. Reeve, eds. *Readings in
Ancient Greek Philosophy*. Third Edition, (Indianapolis: Hackett
Publishing Company, 2005), p645-654.

Constitutional Rights Foundation. "St. Thomas Aquinas, Natural
Law, and the Common Good." http://www.crf-usa.org/bill-of-
rights-in-action/bria-22-4-c-st.-thomas-aquinas-natural-law-and-the-
common-good.html

Dawson, Virginia. *Nature's enigma: the problem of the polyp in the
letters of Bonnet, Trembley and Reaumur*. Philadelphia: American
Philosophical Society. Memoirs Series, vol. 174, 33, 1987.
http://books.google.com/books?id=ehQyWegCmYUC&pg=PA33&l
pg=PA33&dq=Rosenfield,+From+Beast-Machine+to+Man-
Machine&source=bl&ots=dcd7WCBiO4&sig=tDRnIDwyuNSgBFW
Hiqvqb8VC8FI&hl=en&ei=Y0snTYTOF8Kt8AbZnMn_AQ&sa=X&oi

=book_result&ct=result&resnum=8&ved=0CDEQ6AEwBw#v=onep
age&q=Rosenfield%2C%20From%20Beast-Machine%20to%20Man-
Machine&f=false

Demark-Wahnefried, Wendy, et al., "Flaxseed Supplementation
(Not Dietary Fat Restriction) Reduces Prostate Cancer Proliferation
Rates in Men." *Presurgery, Cancer Epidemiology Biomarkers &
Prevention,* 17, 3577-3587. December 1, 2008.

Dennis, Leslie K., et al.. "Problems with the Assessment of Dietary
Fat in Prostate Cancer Studies." *American Journal of Epidemiology,*
160(5):436-444.2004.
http://aje.oxfordjournals.org/cgi/content/full/160/5/436.

Descartes, René, "Animals are Machines," reprinted from *Passions
of the Soul* (1649). *Journal of Cosmology,* Vol. 14, 2011.
http://journalofcosmology.com/Consciousness136.html

Dowe, Phil. *Galileo, Darwin, and Hawking*: *The Interplay of Science,
Reason, and Religion.* (Wm. B. Eerdmans Publishing, 2005), 24, 25.
http://books.google.com/books?id=CJlmSpOpODoC&q=doggedly+l
iteral+minded#v=snippet&q=doggedly%20literal%20minded&f=fals
e
http://books.google.com/books?id=CJlmSpOpODoC&dq=Augustin
e,+scriptures+can+be+taken+metaphorically&source=gbs_navlinks_
s

DrugRecalls.com. "Rezulin Linked to Liver Failure and Heart
Disease." PCRM Action Alert.
http://www.drugrecalls.com/rezulin.html

Encyclopaedia Britannica, "Robert Koch,"
http://www.britannica.com/EBchecked/topic/320834/Robert-
Koch#toc3949.

Festing, Sally. "Animal Experiments: The Long Debate." *The New*
Scientist, 1989.

http://books.google.com/books?id=opeJdTsCCrMC&pg=PA54&lpg=
PA54&dq=historical+vivisection+on+dogs&source=bl&ots=WpFQs0
8jqy&sig=zhjeCk_4CpGPQVnnh3WeROPkabQ&hl=en&ei=7gsvTdT
bI8qr8AbL4L24CQ&sa=X&oi=book_result&ct=result&resnum=7&v
ed=0CDQQ6AEwBg#v=onepage&q=historical%20vivisection%20on
%20dogs&f=false

Forsham, Peter F. "Milestones in the 60 Year History of Insulin
(1922-1982)." *Diabetes Care*, Vol. 5, Suppl. 2. November-December,
1982.
http://care.diabetesjournals.org/content/5/Supplement_2/1.full.pdf

Foster, Michael. *Claude Bernard.* New York: Longman, Greens & Co.,
1899.
http://books.google.com/books?id=cGICAAAAYAAJ&dq=Claude+
Bernard+on+his+death+bed&source=gbs_navlinks_s.

FreeEssays.cc. "Aristotle, A Comprehensive View on Nature and
Society." http://www.freeessays.cc/db/35/prz50.shtml

Freelance Commentaries. "Animal Numbers in Research."
http://www.freelancecommentaries.com/animal-numbers-in-
research-l

Freedman, David H.). "20 Things you didn't know about
autopsies." *Discovery* 9 (September 2012).

Garfalk, Connie. "Help, My Cat Loves Me." Connie Garfalk's blog
Offbeat Cats. http:/www.offbeat-cats.com/feature_feelings_e.html

Gennaro, Rocco J. "Animals, Consciousness, and I-thoughts."
http://www.usi.edu/libarts/phil/gennaro/papers/AnimalsforLurzEd
.pdf

Gennaro, Rocco J. "Higher-Order Thoughts, Animal Consciousness,
and Misrepresentation: A Reply to Carruthers and Levine" in
Higher-Order Theories of Consciousness, an anthology. John

Benjamins, 2004.
http://www.usi.edu/libarts/phil/gennaro/papers/JohnBenjch3.pdf

Greek, Ray, M.D. "The Discovery and Development of Penicillin." *all-creatures.org*. http://www.allcreatures.org/articles/ar-penicillin.html

Gruen. Lori. "The Moral Status of Animals." *Stanford Encyclopedia of Philosophy*. September 13, 2010.
http://plato.stanford.edu/entries/moral-animal/

Guerrini, Anita. *Experimenting with Humans and Animals*. Baltimore: The Johns Hopkins Press. 2003.

Guido Giglioni."What Ever Happened to Francis Glisson? Albrecht Haller and the Fate of Eighteenth-Century Irritability." *Science in Context* 21(4), 465–493, 2008.
http://www.fcsh.unl.pt/chc/pdfs/nature1.pdf

Hamilton, Susan . "On the Cruelty to Animals Act, 15 August 1876." http://www.branchcollective.org/?ps_articles=susan-hamilton-on-the-cruelty-to-animals-act-15-august-1876.

Hariz, Marwan I., M.D., Ph.D., Patric Blomstedt, M.D., Ph.D., and Ludvic Zrinzo, M.D., M.Sc. "Deep Brain Stimulation between 1947 and 1987: The Untold Story." *NCBI*.
http://www.ncbi.nlm.nih.gov/pubmed/20672911

Hart, Donna and Robert W. Sussman. *Man the hunted: Primates, Predators, And Human Evolution*. Westview Press, Cambridge, MA, 2005.

Hart, Lynette A., Mary W. Wood and Benjamin J. Hart. *Why Dissection?* (Oxford U.K.: Greenwood Press, 2008)
http://books.google.com/books?id=jO5eQfIkJaQC&q=Michelangelo #v=snippet&q=Michelangelo&f=true

Hauck Center for the Albert B. Sabin Archives. "Sabin Sundays and His Oral Polio Vaccine," and "A Biography of Dr. Sabin." http://sabin.uc.edu/

Herbermann, Charles George, Ph.D., LL.D., Edward Aloysius Pace, Ph.D., D.D., Conde Benoist Pallen, Ph..D., LL.D., Thomas J. Shahan, D.D., and John J. Wynne, S.J., eds. *The Catholic Encyclopedia*, Volume 10. New York: The Universal Knowledge Foundation, 1913. http://books.google.com/books?id=RmoQAAAAIAAJ&pg=PA127&l pg=PA127&dq=History+of+Anatomy+in+the+school+of+Padua&sou rce=bl&ots=fjLWf-bwIL&sig=z8vHJkBQzfiGX4yjgQMVah75zTE&hl=en&ei=nYS1Tbzs HsXh0QGz34WIBQ&sa=X&oi=book_result&ct=result&resnum=9&v ed=0CFQQ6AEwCA#v=onepage&q=History%20of%20Anatomy%2 0in%20the%20school%20of%20Padua&f=false

Huffman, Carl."Alcmaeon." *Stanford Encyclopedia of Philosophy*. April 28, 2008. http://plato.stanford.edu/entries/alcmaeon/#Dissec

Hume, David. "Of the Reason of Animals." *A Treatise of Human Nature*, Part III, Section xvi. http://www.animal-rights-library.com/texts-c/hume01.htm

Hunter, Graeme. "Boethius's Complaint: Can the Christian Find Consolation Without Christ?" Pontifical John Paul II Institute. *Touchstone, A Journal of Mere Christianity*, 2004. http://www.touchstonemag.com/archives/article.php?id=17-03-025-f

Huxley, Aldous. *The Perennial Philosophy*. New York: HarperCollins, 2012. http://books.google.com/books?id=l1fs25HbCY0C&dq=For+in+this+ breaking+through+I+perceive+what+God+and+I+are+in+common.+ +There+I+am+what+I+was.++There+I+neither+increase+nor+decreas e.++For+there+I+am+the+immovable+which+moves+all+things&q=F or+in+this+breaking+through+I+perceive+what+God+and+I+are+in+ common.++There+I+am+what+I+was.++There+I+neither+increase+n or+decrease.++For+there+I+am+the+immovable+which+moves+all+things#v=onepage&q&f=false

In Defense of Animals. "Top 10 Reasons Why Animal Research Is A Cruel Joke." http://idausa.org/ridiculousresearch/

Ingeborg A Brouwer, et al. "Dietary Linolenic Acid Is Associated with Reduced Risk of Fatal Coronary Heart Disease, but Increased Prostate Cancer Risk: A Meta-Analysis." *The American Society for Nutritional Sciences J. Nutr* 134:919-922. April 2004.

Institut Pasteur. "Louis Pasteur and Rabies Vaccination." http://www.pasteur.fr/ip/easysite/pasteur/en/press/press-kits/rabies/louis-pasteur-and-rabies-vaccination

International Vegetarian Union. "Ancient Greece and Rome, Plato (?427=?347 BC." http://www.ivu.org/history/greece_rome/plato.html

International Vegetarian Union." North America: Late 20 Century, Isaac Bashevis Singer (1904-1991)." Under Quotes. http://www.ivu.org/history/northam20b/singer.html

Irving, David. *The Protein Myth: Significantly Reducing the Risk of Cancer, Heart Disease, Stroke, and Diabetes While Saving the Animals and Building a Better World*. Arlesford, Hants, UK, O-Books, 2011.

James, Walene. "Immunization: The Reality Behind The Myth." 1988. http://www.whale.to/a/krasner1.html

Jamieson, Dale, and Marc Bekoff. "Carruthers on Nonconscious Experience." *Analysis*, Vol. 52, No. 1, 23-28. January1992. http://as.nyu.edu/docs/IO/1192/JamiesonBekoff-carruthers1992.pdf

Jenkins, Philip. *The Next Christendom: The Coming of Global Christianity*. Oxford University Press, 2002.

http://books.google.com/books?id=zeeVzDmeZhEC&q=billion#v=sn
ippet&q=billion&f=false

John of Salisbury. *Frivolities of Courtiers and Footprints of Philosophers*,
Being a Translation of the First, Second and Third Books and
Selections from the Seventh and Eight Books of the *Policraticus*
[1159] of John of Salisbury, Joseph Pike, trans. University of
Minnesota, 1938. http://www.animalrightshistory.org/0485-1450-
animal-rights/medieval-j/john-of-salisbury/12thc-policraticus-
fortune.htm

Julian Cope Presents The Modern Antiquarian. "Phaistos: Ancient
Village, Settlement, Misc. Earthwork."
http://themodernantiquarian.com/site/10857/phaistos.html#fieldnot
es

Kaplan, Giesela, and Lesley J. Roger. "Elephants That Paint, Birds
That Make Music: Do Animals Have an Aesthetic Sense?" *Cerebrum*.
The Dana Foundation. October 1, 2006.
http://www.dana.org/news/cerebrum/detail.aspx?id=74&p=1

Karsner, Gary, and Barry Mesh. "The Salk Vaccine And The
"Disappearance" of Paralytic Polio--Is Paralysis a Viral Disease?"

Katu.com. "Father: Son who burned himself alive was a troubled
genius." January 28, 2010.
http://www.katu.com/news/local/82986637.html

Katz, Eliot M. "Dogs in South Korea: Man's Best Friend...or
Dinner?" *In Defense of Animals*.
http://ida.convio.net/site/MessageViewer/&printer_friendly=1?em_i
d=18721.0&dlv_id=21121

Kendricks, T. D. *Druids and Druidism*. Dover Publications, Inc., 2003.
http://books.google.com/books/about/Druids_and_Druidism.html?i
d=V5G1SwrZDqUC

Kete, Kathleen. *The Beast in the Boudoir: Petkeeping in Nineteenth-Century Paris*. Berkeley: University of California Press, 1994.

Koinski, Andrea, and Barbara Olsen. "The Burkert Interpretation of Animals Sacrifice."
http://inside.bard.edu/academic/specialproj/ritual/Rituals/Burkert/00.html

Kruta, Vlasislav. "Unzer, Johan August." *Encyclopedia.com* .
http://www.encyclopedia.com/doc/1G2-2830904418.html

Lalonde. Gerald V. *Horos Dios: an Athenian Shrine and Cult of Zeus*.
Leiden, the Netherlands: Koninklijke Brill N.V., 2006.
http://books.google.com/books?id=sO8E8Bik1a4C&pg=PA75&lpg=
PA75&dq=animal+sacrifice+in+Greece+during+the+4th+century+BC
&source=bl&ots=stOBZsWJXJ&sig=7mqR8qJ1To93XxS6soce6PFVib
E&hl=en&ei=5BuqTdvkCqKx0QHc2e35CA&sa=X&oi=book_result&
ct=result&resnum=3&ved=0CCYQ6AEwAg#v=onepage&q&f=false

Lang, Olivia. "Hindu sacrifice of 250,000 animals begins." *The Guardian*. November 24, 2009.
http://www.guardian.co.uk/world/2009/nov/24/hindu-sacrifice-
gadhimai-festival-nepal

Leaf, Alexander. *"Dietary Prevention of Coronary Heart Disease: The Lyon Diet Heart Study."*
http://circ.ahajournals.org/cgi/content/full/99/6/733#R9

Leaf, Alexander, Jing X. Kang, and Yong-Fu Xiao. "Omega-3 Fatty Acids and Ventricular Arrhythmias." In *Nutrition and Fitness: Obesity, the Metabolic Syndrome, Cardiovascular Disease, and Cancer*, World Rev Nutr Diet, vol 94, pp 129-138 (DOI: 10.1159/000088226), edited by AP Simopoulos. Basel, Karger, 2005.

Lewisohn, Richard. "The Importance Of The Proper Dosage Of Sodium Citrate In Blood Transfusion." *Annals of Surgery*, 64(5): 618–

623. November, 1916.
http://www.ncbi.nlm.nih.gov/pmc/articles/PMC1426274/

Lokhorst, Gert-Jan. "Descartes and the Pineal Gland." *Stanford Encyclopedia of Philosophy*. November 5, 2008.
http://plato.stanford.edu/entries/pineal-gland/#3.3

Longrigg, James. Greek Rational Medicine: Philosophy and Medicine from Alcmaeon to the Alexandrians. Routledge, November 1, 2002.
http://books.google.com/books?id=TT5lzingflYC&dq=Alcmaeon+excision+of+eyeball&source=gbs_navlinks_s

Look, Brandon C. "Notes on St. Augustine," Classroom notes for History of Philosophy I, University of Kentucky. 2007.
http://www.uky.edu/~look/Phi%20260-Augustine.pdf

Loukas, Marios, and Alexis Lanteri, et al. "Anatomy in Ancient India: A Focus on the Susruta Samhita." *Journal of* Anatomy, 217(6): 646-650. December, 2010.
http://www.ncbi.nlm.nih.gov/pmc/articles/PMC3039177/

Lurz, Robert W. "The philosophy of animal minds: an introduction." In *The Philosophy of Animal Minds*, edited by Robert W. Lurz. Cambridge University Press, UK, 2009.

Maehle, Andreas-Holger. "Literary Responses to Animal Experimentation in Seventeenth and Eighteenth-Century Britain." *Medical History*, 1990, 34: 27-5 1.
http://www.ncbi.nlm.nih.gov/pmc/articles/PMC1035999/pdf/medhist00056-0031.pdf

Markus, Führer. "Albert the Great." *Stanford Encyclopedia of Philosophy*." April 20, 2012. http://plato.stanford.edu/entries/albert-great/

Martin, Brian. "How to attack a scientific theory and get away with it (usually): the attempt to destroy an origin-of-AIDS hypothesis." In *Science as Culture,* Vol. 19, No. 2, 215-239. June 2010. http://www.bmartin.cc/pubs/10sac.html

Mason, Stephen F. *A History of the Sciences.* New York: Collier Books, 1977.

Matthews, Robert A.J. "Medical progress depends on animal models – doesn't it?" *J R Soc Med,*101(2): 95–98. February 2008. http://www.ncbi.nlm.nih.gov/pmc/articles/PMC2254450/

McLaren, Warren. "Half of World Crop is Feeding Animals, Not People." *Treehugger.com.* June 22, 2010. http://www.treehugger.com/files/2010/06/half-of-world-crop-feeding-animals-not-people.php *Food and Agriculture*

Medical Advances and Animal Research: The contribution of animal science to the medical revolution: some case histories. RDS: Understanding Animal Research in Medicine and Coalition for Medical Progress, 2007. http://www.pro-test.org.uk/MAAR.pdf

Medieval Science, Technology, and Medicine: An Encyclopedia. Edited by Thomas F. Glick, Steven John Livesy, and Faith Wallis. New York: Routledge, 2005. http://books.google.com/books?id=SaJlbWK_-FcC&pg=PA33&lpg=PA33&dq=Dissection+in+Salerno+in+the+14th+century&source=bl&ots=7lmdPvJg2D&sig=AwIAO1K6WRIvavN3t-rLqHg-5rw&hl=en&sa=X&ei=bHtIUuLlNInb4AOZ_YGwDA&ved=0CDgQ6AEwAw#v=onepage&q=Dissection%20in%20Salerno%20in%20the%2014th%20century&f=false

Mendelson, Michael. "Saint Augustine." *Stanford Encyclopedia of Philosophy.*" November 12, 2010 http://plato.stanford.edu/entries/augustine/#Leg

Middleton, Michael. "Faith of our Fathers: Successors of the Apostles." http://trushare.com/0111AUG04/AU04MIDD.htm

Miller, Neil Z. "The polio vaccine: a critical assessment of its arcane history, efficacy, and long-term health-related consequences." Thinktwice Global Vaccine Institute. N.Z. Miller/Medical Veritas 1, 2004. http://www.thinktwice.com

Norris, Frederick, and Donald Harrison. *The Anatomy and Physiology of the Mammalian* Larynx. Cambridge: Cambridge University Press, 1995.
http://books.google.com/books?id=bZBbTNdx4HoC&pg=PA5&lpg=PA5&dq=Fabricius,+animal+research&source=bl&ots=oKuapsbjRD&sig=3YBOxxr3v1fJ-6Niotj8f4llUDs&hl=en&ei=aH-1TZT2LIO3tgf29tnpDg&sa=X&oi=book_result&ct=result&resnum=4&ved=0CDoQ6AEwAw#v=onepage&q=Fabricius%2C%20animal%20research&f=false

Nova Science Now. "How Smart are Dogs." PBS. Feb. 11, 2011.
http://www.pbs.org/wgbh/nova/nature/how-smart-dogs.html

Nutton , Vivian. "Logic, Learning, and Experimental Medicine. Science 5556 (2992).
http://www.sciencemag.org/content/295/5556/800.full

Oklahoma State University Center for Health Services. "Animals in Research and Teaching."
http://www.cvm.okstate.edu/index.php?option=com_content&view=article&id=544&Itemid=335

Olmsted, J.M.D. "The Influence of Claude Bernard on Medicine in the United States and England," Part I. *California and Western Medicine*, Vol 42, No. 2, February 1935.
http://www.ncbi.nlm.nih.gov/pmc/articles/PMC1752078/?page=2

Organization of the United Nations. "Livestock's Long Shadow." Rome, 2007. http://www.fao.org/docrep/010/a0701e/a0701e00.HTM

Ortiz, Edward. "Science Hero: Frederick Banting." *Science Heroes.* http://myhero.com/go/hero.asp?hero=Banting

Otts, Laura. "Howled Out of the Country: Wilkie Collins and H.G. Wells Retry David Ferrier," http://www.palgrave.com/PDFs/0230520944.pdf

Parker-Pearson, Mike, M.D. "The Practice of Human Sacrifice," *BBC: History.* http://www.bbc.co.uk/history/ancient/british_prehistory/human_sacrifice_01.shtml

Patterson, Charles. *Eternal Treblinka: Our Treatment of Animals and the Holocaust.* New York: Lantern Books, 2002. http://books.google.com/books?id=zkvY1-t3VxMC&dq=Charles+Patterson,+Eternal+Treblinka&printsec=frontcover&source=bn&hl=en&ei=pqhcTIHYCoP78Abu5Nz1Ag&sa=X&oi=book_result&ct=result&resnum=4&ved=0CCUQ6AEwAw#v=onepage&q&f=false

Phil, Dowe. *Galileo, Darwin, and Hawking: The Interplay of Science, Reason, and Religion.* Wm. B. Eerdmans Publishing, 2005. http://books.google.com/books?id=CJlmSpOpODoC&dq=Augustine,+scriptures+can+be+taken+metaphorically&source=gbs_navlinks_s

Phoenician International Research Center. "Tertullian of Carthage, Early Church Father." http://phoenicia.org/tertullian2.html#n25

"Pierre Belon's Early Natural History of Birds." From the Graphic Arts Collection, Princeton University Library, Princeton, New Jersey. Posted by Julie Melby April 16, 2010.

Pippin, John J. "PLoS takes a step backward." In *PLoS Med* 2(8): e278. 2005.

http://www.plosmedicine.org/article/info:doi/10.1371/journal.pmed.
0020278

Plotkin, Stanley A., Walter A. Orenstein, and Paul. A. Offit.
Vaccines. London, Amsterdam, New York: Elsevier Health Services,
2008.
http://books.google.com/books?id=BFQq2-
fIAJ8C&pg=PA3&lpg=PA3&dq=Pasteur,+anthrax+demonstration,+2
5+sheep,+a+goat+and+several+cows&source=bl&ots=jfcNuGjz-
g&sig=IrSafxQO6JT4FAr5OQB4SBCUZEA&hl=en&ei=dI0cTuHCKu
m30AGrzonHBw&sa=X&oi=book_result&ct=result&resnum=2&ved
=0CCMQ6AEwAQ#v=onepage&q&f=false

Potter, Will. "Big Ag Wants to Rewrite the Law So That You'll
Never See This." Will Potter's blog *Green is the New Red*. February
22, 2013.
http://www.greenisthenewred.com/blog/new-ag-gag-bills-targets-
whistleblowers-investigators-journalists/6736/? utm_
source=GreenIsTheNewRed+Newsletter&utm_medium=email&ut
m_campaign=3a394e91cb-RSS_EMAIL_CAMPAIGN_2

Potter, Will. "Dairy Industry Magazine Compares Undercover
Investigations to Cross Burning," Will Potter's blog *Green is the New
Red*. January 5, 2012.
http://www.greenisthenewred.com/blog/undercover-investigations-
hatecrimes/5511/?utm_source=GreenIsTheNewRed+Newsletter&ut
m_medium=email&utm_campaign=7fdfcd0301-
RSS_EMAIL_CAMPAIGN_2

Powell, Alvin. "John Enders Breakthrough Led to Polio Vaccine."
The Harvard University Gazette. October 8, 1998.
http://www.news.harvard.edu/gazette/1998/10.08/JohnEndersBreak
.html.

Preece, Rod. *Sins of the Flesh: A History of Ethical Vegetarian Thought*.
Vancouver: UBC Press, 2008.

http://books.google.com/books?id=uMnubkF5HjAC&dq=Was+John+Stuart+Mill+a+vegetarian&q=Gassendi#v=onepage&q&f=false

Prioreschi, Plinio. *A History of Medicine: Greek Medicine*. Omaha, NE: Horatius Press, 1996.
http://books.google.com/books?id=HaX733MnZZ4C&pg=PA417&lpg=PA417&dq=Aristotle+strangled+animals&source=bl&ots=MApxlTEfTu&sig=bm2Qd-kVwkGsWEbFtkQerbrP62Q&hl=en&ei=K0isTYOeAsPKgQes6KX0BQ&sa=X&oi=book_result&ct=result&resnum=2&ved=0CBsQ6AEwAQ#v=onepage&q=Aristotle%20strangled%20animals&f=false

Public Discourse. "St. Anselm of Canterbury (1033-1109)." Posted by Publisher Professional. http://public-discourse.blogspot.com/2010/01/st-anselm-of-canterbury-10331109.html

Quotes on Animal Vivisection. "The Samuel Johnson Sound Bite Page." http://www.samueljohnson.com/animalv.html

Ray Stedman.org. "Help for Elders." November 8, 1981. Ray Stedman blog. http://raystedman.org/new-testament/timothy/help-for-elders

Ross, Greg. "An Interview with Marc Hauser." *American Scientist ,* Volume 100, No. 1. January-February, 2012.
http://www.americanscientist.org/bookshelf/pub/marc-hauser

Rudacille, Deborah. *The Scalpel and the Butterfly*. Berkeley: University of California Press, 2001.
http://books.google.com/books?id=BabamiCYEdUC&q=rabbit#v=snippet&q=rabbit&f=false

Safer Medicines. "Animal Testing – MPs, GPs and scientists demand evaluation."
http://www.safermedicines.org/news.php?pid=61

Safer Medicines. "Doctors fear animal experiments endanger patients." http://www.safermedicines.org/news.php?pid=64

Sagan, Carl, and Ann Druyan. *Shadows of Forgotten Ancestors*. Random House Digital, Inc., 2011. http://books.google.com/books?id=DjjWea3fgO8C&vq=the+annals+of+primate+ethics&source=gbs_navlinks_s

Salisbury, Joyce E., Dr. *Women in the Ancient World*. Santa Barbara, CA: ABC-CLIO, Inc., 2001. http://books.google.com/books?id=HF0m3spOebcC&pg=PA144&lpg=PA144&dq=Aristotle+and+Herophilus&source=bl&ots=q0Hnmwx-fz&sig=iqw4y2OnSoTpz99HN8ReG17Q0_Y&hl=en&ei=zVesTbKxAofx0gGCt4XCAw&sa=X&oi=book_result&ct=result&resnum=4&ved=0CCMQ6AEwAw#v=onepage&q=Aristotle%20and%20Herophilus&f=false

Salk Institute for Biological Studies. "Discovery Timeline," http://www.salk.edu/about/discovery_timeline.html

Santiago, Arango Muñoz. "Review of The Philosophy of Animal Minds, Robert Lurz (ed).Cambridge: CUP." Acedemia.edu. http://www.academia.edu/239035/Review_of_The_Philosophy_of_Animal_Minds_Robert_Lurz_ed_._Cambridge_CUP

Schaus, Margaret C. *Women and gender in medieval Europe: an encyclopedia*. New York: Routledge, Taylor & Francis, 2006. http://books.google.com/books?id=aDhOv6hgN2IC&dq=Vigri

Schopenhauer, Arthur. *The World as Will and Representation*. Translated by E.F.J. Payne. Selections by Peter Myers. October 8, 2010. http://mailstar.net/schopenhauer.html

Science. "Panel Nixes Congo Trials as AIDS Source." October 30, 1992. http://www.sciencemag.org/content/258/5083/738.4.extract

SHARAN (Sanctuary for Health and Reconnection to Animals and Nature). "Animal Sentience." http://sharan-india.org/animals/animal-sentience/

Sharpe, Dr. Robert. "Part 1. 'Animal Experimentation: A Failed Technology.'" *Animals Against Vivisectors*. http://animals-against-vivisectors.over-blog.org/pages/The_failure_of_vivisection-2012641.html

Shattuck, George B. M.D., and Abner Post, M.D., Eds. The Boston Medical and Surgical Journal. Houghton, Mifflin and Company: The Riverside Press, 1881. http://books.google.com/books?id=o5wEAAAAQAAJ&pg=PA203&lpg=PA203&dq=Democritus+as+a+vivisector&source=bl&ots=HGtbrbfXF9&sig=qQmiXtY4dFTBnXWiXXT4gqSd-gU&hl=en&sa=X&ei=L5gvUfPNM6Xw0gHCyoGICQ&ved=0CD8Q6AEwAw#v=onepage&q=Democritus%20as%20a%20vivisector&f=false

Sheldrake, Rupert. "Extended Mind, Power, & Prayer: Morphic Resonance and the Collective Unconscious." *Psychological Perspectives*, Part III. Spring, 1988. http://www.sheldrake.org/Articles&Papers/papers/morphic/morphic3_paper.html

Sheldrake, Rupert. *The Rebirth of Nature: Science and God*. Rochester, Vermont: Park Street Press, 1994.

Shevelow, Kathryn. *For the Love of Animals: The Rise of the Animal Protection* Movement. New York: Henry Holt and Company, LLC, 2008.

Singer, Peter. *Animal Liberation: A New Ethics For Our Treatment of Animals*. New York: Avon Books, 1977.

Smith, Jane A.. "A Question of Pain in Invertebrates." *Institute for Laboratory Animals Journal*, 33 (1-2). 1991.
http://www.abolitionist.com/darwinian-life/invertebrate-pain.html

Sneddon, Lynne U., Victoria A. Braithwaite, and Michael J. Gentle. "Do fishes have nociceptors? Evidence for the evolution of a vertebrate sensory system." *The Royal Society.* Dec. 5, 2002.
http://rspb.royalsocietypublishing.org/content/270/1520/1115.full.pdf

Snyder, Laura J. "William Whewell." *Stanford Encyclopedia of Philosophy.* November 12, 2012.
http://plato.stanford.edu/entries/whewell/

Spielvogel, Jackson J. *Western Cviilization*. Vol. II Since 1500. Boston: Wadsworth Publishing, 1996.
St. Augustine. *Confessions* "Book Four" and "Book Seven."
http://www.ourladyswarriors.org/saints/augcon4.htm

Spikins, Penny, et al. *The Prehistory of Compassion*. Blurb Inc., 2010.

Steintrager, James A. *Cruel Delight : Enlightenment Culture and the Inhuma.* Bloomington : Indiana University Press, 2004.

Stop White Coat Welfare. "The Scientific Argument Against Animal Testing." http://www.whitecoatwelfare.org/aat-text.shtml

Storch, Gregory A. "Diagnostic Virology." Journals of the Royal Society and Tropical Medicine and Hygiene, Vol. 31, Issue 3, pp. 739-751. http://cid.oxfordjournals.org/content/31/3/739.full#sec-2

Stutdmann, Paul. *Aristotle's Categories. Stanford Encyclopedia of Philosophy.* September 7, 2007.
http://plato.stanford.edu/entries/aristotle-categories/

Tangley, Laura. "Animal Emotions." U.S. News and World Report. October 22, 2000.

http://www.usnews.com/usnews/culture/articles/001030/archive_01
0364_3.htm

The Bible. Kings James Version.

The Bible. The New Revised Standard Version.

The European Union Times. "Animal rights advocate says: Korea
Should Stop Eating Man's Best Friends." January 25, 2010.
http://www.eutimes.net/2010/01/animal-rights-advocate-says-
korea-should-stop-eating-mans-best-friends/

The House of Lords, Session 2001-2002. "Select Committee on
Animals in Scientific Procedures," Volume I, Report. July 16, 2002.
http://www.publications.parliament.uk/pa/ld200102/ldselect/ldani
mal/150/150.pdf

The National Humane Education Society. "Research Issues, U.S.
Agencies and Animal Testing."
http://www.nhes.org/articles/view/750

The New York Review of Books. "The Dog in the Lifeboat: An
Exchange, Tom Regan, reply by Peter Singer." (in response to *Ten
Years of Animal Liberation* from the January 17, 1985 issue).
http://www.nybooks.com/articles/archives/1985/apr/25/the-dog-in-
the-lifeboat-an-exchange/?pagination=false

The Roman Empire in the First Century. "Titus and Domitian."
PBS.
http://www.pbs.org/empires/romans/empire/titus_domitian.html

The Telegraph. "Resist animal rights extremism, top scientists
urge." August 24, 2005.
http://www.telegraph.co.uk/news/1496846/Resist-animal-rights-
extremism-top-scientists-urge.html

The Wistar Institute, "No Aids-Related Viruses or Chimpanzee DNA Found in 1950s Era Polio Vaccine." http://www.wistar.org/news_info/pressreleases/pr_9.11.00.html

Thompson, D'Arcy Wentworth, trans. *Aristotle*: *Historia Animalium*. Oxford: Clarendon Press, 1910. Book I, No. 17, Electronic Text Center, University of Virginia Library, http://etext.virginia.edu/etcbin/toccer-new2?id=AriHian.xml&images=images/modeng&data=/texts/englis h/modeng/parsed&tag=public&part=all

Tynes, Valarie V., DMV. "Drug Therapy in Pet Rodents." In *Vet Med*, 93[11]:988-991. November 1998. http://www.vspn.org/vspnsearch/aow/drugtherapyinpetrodents.ht m

Vallery-Radot, Rene. *The Life of Pasteur.* New York: Doubleday, Page & Company, 1915. http://www.pasteurbrewing.com/documents/The%20Life%20of%20 Pasteur%20-%20Rene%20Vallery-Radot%20(English).txt

Van der Voet, Hertwich, S, Suh, S, A. Tukker, M. Huijbregts, P. Kazmierczyk, M. Lenzen, J. McNeely and Y. Moriguchi. "Assessing the Environmental Impacts of Consumption and Production: Priority Products and Materials, A Report of the Working Group on the Environmental Impacts of Products and Materials to the International Panel for Sustainable Resource Management." UNEP, 2010 . http://www.unep.org/resourcepanel/documents/pdf/PriorityProduc tsAndMaterials_Report_Full.pdf

Vegan Activist. http://veganactivist.wordpress.com/2010/02/28/was-pythagoras-vegetarian/

Vitello, Paul. "Alexander Leaf dies at 92; Linked Diet and Health." The New York Times. January 6, 2013.

http://www.nytimes.com/2013/01/07/us/alexander-leaf-dies-at-92-linked-diet-and-health.html?_r=0

West Coast Odysseus. "Euripides' *Bacchae.*" January 13, 2009. http://nathanbauman.com/odysseus/?p=412

Woolf , Greg. *Ancient Civilizations*. San Diego:Thunder Bay Press, 2005.

Yarri, Dana. *The Ethics of Animal Experimentation: A Critical Analyss and Constructive Christian Proposal.* New York: Oxford University Press," 2005. http://books.google.com/books/about/The_Ethics_of_Animal_Experimentation_A_C.html?id=DkNJXIWbhtEC

Ullucci, Daniel C. *The Christian Rejection of Animal Sacrifice*. Oxford Scholarship online, 2011. http://www.oxfordscholarship.com/view/10.1093/acprof:oso/9780199791705.001.0001/acprof-9780199791705

Index

A

abolition movement, 21
Academie of Sciences, 99
Academy of Medical Sciences, 114
addiction testing, 105, 106, 182
adultery, 36
African Americans, 22
Albert the Great, 53, 57, 204, 216, 245
Alcmaeon of Croton, 17, 216, 240
Alexander the Great, 18d
Alexandria, 28, 31, 216, 240
Alzheimer's Disease, 58, 106, 136, 199
Alzheimer's research, 115
American Vegetarian Society, 8, 83
Americans for Medical Progress, 112, 113
amygdale, 191
anal electrocutions, 197
anatomist, 62, 63, 69, 75, 78, 195
ancient Greeks, 9, 11, 15
Andes, foothills, 183
Anecdotal evidence, 141, 143, 160
anesthesia,
    discovery of, 99, 112, 113
    experiments conducted without, 4, 33, 63, 64, 78, 87, 88, 89, 99, 110, 157, 179, 196
Anglican church, 70
Animal and Plant Health Inspection Service, 15
animal psychologists, 161, 163, 186
animal sacrifice, 10-15, 22-24, 26, 27 43, 51, 56, 59, 81, 227, 240
Animal Science Association, 114

animal shelters,
    sale of animals to animal research laboratories, 196
animal spirits, 65, 66, 204, 248
Animal Welfare Act, 107
animals' aesthetic appreciation of their environment, 152, 153, 214, 257
animals' expressions of their perceptions, 153
anthrax vaccine for cattle, 99, 100, 101, 107
anthropologists, 29, 148
anthropomorphic sympathies, 8, 143
antivivisection, 80, 84, 85, 86, 87, 89, 95, 110, 120
Anti-vivisection act of 1876, 87, 211, 251
apes, 32, 143, 152, 160, 167, 205, 256
archaeological evidence unavailable, 12, 29, 139, 150, 173
archaeologists, 148
Aristophanes, 10
Aristotle, See Chapter 3,
    Categories, 49, 224, 244
    De Animalibus, 54
    strangled animals, 25
Arundale, George S., xiii
aseptic meningitis, 130
Association for the Advancement of Medicine by Research, 87
Association of the British Pharmaceutical Industry, 114
Aston University of Information Engineering, 115
automata, 65, 67, 163, 164
Averroes, 53, 55

B

Bacon, Francis, 189

baiting sports, 5

Ballestero, Joana and Melchiora, 62

Banting, Frederick, 113, 219, 253

Barnard, Dr. Christian
Good Life, Good Death, 80

Barron, Dr. Moses, 112, 113

bats, 151

Baylor University, 107

beans, soybeans, 188

bees, 165, 199

Bekoff, Marc
Carruthers on nonconscious experience, 158, 213, 257

Belgian Congo, 124

Bell, Charles
theory of nerves, 103

benefits of relating to each species individually, 198

Bentham, Jeremy, 82, 83, 174

Berlin Academy of Sciences,79

Bernard, Claude,
Exhaust experiment and then think, 95, 137
Introduction to the Study of Experimental Medicine, 91, 94, 96, 205, 251

Billman, Professor George E., 185, 188

Birmingham Medical School, 164

Bishop Ambrose of Milan, 48

black currant seed oil, 188

Blavatsky, Madame Helena, 66

blood circulation mistakes,
Galen, Harvey, 180

blood sports, 57, 170

blood transfusion, 114, 115, 212, 253

Boethius, Anicius Manlius Severinus, 48, 52, 53, 54, 215, 246

bowerbirds, 152, 153

Boyle, Robert, 4, 73, 83, 206, 241

brain damage research, 105

British Medical Journal, 87

British Parliament, 78

Browning, Robert, 84

Buddha, 18

bushmeat, 125, 126

C

Calvin, John, 40, 41, 42, 45, 48, 55, 57, 79, 175, 176, 206, 244, 246

Cambridge University, 79

Canadian Broadcasting Corporation, 124

Carlsen, William, 128, 207, 255

Carlyle, Thomas, 87

Carruthers, Peter, See Chapter 13, "Humans in, animals out," 166, 170

Cartesian dualism, 66, 69, 74, 154, 164

castrated monkeys, 5

Catholic Church, 53, 61, 62

Caucasus Mountains, 183

Cavendish, Duchess Margaret
"The Hare," 81, 82

Celts, 11, 12

Center for Veterinary Health Services at Oklahoma State University, 117

center of gaze experiment, 105

Centlivre, Susanna, 74

cetaceans, 143, 151

Chain, Sir Ernst Boris, 117, 118

Chinese, 11, 22, 180

Chloramphenicol, 135

chloroform, 63, 99, 101

cholera vaccine for chickens, 99

church fathers, 35, 36, 39, 48, 53, 57, 59

Cicero, 48

circuses, 7, 57, 158, 170, 197

Class B animal dealers, 196

clocks, 65, 67, 69, 74, 157

methane gas, xi
methylmercury found in fish, 187
mice, 4, 103, 106, 107, 110, 117, 118, 119, 121, 128, 135
Mill, John Stuart, 82
millions of deaths from cancer, 8, 122
Minoans, 10
miracles, 3, 63
mirror self-recognition, 143
miserable, dark cellars, 98
Mitchell, Silas Weir, 95
Moniteur Universel, 96
Montaigne, Michel de, 30, 33, 81
Mormons, 76
Moses, 11, 36, 37, 38, 42, 43, 45, 59, 60, 65
multiple sclerosis, 136
musicians, 23

N

National Aeronautics and Space Administration (NASA), 104
National Association for Biomedical Research, 107
National Cancer Institute (NCI), 127
National Institute for Occupational Safety and Health, 104
National Institute of Environmental Health Sciences, 104
National Institute of Mental Health, 5, 106
National Institutes of Health (NIH), 2, 102, 104, 107, 126, 144, 145, 188, 191
National Toxicology Program, 104
Native Americans, 22
Nazis, 30, 98
Nepal, 13
New England Journal, The, 183
New Right in England, 161

New Testament, 35, 36, 42, 44, 46, 51, 202
New York University, 110, 206, 240
Newton, Isaac, 71, 189
Nicholas Ungar Furs, 14
Nietzsche, Friedrich, 48
Nobel Prize, 98, 101, 116-119, 121, 255
nonconsciousness, 155-159
non-paralytic polio, 130
nonsteroidal anti-inflammatory drugs, 134
Nurse, Sir Paul, 116
nuts, walnuts, 188

O

Occupational Health and Safety Administration., 104
Ohio University, 106, 185
Old Testament, 11, 36, 37, 42, 44, 46, 47, 58, 65
omega 3 fatty acids
avoiding risk of diseased fish, **188**
OPV (Oral Polio Vaccine), 121, 123, 124, 125, 212, 255
Oregon Health and Science University, 106
Origins of AIDS, The, 125, 256
Original Sin, 48
Osborne, Thomas, 135
Osvath, Mathias, Current Biology, 143
overall statistical number of polio cases, 129

P

Padua University, 62
Paleolithic burials, 10
Pardies, Père Ignaz-Gaston, 69
Parker-Pearson, Dr. Mike, 14, 219, 240

Thalidomide, 134

The Great Assumers, 34, 40, 116

Theophrastus, 22, 81, 73, 74

theory of blood circulation
  known by ancient Chinese, 180

Theosophy, 66

Third Eye, The, 66

Times of London, 85

Titus Vestricius Spurinna, 12

trapping, 7, 57, 158, 197

treadmill for dogs,
  cardiac death experiments, 185

tropism, 164

Trull, Frankie, 107

Tweedle, John, 83, 174

Tylenol kills cats, 135

Type 1 diabetes, 132

Type 2 diabetes, 132, 135

U

U.S. Congress, 107

U.S. Presidents, 21

unique character and value of
  each species, 198

United Nations, 218, 239

United States Court of Appeals of
  the 7th Circuit, 161

United States Department of
  Agriculture (USDA), 15, 107

universities, 26, 53, 61, 64, 101,
  103, 106, 107, 112, 138, 187, 198

University of Bologna, 61

University of California San
  Francisco, 2, 105

University of Connecticut, 105,
  106

University of Halle, 75

University of Michigan, 107, 162

University of Minnesota, 106, 214,
  251

University of North Carolina, 110

University of Pennsylvania, 107

University of Southern Indiana,
  168

University of Virginia, 106, 226,
  243

University of Washington, 107

University of Wisconsin, 5, 107,
  109

University of Wollongong, 125

Unzer, Johann August, 75, 76, 215,
  250

V

Vegetarian Society in Britain, 83

Ventricular Arrhythmias, 183, 186,
  215, 260

Vesalius, Andreas, 62, 63

veterinary school of Turin, 100

veterinary schools, 75

Victoria Street Society, 84, 86, 87,
  88, 89, 92

violent manner in which nations
  interact, 198

Vioxx, 135

Virchow, Rudolf, 85

Virgin Mary, 70

virtually every medical
  achievement of the last century
  has depended directly or
  indirectly on research with
  animals, 115, 116, 117,

vocalizations, 151, 153

Voltaire, 68

W

wagging finger warning, 197

Wagner, Richard, 82, 174

Waksman, Selman Abraham, 119,
  120

weapons and military research,
  104

Weller, Dr. Thomas H., 120

Wells, M.J., 164

whales, 151

Whewell, William, 189, 224, 261

whistle blowers, 192

References

Preface

[1] *Food and Agriculture Organization of the United Nations*, "Livestock's Long Shadow" (Rome, 2007), 267-284,
http://www.fao.org/docrep/010/a0701e/a0701e00.HTM

[2] UNEP, E. Hertwich, E. Van der Voet, S. Suh, S, A. Tukker, M. Huijbregts, P. Kazmierczyk, M. Lenzen, J. McNeely and Y. Moriguchi, "**Assessing the Environmental Impacts of Consumption and Production: Priority Products and Materials**, A Report of the Working Group on the Environmental Impacts of Products and Materials to the International Panel for Sustainable Resource Management," (UNEP, 2010), p. 80.
http://www.unep.org/resourcepanel/documents/pdf/PriorityProductsAndMaterials_Report_Full.pdf. See also Warren McLaren, "Half of World Crop is Feeding Animals, Not People," *Treehugger.com* June 22, 2010. http://www.treehugger.com/files/2010/06/half-of-world-crop-feeding-animals-not-people.php
http://www.unep.org/resourcepanel/documents/pdf/PriorityProductsAndMaterials_Report_Full.pdf

Chapter 1

[1] Eliot M. Katz, "Dogs in South Korea: Man's Best Friend…or Dinner?" *In Defense of Animals*,
http://ida.convio.net/site/MessageViewer/&printer_friendly=1?em_id=18721.0&dlv_id=21121

[2] *The European Union Times*, "Animal rights advocate says: Korea Should Stop Eating Man's Best Friends" (January 25, 2010),
http://www.eutimes.net/2010/01/animal-rights-advocate-says-korea-should-stop-eating-mans-best-friends/

[3] David Irving, *The Protein Myth: Significantly Reducing the Risk of Cancer, Heart Disease, Stroke, and Diabetes While Saving the Animals and Building a Better World* (Arlesford, Hants, UK, O-Books, 2011), 247, 248.

[4] Donna Hart and Robert W. Sussman, *Man the hunted: Primates, Predators, And Human Evolution*," (Westview Press, Cambridge, MA, 2005).

[5] Ibid.

[6] Anita Guerrini, *Experimenting with Humans and Animals* (Baltimore: The Johns Hopkins Press, 2003), 38.

[7] Irving, p. 317.

[8] In Defense of Animals, "Top 10 Reasons Why Animal Research Is A Cruel Joke." http://idausa.org/ridiculousresearch/

[9] Irving, for additional examples of unnecessary animal research see Appendix III.

[10] Kathryn Shevelow, *For the Love of Animals: The Rise of the Animal Protection Movement* (New York: Henry Holt and Company, LLC, 2008), 7. 8.

[11] Ibid.

[12] Ibid., 133, 134.

[13] Louis Breger, *Dostoievsky: The Author As Psychoanalyst* (New York: New York University, 1989), 2,
http://books.google.com/books/about/Dostoevsky.html?id=jJqMm3fh9tIC
[14] Dan Cantrell, "Dostoievsky and Psychology,"
http://www.fyodordostoevsky.com/essays/m-cantrell.html
[15] Shevelow, 133, 134.
[16] Rob Preece, Awe for the Tiger, Love for the Lamb, (UBC Press, 2002), 327.
http://books.google.com/books?id=i1mXs6qrRDcC&printsec=frontcover&source=gbs_ge_summary_r&cad=0#v=snippet&q=Dickens&f=true
[17] Ibid., 241-242, 268-269, 277-178, 280.
[18] Ibid., 11.
[19] American Vegetarian Convention New York City 1850, from the Vegetarian Advocate (London), July 1, 1850,
http://www.ivu.org/congress/1850/convention.html
[20] It has been theorized that language began when the high position of the larynx in the vocal tract dropped creating an expanded pharynx (the five inch tube that starts at the nose and descends to the esophagus) which would allow the tongue the freedom of movement necessary for articulating vowel and consonant sounds. An ongoing debate continues as to when this would have occurred. This author presently accepts the argument that it would have started about 150 thousand years ago and took an additional 100,000 years for humans to really develop language that was adequate to express the interior and exterior worlds of their life experience.

Chapter 2

[1] *Julian Cope Presents The Modern Antiquarian*, "Phaistos: Ancient Village, Settlement, Misc. Earthwork,"
http://themodernantiquarian.com/site/10857/phaistos.html#fieldnotes
[2] *About.com*, "Lefkandi," See Toumba,
http://archaeology.about.com/gi/o.htm?zi=1/XJ&zTi=1&sdn=archaeology&cdn=education&tm=115&gps=263_101_796_367&f=10&tt=8&bt=0&bts=0&zu=http%3A//faculty.vassar.edu/jolott/old_courses/crosscurrents2001/Lefkandi/
[3] Richard Hamilton, Review of "Dennis D. Hughes, *Human Sacrifice in Ancient Greece*, Bryn Mawr Classical Review 03.01.25 html,
http://bmcr.brynmawr.edu/1992/03.01.25.html
[4] *West Coast Odysseus*, "Euripides' *Bacchae*" (January 13, 2009),
http://nathanbauman.com/odysseus/?p=412
[5] Greg Woolf, *Ancient Civilizations* (San Diego:Thunder Bay Press, 2005), 332.
[6] T.D. Kendricks, *Druids and Druidism*, (Dover Publications, Inc., 2003),
http://books.google.com/books/about/Druids_and_Druidism.html?id=V5G1SwrZDqUC
[7] Mike Parker-Pearson, M.D., "The Practice of Human Sacrifice," *BBC: History*,
http://www.bbc.co.uk/history/ancient/british_prehistory/human_sacrifice_01.shtml

[8] Greta Nilsson, "Persecution and Hunting: Roman Slaughters," Endangered Species Handbook, 1983, Animal Welfare Institute, Washington, D.C. PDF (1983). http://www.endangeredspecieshandbook.org/persecution_roman.php

[9] John T. Ramsey, "'Beware the Ides of March!': an astrological prediction?" *The Classical Quarterly* (New Series), 50: 440-454 (2000), http://journals.cambridge.org/action/displayAbstract?fromPage=online&aid=3648424

[10] Daniel C. Ullucci, *The Christian Rejection of Animal Sacrifice*, Oxford Scholarship online, 2011, http://www.oxfordscholarship.com/view/10.1093/acprof:oso/9780199791705.001.0001/acprof-9780199791705

[11] The Bible, Matthew 9:13, New Revised Standard Edition.

[12] Candice Bailey, "Muti killings is a way of life in rural areas," *IOL News*, January 16, 2010, http://www.iol.co.za/news/south-africa/muti-killings-is-a-way-of-life-in-rural-areas-1.470603

[13] Olivia Lang, "Hindu sacrifice of 250,000 animals begins," *The Guardian* , November 24, 2009, http://www.guardian.co.uk/world/2009/nov/24/hindu-sacrifice-gadhimai-festival-nepal

[14] Parker-Pearson.

[15] *Katu.com*, "Father: Son who burned himself alive was a troubled genius," January 28, 2010, http://www.katu.com/news/local/82986637.html

[16] Dana Yarri, *The Ethics of Animal Experimentation: A Critical Analysis and Constructive Christian Proposal,* (New York: Oxford University Press, 2005), 15, http://books.google.com/books/about/The_Ethics_of_Animal_Experimentation_A_C.html?id=DkNJXIWbhtEC

[17] Ibid.

[18] Tzachi Zamir, *Ethics and the Beast: A Speciesist Argument for Animal Liberation*, (Princeton, NJ: Princeton University Press, 2007), p. 80, http://books.google.com/books?id=heMuF5gaGo0C&pg=PP1&lpg=PP1&dq=Tzachi+Zamir,+Ethics+and+the+Beast&source=bl&ots=EjxfHpdiTf&sig=M-qqNuIFzBZGa3ivEPU3U1fwkTg&hl=en&sa=X&ei=4IT2Ua6kG5j_4AOz44CYBw&ved=0CF8Q6AEwCA#v=onepage&q=200%20million&f=false

[19] American Antif-Vivisection Society, "Genetic Engineering," http://www.aavs.org/site/c.bkLTKfOSLhK6E/b.6457025/k.EB0B/Genetic_Engineering.htm

Chapter 3

[1] Carl Huffman, "Alcmaeon," *Stanford Encyclopedia of Philosophy* (April 28, 2008), http://plato.stanford.edu/entries/alcmaeon/#Dissec

[2] James Longrigg, Greek Rational Medicine: Philosophy and Medicine from Alcmaeon to the Alexandrians (Routledge, November 1, 2002), p. 58, http://books.google.com/books?id=TT5lzingflYC&dq=Alcmaeon+excision+of+eyecball&source=gbs_navlinks_s

[3] Shattuck, George B. M.D., and Abner Post, M.D., Eds, The Boston Medical and Surgical Journal, (Houghton, Mifflin and Company: The Riverside Press, 1881).

For 17th century sources see Robert Burton's History of Melancholy, editions 1631 and 1638.
http://books.google.com/books?id=o5wEAAAAQAAJ&pg=PA203&lpg=PA203&dq=Democritus+as+a+vivisector&source=bl&ots=HGtbrbfXF9&sig=qQmiXtY4dFTBnXWiXXT4gqSd-gU&hl=en&sa=X&ei=L5gvUfPNM6Xw0gHCyoGICQ&ved=0CD8Q6AEwAw#v=onepage&q=Democritus%20as%20a%20vivisector&f=false

[4] Istvan Bodnar, "Aristotle's Natural Philosophy," *Stanford Encyclopedia of Philosophy* (Dec. 31, 2009), http://plato.stanford.edu/entries/aristotle-natphil/

[5] *FreeEssays.cc*, "Aristotle, A Comprehensive View on Nature and Society," http://www.freeessays.cc/db/35/prz50.shtml

[6] Aldous Huxley, The Perennial Philosophy, (New York: HarperCollins, 2012), 25,
http://books.google.com/books?id=l1fs25HbCY0C&dq=For+in+this+breaking+through+I+perceive+what+God+and+I+are+in+common.++There+I+am+what+I+was.++There+I+neither+increase+nor+decrease.++For+there+I+am+the+immovable+which+moves+all+things&q=For+in+this+breaking+through+I+perceive+what+God+and+I+are+in+common.++There+I+am+what+I+was.++There+I+neither+increase+nor+decrease.++For+there+I+am+the+immovable+which+moves+all+things#v=onepage&q&f=false

[7] Arthur Schopenhauer, *The World as Will and Representation*, Translated by E.F.J. Payne, Selections by Peter Myers, October 8, 2010,
http://mailstar.net/schopenhauer.html

[8] Wildman, Lesley, "Aristotle (384-322 BCE)," Wildman's Weird Wild Web, under Hierarchy of Being,
http://people.bu.edu/wwildman/WeirdWildWeb/courses/wphil/lectures/wphil_theme03.htm#Explaining the World: Aristotle's Enhanced Hierarchy of Being

[9] Rupert Sheldrake, "Extended Mind, Power, & Prayer: Morphic Resonance and the Collective Unconscious," *Psychological Perspectives*, Part III, (Spring, 1988), 19(1) 64-78,
http://www.sheldrake.org/Articles&Papers/papers/morphic/morphic3_paper.html

[10] Stephen F. Mason, *A History of the Sciences*, (New York: Colier Books, 1977), p. 58.

[11] Wildman, Lesley, "Aristotle (384-322 BCE)," Wildman's Weird Wild Web, http://people.bu.edu/wwildman/WeirdWildWeb/courses/wphil/lectures/wphil_theme03.htm#Explaining the World: Aristotle's Enhanced Hierarchy of Being

[12] S. Marc Cohen, Patricia Curd, and C.D.C. Reeve, eds., *Readings in Ancient Greek Philosophy*, Third Edition, (Indianapolis: Hackett Publishing Company, 2005), p645-654.

[13] Matthew Brendan Boyle, *Kant and the Significance of Self-Consciousness* (2005), Doctor of Philosophy Dissertation, University of Pittsburgh, pp. 2,3, http://d-scholarship.pitt.edu/9302/1/boylemb_etd2005.pdf

[14] Anita Guerrini, *Experimenting with Humans and Animals* (Baltimore: The Johns Hopkins Press, 2003), 7, 10, 11.

[15] Margaret C..Schaus, *Women and gender in medieval Europe: an encyclopedia* (New York: Routledge, Taylor & Francis, 2006), 35,
http://books.google.com/books?id=aDhOv6hgN2IC&dq=Vigri

[16] Guerrini, 11.

[17] *International Vegetarian Union*, "Ancient Greece and Rome, Plato (?427=?347 BC)," http://www.ivu.org/history/greece_rome/plato.html

[18] For a brief discussion of whether or not Plato was a vegetarian, see http://www.suite101.com/content/vegetarian-philosophers--list-of-vegetarian-thinkers-a340397

[19] For a discussion of attempts to discredit the belief that Pythagoreans were vegetarian, notably by Aristotle, see Vegan Activist, http://veganactivist.wordpress.com/2010/02/28/was-pythagoras-vegetarian/

[20] Andrea Koinski and Barbara Olsen, "The Burkert Interpretation of Animals Sacrifice," http://inside.bard.edu/academic/specialproj/ritual/Rituals/Burkert/00.html

[21] Gerald V. Lalonde, *Horos Dios: an Athenian Shrine and Cult of Zeus*, (Leiden, the Netherlands: Koninklijke Brill N.V., 2006), 76, http://books.google.com/books?id=sO8E8Bik1a4C&pg=PA75&lpg=PA75&dq=animal+sacrifice+in+Greece+during+the+4th+century+BC&source=bl&ots=stOBZsWJXJ&sig=7mqR8qJ1To93XxS6soce6PFVibE&hl=en&ei=5BuqTdvkCqKx0QHc2e35CA&sa=X&oi=book_result&ct=result&resnum=3&ved=0CCYQ6AEwAg#v=onepage&q&f=false

[22] Ibid., 77.

[23] Ibid., 119.

[24] Ibid., 18.

[25] Ibid., 21.

[26] Koinski and Olsen

[27] Lalonde, 18.

[28] Guerrini, 7.

[29] Ibid., 10.

[30] Aristotle, *Historia Animalium*, D'Arcy Wentworth Thompson, trans. (Oxford: Clarendon Press, 1910), Book I, No. 17, Electronic Text Center, University of Virginia Library, http://etext.virginia.edu/etcbin/toccer-new2?id=AriHian.xml&images=images/modeng&data=/texts/english/modeng/parsed&tag=public&part=all

[31] Guerrini, 8.

[32] Ibid., Book III, 3.

[33] Plinio Prioreschi, *A History of Medicine: Greek Medicine*, (Omaha, NE: Horatius Press, 1996), 413, 414, http://books.google.com/books?id=HaX733MnZZ4C&pg=PA417&lpg=PA417&dq=Aristotle+strangled+animals&source=bl&ots=MApxlTEfTu&sig=bm2Qd-kVwkGsWEbFtkQerbrP62Q&hl=en&ei=K0isTYOeAsPKgQes6KX0BQ&sa=X&oi=book_result&ct=result&resnum=2&ved=0CBsQ6AEwAQ#v=onepage&q=Aristotle%20strangled%20animals&f=false

Chapter 4

[1] Anita Guerrini, *Experimenting with Humans and Animals* (Baltimore: The Johns Hopkins Press, 2003), 8.

[2] Joyce E. Salisbury, Dr., *Women in the Ancient World*, (Santa Barbara, CA: ABC-CLIO, Inc., 2001), 144, http://books.google.com/books?id=HF0m3spOebcC&pg=PA144&lpg=PA144&dq=Aristotle+and+Herophilus&source=bl&ots=q0Hnmwx-fz&sig=iqw4y2OnSoTpz99HN8ReG17Q0_Y&hl=en&ei=zVesTbKxAofx0gGCt4XCAw&sa=X&oi=book_result&ct=result&resnum=4&ved=0CCMQ6AEwAw#v=onepage&q=Aristotle%20and%20Herophilus&f=false

[3] Marios Loukas, Alexis Lanteri, et al., "Anatomy in Ancient India: A Focus on the Susruta Samhita," Journal of Anatomy, December, 2010, 217(6): 646-650, http://www.ncbi.nlm.nih.gov/pmc/articles/PMC3039177/

[4] Guerrini, 12.

[5] Ibid, 9.

[6] Ibid.

[7] Ibid, 8.

[8] Rupert Sheldrake, *The Rebirth of Nature: Science and God*, (Rochester, Vermont: Park Street Press, 1994), 36.

[9] Donna Hart and Robert W. Sussman, *Man the hunted: Primates, Predators, And Human Evolution*," (Westview Press, Cambridge, MA, 2005).

[10] Peter Singer, *Animal Liberation: A New Ethics For Our Treatment of Animals*, (New York: Avon Books, 1977), 206, 207.

[11] Kathryn Shevelow, *For the Love of Animals: The Rise of the Animal Protection Movement* (New York: Henry Holt and Company, LLC, 2008), 29.

[12] Charles Patterson, *Eternal Treblinka: Our Treatment of Animals and the Holocaust* (New York: Lantern Books, 2002), 7, 8, http://books.google.com/books?id=zkvY1-t3VxMC&dq=Charles+Patterson,+Eternal+Treblinka&printsec=frontcover&source=bn&hl=en&ei=pqhcTIHYCoP78Abu5Nz1Ag&sa=X&oi=book_result&ct=result&resnum=4&ved=0CCUQ6AEwAw#v=onepage&q&f=false

[13] Guerrini, 6, 7.

[14] Prioreschi, *A History of Medicine*, 418.

[15] Vivian Nutton, "Logic, Learning, and Experimental Medicine," Science 5556 (2992), 800-801, http://www.sciencemag.org/content/295/5556/800.full

[16] Guerrini, p. 18.

[17] Ibid., pp. 16-18.

[18] Ibid., 18.

Chapter 5

[1] *Phoenician International Research Center*, "Tertullian of Carthage, Early Church Father." http://phoenicia.org/tertullian2.html#n25

[2] The Bible, Luke 2:4, New Revised Standard Version.

[3] Ibid., Jude 1:8.

[4] Ibid., John 8:7, St. James version.

[5] The Bible, John 8:11, New Revised Standard Version..

[6] Ibid., Galatians 3:23-28,

[7] Ibid., Deuteronomy 25:4; I Corinthians 9:9-10.

[8] Ibid., I Corinthians 9:9-10

[9] Ray Stedman.org, "Help for Elders," November 8, 1981,
www.raystedman.org/new-testament/timothy/help-for-elders

[10] John Calvin, *The First Epistle of Paul the Apostle to the Corinthians*, trans. By
John W. Fraser, ed. by David Wishart Torrance and Thomas Forsyth Torrance,
Wm. B. Eerdmans Publishing, 1996, http://books.google.com/books?id=--
9jl1EjJtkC&dq=Therefore+that+humane+treatment+of+oxen+ought+to+be+an+i
ncentive,+moving+us+to+treat+each+other+with+consideration+and+fairness&so
urce=gbs_navlinks_s

[11] The Bible, Genesis 1:20-25, New Revised Standard Version.

[12] Ibid, 1:28.

[13] The Bible, Leviticus 2:1; 9:3-4; and 8-9, New Revised Standard Version.

[14] Ibid., John 1:17.

[15] Ibid., Isaiah 66:3 and Matthew 9:13.

[16] Ibid., Exodus 32:14.

[17] Ibid., Genesis 18:22-33.

[18] Ibid., I Corinthians 15:38-40.

[19] Ibid., Ecclesiastes 3:18-22.

[20] Ibid., Exodus 23:4 and 23:12.

[21] Ibid., Deuteronomy 22:10.

[22] Ibid., Psalm 145: 9 and 16; Psalm 36:6.

[23] Ibid., Proverbs 12:10.

[24] Ibid., Genesis 49: 5-7.

[25] Ibid., Luke 12:6.

[26] Ibid., Matthew 10:29.

[27] Ibid., Luke 13:15; 14:5.

[28] Ibid., Matthew 18: 12-14.

[29] Ibid., Matthew 23:37.

[30] Ibid., I John 1:29.

[31] Ibid., Matthew 3:16.

[32] Ibid., Matthew 11:11.

[33] Ibid., Hosea 2:18. For a discussion, see Martin V. Cisneros, "Hosea 2:18: God's
New Covenant Between Man and Animal," all-creatures.org, http://www.all-
creatures.org/discuss/hosea2.18-mvc.html

[34] Ibid., Romans 9:25.

[35] Christianity in View, *Timeline of Paul's Ministry*,
http://christianityinview.com/paulstimeline.html

[36] Michael Mendelson, "Saint Augustine," *Stanford Encyclopedia of Philosophy*
(November 12, 2010), http://plato.stanford.edu/entries/augustine/#Leg

[37] St. Augustine, *Confessions*, "Book Seven,"
http://www.ourladyswarriors.org/saints/augcon4.htm

[38] Ibid., "Book Four."

[39] Paul Stutdmann, , *Aristotle's Categories*, *Stanford Encyclopedia of Philosophy*
(September 7, 2007), http://plato.stanford.edu/entries/aristotle-categories/

[40] Brandon C. Look, "Notes on St. Augustine," *History of Philosophy I*,
(University of Kentucky, 2007, http://www.uky.edu/~look/Phi%20260-
Augustine.pdf

[41] Anita Guerrini, *Experimenting with Humans and Animals* (Baltimore: The Johns Hopkins Press, 2003), 20.

[42] Ibid., 20, 21.

[43] Ibid.

[44] Peter Singer, *Animal Liberation: A New Ethics For Our Treatment of Animals*, (New York: Avon Books, 1977), 199.

[45] The Bible, Luke 14:5

[46] Ibid., Mark 11:15.

[47] Boethius contended he was brought down by deceit. Graeme Hunter, "Boethius's Complaint: Can the Christian Find Consolation Without Christ?" Pontifical John Paul II Institute, Touchstone, A Journal of Mere Christianity (2004), http://www.touchstonemag.com/archives/article.php?id=17-03-025-f

[48] *Public Discourse*, "St. Anselm of Canterbury (1033-1109)," Posted by Publisher Professional, http://public-discourse.blogspot.com/2010/01/st-anselm-of-canterbury-10331109.html

[49] Singer, 205.

[50] Guerrini, 21.

[51] Markus Führer, "Albert the Great," *Stanford Encyclopedia of Philosophy* (April 20, 2012), http://plato.stanford.edu/entries/albert-great/

[52] Albert the Great, *Questions Concerning Aristotle's on Animals*, translated by Irven M. Resnick and \ Kenneth F. Kitchell Jr., in *The Fathers of the Church, Medieaval Continuation* (The Catholic University of America Press, 1984) , 3. http://books.google.com/books?id=vCFFpzofHqIC&pg=PA38&source=gbs_toc_r&cad=3#v=onepage&q&f=true

[53] Ibid., 6.

[54] Ibid., 39.

[55] Ibid., 38.

[56] Melissa S. Atkinson, "Aristotle and Aquinas: Intrinsic Morality versus God's Morality," Rebirth of Reason. http://rebirthofreason.com/Articles/atkinson/Aristotle_and_Aquinas_Intrinsic_Morality_versus_Gods_Morality.shtml

[57] Führer.

[58] Constitutional Rights Foundation, "St. Thomas Aquinas, Natural Law, and the Common Good." http://www.crf-usa.org/bill-of-rights-in-action/bria-22-4-c-st.-thomas-aquinas-natural-law-and-the-common-good.html

[59] Guerrini, 47. This belief has been carried on for centuries. In the 17th century, the Jesuit Gabriel David, who thought that animal experimentation was extremely cruel, also objected to cruel behavior toward animals on the grounds that it could cause human beings to be cruel to other humans, an idea he stated in his *Voyage to the World of Descartes* (1690).

[60] Singer, 202.

[61] Ibid., 201, 203.

[62] In 1970, Richard Ryder , one of the pioneers of the philosophy of animal liberation in Great Britain, was taking his bath one day when the term "speciesism" sprang into his mind as the perfect term for defining the human prejudice against other species that is based on species differences. With speciesism, the Homo sapiens species regards itself as fundamentally superior to

all other species which are granted rights only insofar as human beings decide to grant them. Animals should, consequently, be seen as slaves, mere objects to be used in whatever manner human beings decide.

[63] Singer, 203.

[64] Philip Jenkins, *The Next Christendom: The Coming of Global Christianity* (Oxford University Press, 2002), p. 2, http://books.google.com/books?id=zeeVzDmeZhEC&q=billion#v=snippet&q=billion&f=false

[65] Ibid., Hosea 2:16-18,

[66] Ibid., Isaiah 11:6-9.

[67] Ibid., Job 5:23.

[68] Ibid., Matthew 22:37-40.

[69] Ibid., Matthew 9:13

Chapter 6

[1] Criticisms of Medieval Medicine, "Critique of Medieval Anatomy, physiology, and treatment in approach to disease," http://www.calvin.edu/academic/medieval/medicine/defense/critique.htm

[2] Lynette A. Hart, Mary W. Wood and Benjamin J. Hart, Why Dissection? (Oxford U.K.: Greenwood Press, 2008), 19, http://books.google.com/books?id=jO5eQflkJaQC&q=Michelangelo#v=snippet&q=Michelangelo&f=true

[3] *Medieval Science, Technology, and Medicine: An Encyclopedia*, edited byThomas F. Glick, Steven John Livesy, and Faith Wallis, (New York: Routledge 2005) 33, http://books.google.com/books?id=SaJlbWK_-FcC&pg=PA33&lpg=PA33&dq=Dissection+in+Salerno+in+the+14th+century&source=bl&ots=7lmdPvJg2D&sig=AwIAO1K6WRIvavN3t-rLqHg-5rw&hl=en&sa=X&ei=bHtIUuLlNInb4AOZ_YGwDA&ved=0CDgQ6AEwAw#v=onepage&q=Dissection%20in%20Salerno%20in%20the%2014th%20century&f=false

[4] Criticisms of Medieval Medicine.

[5] *Medieval Science, Technology, and Medicine*, 33.

[6] Charles George Herbermann, Ph.D., LL.D., Edward Aloysius Pace, Ph.D., D.D., Conde Benoist Pallen, Ph..D., LL.D., Thomas J. Shahan, D.D., and John J. Wynne, S.J., eds., *The Catholic Encyclopedia*, Volume 10, (New York: The Universal Knowledge Foundation, 1913), 127, http://books.google.com/books?id=RmoQAAAAIAAJ&pg=PA127&lpg=PA127&dq=History+of+Anatomy+in+the+school+of+Padua&source=bl&ots=fjLWf-bwIL&sig=z8vHJkBQzfiGX4yjgQMVah75zTE&hl=en&ei=nYS1TbzsHsXh0QGz34WIBQ&sa=X&oi=book_result&ct=result&resnum=9&ved=0CFQQ6AEwCA#v=onepage&q=History%20of%20Anatomy%20in%20the%20school%20of%20Padua&f=false

[7] Hart, 19.

[8] *Medieval Science, Technology, and Medicine*, 33.

[9] Hart, 20.

[10] David H. Freedman, "20 Things you didn't know about autopsies,"*Discovery* 9 (September 2012) , 72.

[11] Donald Frederick and Norris Harrison, *The Anatomy and Physiology of the Mammalian Larynx* (Cambridge: Cambridge University Press, 1995), p4- 6. http://books.google.com/books?id=bZBbTNdx4HoC&pg=PA5&lpg=PA5&dq=Fa bricius,+animal+research&source=bl&ots=oKuapsbjRD&sig=3YBOxxr3v1fJ-6Niotj8f4llUDs&hl=en&ei=aH-1TZT2LIO3tgf29tnpDg&sa=X&oi=book_result&ct=result&resnum=4&ved=0CD oQ6AEwAw#v=onepage&q=Fabricius%2C%20animal%20research&f=false

[12] Herbermann, et al, 127. http://books.google.com/books?id=RmoQAAAAIAAJ&pg=PA127&lpg=PA127 &dq=History+of+Anatomy+in+the+school+of+Padua&source=bl&ots=fjLWf-bwIL&sig=z8vHJkBQzfiGX4yjgQMVah75zTE&hl=en&ei=nYS1TbzsHsXh0QG z34WIBQ&sa=X&oi=book_result&ct=result&resnum=9&ved=0CFQQ6AEwCA #v=onepage&q=History%20of%20Anatomy%20in%20the%20school%20of%20 Padua&f=false

[13] "Pierre Belon's Early Natural History of Birds," from the Graphic Arts Collection, Princeton University Library, Princeton, New Jersey, posted by Julie Melby April 16, 2010. http://blogs.princeton.edu/graphicarts/2010/04/the_first_natural_history_of_b.htm l

[14] Frederick and Harrison, 4.

[15] Anita Guerrini, *Experimenting with Humans and Animals*, 46

[16] Ibid.

[17] Ibid., 23.

[18] Ibid., 23.

[19] Ibid., 28, 29

[20] Ibid., 81.

[21] Rupert Sheldrake, *The Rebirth of Nature: Science and God*, 49.

[22] Ibid., 45.

[23] Ibid.

[24] Ibid., 49.

[25] Jackson J. Spielvogel, *Western Civilization*, Vol. II Since 1500 (Boston: Wadsworth Cengage Advantage, 2012), 568. http://books.google.com/books?id=zAsnJ4hU974C&printsec=frontcover&vq=the +mind+cannot+be+doubted,+but+the+body+and+material+world+can&source=g bs_ge_summary_r&cad=0#v=onepage&q=the%20mind%20cannot%20be%20dou bted%2C%20but%20the%20body%20and%20material%20world%20can&f=false

[26] Vivian Nutton, "Logic, Learning, and Experimental Medicine," Science 5556 (2992), 800-801, http://www.sciencemag.org/content/295/5556/800.full

[27] Ibid.

[28] Gert-Jan Lokhorst, "Descartes and the Pineal Gland," *Stanford Encyclopedia of Philosophy* (November 5, 2008), http://plato.stanford.edu/entries/pineal-gland/#3.3

[29] Guerrini, 37.

[30] The Bible, Deuteronomy 12:23-24, New Revised Standard Version.

[31] "In the original use of the term, in its ancient and medieval Latin form, *spiritus animalis*, the word *animal* means "of the mind" or "animating." It refers to a basic mental energy and life force….The term *animal spirits* originated in ancient times, and the works of the ancient physician Galen (ca. 130-ca. 200) have been widely quoted ever since as a source for it. The term was commonly used in medicine through medieval times and up until Robert Burton's *The Anatomy of Melancholy* (1632) and Rene Descartes' *Traité de l'Homme* (1664). There were said to be three spirits: the **spiritus vitalis** that originated in the heart, the **spiritus naturalis** that originated in the liver, and the *spiritus animalis* that originated in the brain. The philosopher George Santayana (1923) built a system of philosophy around the centrality of 'animal faith,' which he defined as 'a pure and absolute spirit, an imperceptible cognitive energy, whose essence is intuition.'" Quoted from George Akerlof and Robert Shiller, *Animal Spirits: How human psychology drives the economy and why it matters for global capitalism* (Princeton University Press, 2009), 3-4, 177-178 in "'Animal Spirits' explained,'" Larry Willmore blog Thought du jour, http://larrywillmore.net/blog/2010/10/10/animal-spirits-explained/

[32] René Descartes, "Animals are Machines," reprinted from *Passions of the Soul* (1649). *Journal of Cosmology*, Vol. 14, 2011. http://journalofcosmology.com/Consciousness136.html

[33] Ibid.

[34] Sheldrake, *The Rebirth of Nature*, 53.

[35] Ibid.

[36] Singer, Animal Liberation, 209.

[37] Irving, *The Protein Myth*, 241.

[38] Sheldrake, *The Rebirth of Nature,* 53.

[39] Rod Preece, *Sins of the Flesh: A History of Ethical Vegetarian Thought,* (Vancouver: UBC Press, 2008), 193, http://books.google.com/books?id=uMnubkF5HjAC&dq=Was+John+Stuart+Mill+a+vegetarian&q=Gassendi#v=onepage&q&f=false

[40] Virginia Park Dawson, *Nature's enigma: the problem of the polyp in the letters of Bonnet, Trembley and Reaumur* (Philadelphia: American Philosophical Society (1987)), Memoirs Series, vol. 174, 33, http://books.google.com/books?id=ehQyWegCmYUC&pg=PA33&lpg=PA33&dq=Rosenfield,+From+Beast-Machine+to+Man-Machine&source=bl&ots=dcd7WCBiO4&sig=tDRnIDwyuNSgBFWHiqvqb8VC8FI&hl=en&ei=Y0snTYTOF8Kt8AbZnMn_AQ&sa=X&oi=book_result&ct=result&resnum=8&ved=0CDEQ6AEwBw#v=onepage&q=Rosenfield%2C%20From%20Beast-Machine%20to%20Man-Machine&f=false

[41] Dawson, 32.

[42] Ibid., 34.

[43] Ibid., 35.

[44] Ibid., Matthew 10:29.

[45] Kathryn Shevelow, *For the Love of Animals: The Rise of the Animal Protection Movement* (New York: Henry Holt and Company, LLC, 2008), 37.

[46] Sheldrake, *The Rebirth of Nature,* 49.

[47] Ibid., 53.

Chapter 7

[1] Anita Guerrini, *Experimenting with Humans and Animals* (Baltimore: The Johns Hopkins Press, 2003), 45

[2] Kathryn Shevelow, *For the Love of Animals: The Rise of the Animal Protection Movement* (New York: Henry Holt and Company, LLC, 2008), 141.

[3] Guerrini, 42, 43, 45.

[4] Andreas-Holger Maehle, "Literary Responses to Animal Experimentation in Seventheeth and Eioghteenth-Century Britain," *Medical History*, 1990, 34: 27-5 1. http://www.ncbi.nlm.nih.gov/pmc/articles/PMC1035999/pdf/medhist00056-0031.pdf

[5] Sally Festing, "Animal Experiments: The Long Debate," *The New* Scientist (1989), 54. http://books.google.com/books?id=opeJdTsCCrMC&pg=PA54&lpg=PA54&dq=historical+vivisection+on+dogs&source=bl&ots=WpFQs08jqy&sig=zhjeCk_4CpGPQVnnh3WeROPkabQ&hl=en&ei=7gsvTdTbI8qr8AbL4L24CQ&sa=X&oi=book_result&ct=result&resnum=7&ved=0CDQQ6AEwBg#v=onepage&q=historical%20vivisection%20on%20dogs&f=false

[6] Anita Guerrini, *Experimenting with Humans and Animals* (Baltimore: The Johns Hopkins Press, 2003), 72.

[7] Vlasislav Kruta, "Unzer, Johan August," *Encyclopedia.com* , http://www.encyclopedia.com/doc/1G2-2830904418.html

[8] Festing, 52

[9] Ibid.

[10] Guido Giglioni."What Ever Happened to Francis Glisson? Albrecht Haller and the Fate of Eighteenth-Century Irritability," *Science in Context* 21(4), 465–493 (2008), 472, http://www.fcsh.unl.pt/chc/pdfs/nature1.pdf

[11] Ibid., 52, 53.

[12] Ibid.

[13] James A. Steintrager, *Cruel Delight : Enlightenment Culture and the Inhuman,* (Bloomington : Indiana University Press, 2004), 70.

[14] Festing, 53.

[15] Deborah Rudacille, *The Scalpel and the Butterfly*, (Berkeley: University of California Press, 2001), 25, http://books.google.com/books?id=BabamiCYEdUC&q=rabbit#v=snippet&q=rabbit&f=false

[16] Shevelow, 144.

[17] Ibid., 54.

[18] Singer, *Animal Liberation*, 212.

[19] Shevelow, 259.

[20] Ibid., 212.

[21] Shevelow, 185.

[22] Festing, 54.

[23] W.F., Bynum, *Science and the Practice of Medicine in the Nineteenth Century* (Cambridge, Melbourne: Cambridge University Press, 1994), 98, http://books.google.com/books?id=tv65dPNmdsgC&pg=PA286&lpg=PA286&dq

=Bynum,+Science+and+the+Practice+of+Medicine+in+the+Nineteenth+Century
&source=bl&ots=CjApW9n7-
2&sig=gclYmZrCCQhE2TOYFuSdDeIpt3M&hl=en&ei=DiDBTr-
FHebL0QHe6emrBA&sa=X&oi=book_result&ct=result&resnum=5&ved=0CEU
Q6AEwBA#v=onepage&q&f=true

[24] *SHARAN* (*Sanctuary for Health and Reconnection to Animals and Nature*),
"Animal Sentience," http://sharan-india.org/animals/animal-sentience/

[25] John of Salisbury, *Frivolities of Courtiers and Footprints of Philosophers*,
Being a Translation of the First, Second and Third Books and Selections from the
Seventh and Eight Books of the *Policraticus* [1159] of John of Salisbury, Joseph
Pike, trans. (University of Minnesota, 1938);
http://www.animalrightshistory.org/0485-1450-animal-rights/medieval-j/john-of-
salisbury/12thc-policraticus-fortune.htm

[26] Shevelow, 29.

[27] Singer, 7, 8.

[28] Kathleen Kete, *The Beast in the Boudoir: Petkeeping in Nineteenth-Century
Paris*, (Berkeley: University of California Press, 1994), 15.

[29] Rod Preece, *Sins of the Flesh: A History of Ethical Vegetarian Thought*,
(Vancouver: UBC Press, 2008), 228, 229,
http://books.google.com/books?id=uMnubkF5HjAC&dq=Was+John+Stuart+Mill
+a+vegetarian&q=Gassendi#v=onepage&q&f=false

[30] Singer, 216-220.

[31] Ibid., 219.

[32] Rod Preece, *Sins of the Flesh*.

[33] Ibid., 208

[34] Ibid., 230.

[35] The Roman Empire in the First Century, "Titus and Domitian," PBS,
http://www.pbs.org/empires/romans/empire/titus_domitian.html

[36] Festing, 52.

[37] Lori Gruen. "The Moral Status of Animals," Standford Encyclopedia of
Philosophy, September 13, 2010. http://plato.stanford.edu/entries/moral-animal/

[38] Rob Preece, Awe for the Tiger, Love for the Lamb, (UBC Press, 2002), 308,
310,
http://books.google.com/books?id=i1mXs6qrRDcC&printsec=frontcover&source
=gbs_ge_summary_r&cad=0#v=snippet&q=Dickens&f=true

[39] Ibid., 316.

[40] André Luis de Lima Carvalho and Ricardo Waizbort, Pain beyond the confines
of man: a preliminary introduction to the debate between Frances Power Cobbe
and the darwinists with respect to vivisection in Victorian England (1863-1904),
Hist. cienc. saude-Manguinhos vol.17 no.3 Rio de Janeiro (2010),
http://www.scielo.br/scielo.php?pid=S0104-
59702010000300002&script=sci_arttext&tlng=en

[41] Ibid.

[42] The Times, April 23, 1881, http://www.newspapers.com/newspage/33142884/

[43] Carvalho.

[44] Preece., *Awe for the Tiger*, 273.

[45] Carvalho
[46] Susan Hamilton, "On the Cruelty to Animals Act, 15 August 1876," http://www.branchcollective.org/?ps_articles=susan-hamilton-on-the-cruelty-to-animals-act-15-august-1876.
[47]Laura Otts, "Howled Out of the Country: Wilkie Collins and H.G. Wells Retry David Ferrier," 32, http://www.palgrave.com/PDFs/0230520944.pdf
[48] Preece, *Awe for the Tiger*, 357.
[49]Hamilton.
[50] Preece, 326, 327.
[51] Otts, 27.
[52] Ibid., *Awe for the Tiger*, 35.
[53] Ibid.
[54] Ibid., 42.

Chapter 8

[1] Anita Guerrini, *Experimenting with Humans and Animals* (Baltimore: The Johns Hopkins Press, 2003), 86, 87.
[2] J.M.D. Olmsted, "The Influence of Claude Bernard on Medicine in the United States and England," Part I, *California and Western Medicine*, Vol 42, No. 2 (February 1935), 112, http://www.ncbi.nlm.nih.gov/pmc/articles/PMC1752078/?page=2
[3] Ibid.
[4]Rob Preece, *Awe for the Tiger*, 310-312,
[5] André Luis de Lima Carvalho and Ricardo Waizbort, Pain beyond the confines of man: a preliminary introduction to the debate between Frances Power Cobbe and the darwinists with respect to vivisection in Victorian England (1863-1904), Hist. cienc. saude-Manguinhos vol.17 no.3 Rio de Janeiro (2010), http://www.scielo.br/scielo.php?pid=S0104-59702010000300002&script=sci_arttext&tlng=en
[6]Ibid. (See also Claude Bernard, *An introduction to the study of experimental medicine*, 102)
[7] Kathleen Kete, *The Beast in the Boudoir: Petkeeping in Nineteenth-Century Paris*, (Berkeley: University of California Press, 1994), 142 ftn. 46.
[8] Guerrini, *Experimenting with Humans and Animals*, 85, 91.
[9] Michael Foster, *Claude Bernard* (New York: Longman, Greens & Co., 1899), 204, http://books.google.com/books?id=cGICAAAAYAAJ&dq=Claude+Bernard+on+his+death+bed&source=gbs_navlinks_s.
[10] Deborah Rudacille, *The Scalpel and the Butterfly*, 18, http://books.google.com/books?id=BabamiCYEdUC&q=rabbit#v=snippet&q=rabbit&f=false, 26.
[11] Olmsted, 112.
[12] Dr. Robert Sharpe, "Part 1. 'Animal Experimentation: A Failed Technology,'" *Animals Against Vivisectors*, http://animals-against-vivisectors.over-blog.org/pages/The_failure_of_vivisection-2012641.html

[13] Encyclopaedia Britannica, "Robert Koch,"
http://www.britannica.com/EBchecked/topic/320834/Robert-Koch#toc3949.
[14]Rene Vallery-Radot, Search "136, The Life of Pasteur."
http://www.pasteurbrewing.com/documents/The%20Life%20of%20Pasteur%20-
%20Rene%20Vallery-Radot%20(English).txt
[15] *International Vegetarian Union (IVU)*, "North America: Late 20th Century Isaac
Bashevis Singer (1904-1991)," under Quotes,
http://www.ivu.org/history/northam20b/singer.html
[16] *Institut Pasteur* "Louis Pasteur and Rabies Vaccination,"
http://www.pasteur.fr/ip/easysite/pasteur/en/press/press-kits/rabies/louis-pasteur-
and-rabies-vaccination
[17] Rudacille, 23.
[18] Guerrini,, 96, 97.
[19] Vallery-Radot, Search "240 The Life of Pasteur."
[20] *Encyclopedia.com*, "Louis Pasteur,"
http://www.encyclopedia.com/topic/Louis_Pasteur.aspx
[21] Ibid.
[22] Guerrini, 93.
[23] *Encyclopedia.com*, "Louis Pasteur."
[24] Stanley A. Plotkin, Walter A. Orenstein, Paul. A. Offit, *Vaccines* (London,
Amsterdam, New York: Elsevier Health Services, 2008), 3.
http://books.google.com/books?id=BFQq2-
fIAJ8C&pg=PA3&lpg=PA3&dq=Pasteur,+anthrax+demonstration,+25+sheep,+a
+goat+and+several+cows&source=bl&ots=jfcNuGjz-
g&sig=IrSafxQO6JT4FAr5OQB4SBCUZEA&hl=en&ei=dI0cTuHCKum30AGrz
onHBw&sa=X&oi=book_result&ct=result&resnum=2&ved=0CCMQ6AEwAQ#
v=onepage&q&f=false

Chapter 9

[1]This was the beginning of a major scientific controversy over who would
eventually be credited with discovering the motor and sensory function of certain
nerve fibers, the Englishman Bell, or the Frenchman Magendie. Some historians
have sought to resolve the crisis by calling it the Bell-Magendie law, though
whether that would have pleased Bell, to whom Magendie's methods were crude,
is doubtful. Added to the debate was the claim by Alexander Walker, a
contemporary of Bell, who claimed that his discovery of the spinal nerve roots
had preceded the work of both Bell and Megandie who had not credited him for
his discovery. (See Gillian Rice, "The Bell-Magendie-Walker Controversy,
Medical History (1987) 31: 190-200),
http://europepmc.org/articles/PMC1139711/pdf/medhist00067-0074.pdf
[2] Ibid., 98, 99.
[3] Dana Yarri, The Ethics of Animal Experimentation: A Critical Analysis and
Constructive Christian Proposal, (New York: Oxford University Press, 2005), p.
14.
[4]*The National Humane Education Society*, "Research Issues, U.S. Agencies and
Animal Testing," http://www.nhes.org/articles/view/750

[5] American Anti-Vivisection Society, "Types of Research," Psychology Research, Military Research, Space Research, Genetic Engineering, http://www.aavs.org/site/c.bkLTKfOSLhK6E/b.6446379/k.B75D/Types_of_Rese arch.htm

[6] David Irving, *The Protein Myth*, 232.

[7] Ibid., Appendix III.

[8] Ibid, 243.

[9] In Defense of Animals, "Top 10 Reasons Why Animal Research Is A Cruel Joke." http://idausa.org/ridiculousresearch/

[10] Irving, 237-239.

[11] Ibid., 244, 245, 319.

[12] Ibid., 236, 237. Also http://www.all-creatures.org/saen/fact-anex-2007.html

Chapter 10

[1] Quotes on Animal Vivisection, "The Samuel Johnson Sound Bite Page," http://www.samueljohnson.com/animalv.html

[2] Irving, *The Protein Myth*, *s*ee Appendix III

[3] Peter Carruthers, "Animal Mentality: Its Character, Extent, and Moral Significance," in Tom L. Beauchamp and R.G. Frey eds., *The oxford handbook of animal ethics* (Oxford University Press: 2011), Part IV, Ch. 13, 378. http://www.philosophy.umd.edu/Faculty/pcarruthers/Animal%20mentality%20an d%20value.pdf

[4] *Stop White Coat Welfare*, "The Scientific Argument Against Animal Testing,". http://www.whitecoatwelfare.org/aat-text.shtml

[5] Peter F. Forsham, "Milestones in the 60 Year History of Insulin (1922-1982), Diabetes Care, vol. 5, Suppl. 2, November-December 1982, http://care.diabetesjournals.org/content/5/Supplement_2/1.full.pdf.

[6] Edward Ortiz, "Science Hero: Frederick Banting," *Science Heroes*, http://myhero.com/go/hero.asp?hero=Banting

[7] Forsham.

[8] *Medical Advances and Animal Research: The contribution of animal science to the medical revolution: some case histories*," (RDS: Understanding Animal Research in Medicine and Coalition for Medical Progress, 2007), http://www.pro-test.org.uk/MAAR.pdf

[9] Richard Lewisohn, "The Importance Of The Proper Dosage Of Sodium Citrate In Blood Transfusion," *Annals of Surgery*, (November, 1916), 64(5): 618–623, http://www.ncbi.nlm.nih.gov/pmc/articles/PMC1426274/

[10] Robert A.J Matthews,. "Medical progress depends on animal models – doesn't it?" *J R Soc Med* (February 2008), 101(2): 95–98, http://www.ncbi.nlm.nih.gov/pmc/articles/PMC2254450/

[11] *Animal Welfare Information Center Newsletter*, "The Importance of Animals in Biomedical and Behavioral Research" (Summer 1994), Vol. 5, no. 2, http://www.nal.usda.gov/awic/newsletters/v5n2/5n2phs.htm

[12] Ibid.

[13] *The House of Lords, Session 2001-2002*, "Select Committee on Animals in Scientific Procedures," Volume I, Report (July 16, 2002), 21, http://www.publications.parliament.uk/pa/ld200102/ldselect/ldanimal/150/150.pdf

[14] *The Telegraph*, "Resist animal rights extremism, top scientists urge," August 24, 2005, http://www.telegraph.co.uk/news/1496846/Resist-animal-rights-extremism-top-scientists-urge.html

[15] *Animal Research for Life*,m "Past Research" (EPFIA), 2011. http://www.animalresearchforlife.eu/index.php/en/past-research

[16] *Oklahoma State University Center for Health Services*, "Animals in Research and Teaching," http://www.cvm.okstate.edu/index.php?option=com_content&view=article&id=544&Itemid=335

[17] Ray Greek, M.D., "The Discovery and Development of Penicillin," *all-creatures.org*, http://www.allcreatures.org/articles/ar-penicillin.html

[18] Ibid.

[19] Valarie V. Tynes, DMV, "Drug Therapy in Pet Rodents," *Vet Med* (November 1998), 93[11]:988-991. http://www.vspn.org/vspnsearch/aow/drugtherapyinpetrodents.htm

[20] *American Chemical Society*, "The trials of streptomycin," http://acswebcontent.acs.org/landmarks/antibiotics/trials.html

[21] Irving, *The Protein Myth*, "Science at Work: the Future of Healthcare Research," Chapter 21.

[22] *Medical Advances and Animal Research.*

[23] John J. Pippin, "PLoS takes a step backward," *PLoS Med* 2(8): e278 (2005), http://www.plosmedicine.org/article/info:doi/10.1371/journal.pmed.0020278

[24] *Stop White Coat Welfare.*

[25] Anita Guerrini, *Experimenting with Humans and Animals*, 122.

[26] Salk Institute for Biological Studies, "Discovery Timeline," http://www.salk.edu/about/discovery_timeline.html

[27] Hauck Center for the Albert B. Sabin Archives, "Sabin Sundays and His Oral Polio Vaccine," and "A Biography of Dr. Sabin," http://sabin.uc.edu/

[28] Alvin Powell, "John Enders Breakthrough Led to Polio Vaccine," The Harvard University Gazette (October 8, 1998), http://www.news.harvard.edu/gazette/1998/10.08/JohnEndersBreak.html.

[29] Lawrence K. Altman, "John F. Enders, Virology Pioneer Who Won Nobel Prize, Dies at 88," The New York Times, September 10, 1985.

[30] Gregory A. Storch, "Diagnostic Virology," Journals of the Royal Society and Tropical Medicine and Hygiene, Vol. 31, Issue 3, pp. 739-751, http://cid.oxfordjournals.org/content/31/3/739.full#sec-2

[31] Ibid.

[32] Guerrini, 115.

[33] *Science*, "Panel Nixes Congo Trials as AIDS Source," (October 30, 1992), p738-739. http://www.sciencemag.org/content/258/5083/738.4.extract

[34] *The Wistar Institute*, "No Aids-Related Viruses or Chimpanzee DNA Found in 1950s-Era Polio Vaccine," http://www.wistar.org/news_info/pressreleases/pr_9.11.00.html

[35] Brian Martin, "How to attack a scientific theory and get away with it (usually): the attempt to destroy an origin-of-AIDS hypothesis," Published in *Science as Culture*, Vol. 19, No. 2 (June 2010), p215-239. http://www.bmartin.cc/pubs/10sac.html See also footnote No. 3 which states in reference to the evidence providing proof that leading scientists tried to block the airing of the film *The Origins of Aids*, "I have in my possession copies of this letter signed by Beatrice Hahn, Bette Korber, John Moore, Stanley Plotkin, Mark Wainberg, Robin A. Weiss and Steven Wolinsky. Each letter is individually signed but the text is virtually identical: the letters say 'The signers of this letter are all scientists involved in public health or more specifically the fight against AIDS."

[36] Pippin.

[37] Guerrini. 129.

[38] William Carlsen, "Rogue virus in the vaccine Early polio vaccine harbored virus now feared to cause cancer in humans, " *San Francisco Chronicle*, 2002, http://www.laleva.cc/choice/vaccines/vaccines_whyNOT.html

[39] Neil Z. Miller, "The polio vaccine: a critical assessment of its arcane history, efficacy, and long-term health-related consequences," 251Thinktwice Global Vaccine Institute, N.Z. Miller/Medical Veritas 1 (2004), 239-251, http://www.thinktwice.com

[40] Ibid.

[41] Ibid.

[42] Ibid.

[43] Gary Karsner and Barry Mesh, "The Salk Vaccine And The "Disappearance" of Paralytic Polio- Is Paralysis a Viral Disease?" (Plus Excerpt From, "Immunization: The Reality Behind The Myth" by Walene James (1988).), http://www.whale.to/a/krasner1.html

[44] Ibid.

[45] Ibid.

[46] Ibid.

[47] Irving, Part I.

[48] Marwan Hariz, I. M.D., Ph.D., Patric Blomstedt, M.D., Ph.D., and Ludvic Zrinzo, M.D., M.Sc., "Deep Brain Stimulation between 1947 and 1987: The Untold Story," *NCBI*, http://www.ncbi.nlm.nih.gov/pubmed/20672911

[49] Ibid.

[50] Pippin.

[51] *PCRM Action Alert*, http://support.pcrm.org/site/MessageViewer?em_id=46403.0&printer_friendly=1

[52] *DrugRecalls.com*, "Rezulin Linked to Liver Failure and Heart Disease," http://www.drugrecalls.com/rezulin.html

[53] Irving, p. 195-197.

[54] Ibid.

[55]Safer Medicines, "Animal Testing – MPs, GPs and scientists demand evaluation," http://www.safermedicines.org/news.php?pid=61

[56] Ibid.

[57] Ibid.

[58] Safer Medicines, "Doctors fear animal experiments endanger patients," http://www.safermedicines.org/news.php?pid=64

Chapter 11

[1] Penny Spikins et al, *The Prehistory of Compassion*, (Blurb Inc., 2010), 18-20.

[2] David Hume, "Of the Reason of Animals," *A Treatise of Human Nature*, Part III, Section xvi, http://www.animal-rights-library.com/texts-c/hume01.htm

[3] Kristin Andrews, "Animal Cognition," *Stanford Encyclopedia of Science* (May 6, 2011), http://plato.stanford.edu/entries/cognition-animal/

[4] Robert W. Lurz, "The philosophy of animal minds: an introduction" in Robert W. Lurz, ed., *The Philosophy of Animal Minds* (Cambridge University Press, UK, 2009), p. 13.

[5] Santiago Arango Muñoz, "Review of The Philosophy of Animal Minds, Robert Lurz (ed), Cambridge: CUP," Acedemia.edu, http://www.academia.edu/239035/Review_of_The_Philosophy_of_Animal_Mind s_Robert_Lurz_ed_._Cambridge_CUP

[6] Coco Ballantyne, "Planning of the Apes: Zoo Chimp Plots Rock Attacks on Visitors," *Scientific American* (March 9, 2009), http://www.scientificamerican.com/article.cfm?id= chimpanzee-plans-throws-stones-zoo

Chapter 12

[1] Peter Carruthers, "Animal Subjectivity," *PSYCHE*, 4(3) (April, 1998), http://www.theassc.org/files/assc/2377.pdf

[2] George Mandler, Consciousness Recovered: Psychological functions and origins of conscious thought, (Amsterdam: John Benjamin Publishing, 2002), 70, http://books.google.com/books?id=v6FGA5hUXG8C&pg=PA69&dq=The+Evolu tion+of+Consciousness+by+Euan+MacPhail&hl=en&sa=X&ei=PzDWUfrfH-7A4APGx4GAAQ&ved=0CDMQ6AEwAQ#v=onepage&q&f=true

[3] As previously noted, it has been theorized that language began when the high position of the larynx in the vocal tract dropped creating an expanded pharynx (the five inch tube that starts at the nose and descends to the esophagus) which would allow the tongue the freedom of movement necessary for articulating vowel and consonant sounds. An ongoing debate continues as to when this would have occurred. This author presently accepts the argument that it would have started about 150 thousand years ago and took an additional 100,000 years for humans to really develop language that was adequate to express the interior and exterior worlds of their life experience.

[4] Gisela Kaplan.and Lesley J. Rogers "Elephants That Paint, Birds That Make Music: Do Animals Have an Aesthetic Sense?" Cerebrum, The Dana Foundation, October 1, 2006, http://www.dana.org/news/cerebrum/detail.aspx?id=74&p=1

Chapter 13

[1] Peter Carruthers, *The Animals Issue*: Moral Theory in Practice (Cambridge: Cambridge University Press, 1992), 184

[2] Ibid., 183.

[3] Peter Carruthers, "Brute Experience," *The Journal of Philosophy*, Vol. 86, No. 5 (May, 1989), 258, http://www-personal.umich.edu/~lormand/phil/teach/mind/readings/Carruthers%20-%20Brute%20Experience.pdf

[4] Carruthers, "Animal Subjectivity," *PSYCHE*, 4(3) (April, 1998), http://www.theassc.org/files/assc/2377.pdf

[5] In the article Carruthers illustrates the same condition with two other examples: (1) driving a car and (2) blindsight, a neurological condition.

[6] Carruthers, "Brute Experience."

[7] Dale Jamieson and Marc Bekoff, "Carruthers on Nonconscious Experience," *Analysis*, Vol. 52, No. 1 (January1992), 23-28, http://as.nyu.edu/docs/IO/1192/JamiesonBekoff-carruthers1992.pdf

[8] Peter Carruthers, *The Animals Issue*, 184.

[9] Carruthers, "Animal Subectivity."

[10] *Nova Science Now*, "How Smart are Dogs" PBS (Feb. 11, 2011), http://www.pbs.org/wgbh/nova/nature/how-smart-dogs.html

[11] Carl Cohen, "The Case for the Use of Animals in Biomedical Research," in Richard Sherlock and John D. Morrey, *Ethical issues in biotechnology*, (Lanham, Maryland: Rowman & Littlefield, 2002), 300, http://books.google.com/books?id=mlVh3ysN4ZwC&pg=PA231&lpg=PA231&dq=Richard+Sherlock+and+John+D.+Morrey,&source=bl&ots=3N0FvizTeN&sig=HpMfuuYWjlFuPZga846iGNFxz5U&hl=en&ei=UcbHTrarK6H50gHD4rEL&sa=X&oi=book_result&ct=result&resnum=6&sqi=2&ved=0CFEQ6AEwBQ#v=onepage&q=Richard%20Sherlock%20and%20John%20D.%20Morrey%2C&f=false

[12] Ibid., 3.

[13] *Nova Science Now*.

[14] Carruthers, *The Animals Issue*, 181-185.

[15] Ibid., 58.

[16] Ibid., 56-58.

[17] Jane A..Smith, "A Question of Pain in Invertebrates," *Institute for Laboratory Animals Journal*, 33 (1-2) (1991), http://www.abolitionist.com/darwinian-life/invertebrate-pain.html

[18] Ibid.

[19] Ibid.

[20] Peter Carruthers, "Suffering without subjectivity," http://drum.lib.umd.edu/bitstream/1903/4357/1/Suffering-without-subjectivity.pdf

[21] Peter Carruthers, "Against the Moral Standing of Animals," 1,2,
http://www.philosophy.umd.edu/Faculty/pcarruthers/The%20Animals%20Issue.p
df

[22] Peter Carruthers, "Animal Mentality: Its Character, Extent, and Moral
Significance," in Tom L. Beauchamp and R.G. Frey eds., *The oxford handbook of
animal ethics* (Oxford University Press: 2011), Part IV, 376.
http://www.philosophy.umd.edu/Faculty/pcarruthers/Animal%20mentality%20an
d%20value.pdf

[23] Ibid.

[24] Ibid., 390.

[25] Ibid.

[26] Rocco J. Gennaro, "Animals, Consciousness, and I-thoughts,"
http://www.usi.edu/libarts/phil/gennaro/papers/AnimalsforLurzEd.pdf

[27] Rocco J. Gennaro, "Higher-Order Thoughts, Animal Consciousness, and
Misrepresentation: A
Reply to Carruthers and Levine," in *Higher-Order Theories of Consciousness*,
John Benjamins, 2004,
http://www.usi.edu/libarts/phil/gennaro/papers/JohnBenjch3.pdf

[28] Carruthers, "Animal Mentality," 375.

[29] Ibid.

[30] Ibid., 374.

Chapter 14

[1] Lori Gruen. "The Moral Status of Animals," Standford Encyclopedia of
Philosophy, September 13, 2010. http://plato.stanford.edu/entries/moral-animal/

[2] Ibid.

[3] Ibid.

Chapter 15

[1] Singer, Animal Liberation, 203.

[2] Peter Carruthers, "Animal Mentality: Its Character, Extent, and Moral
Significance," in Tom L. Beauchamp and R.G. Frey eds., *The oxford handbook of
animal ethics* (Oxford University Press: 2011), Part IV, 26.

[3] Carruthers, *The Animals Issue*, 169.

[4] Ibid., 99.

[5] Greg Ross, "An Interview with Marc Hauser," *American Scientist* (January-
February, 2012), Volume 100, No. 1,
http://www.americanscientist.org/bookshelf/pub/marc-hauser

[6] Carl Sagan and Ann Druyan, *Shadows of Forgotten Ancestors* (Random House
Digital, Inc., 2011), 117,
http://books.google.com/books?id=DjjWea3fgO8C&vq=the+annals+of+primate+
ethics&source=gbs_navlinks_s

Chapter 16

[1] Anita Guerrini, *Experimenting with Humans and Animals*, 23.

[2] B. Boon, "Leonarda da Vinci on artherosclerosis and the function of the sinuses of Valsalva," Netherlands Heart Journal, December 17, 2009, 496-499. http://www.ncbi.nlm.nih.gov/pmc/articles/PMC2804084/

[3] Irving, *The Protein Myth*, Chapter 21.

[4] Paul Vitello, "Alexander Leaf dies at 92; Linked Diet and Health," The New York Times, January 6, 2013, http://www.nytimes.com/2013/01/07/us/alexander-leaf-dies-at-92-linked-diet-and-health.html?_r=0

[5] Alexander Leaf, Jing X. Kang, Yong-Fu Xiao, "Omega-3 Fatty Acids and Ventricular Arrhythmias," Simopoulos AP (ed): Nutrition and Fitness: Obesity, the Metabolic Syndrome, Cardiovascular Disease, and Cancer. World Rev Nutr Diet. Basel, Karger, 2005, vol 94, pp 129-138 (DOI: 10.1159/000088226), http://www.google.com/url?sa=t&rct=j&q=&esrc=s&frm=1&source=web&cd=1&ved=0CCkQFjAA&url=http%3A%2F%2Fwww.researchgate.net%2Fpublication%2F7616721_Adolescent_obesity_and_physical_activity%2Ffile%2F9fcfd50fec97504f69.pdf&ei=zWxHUoCrM8Ti4APUq4C4DQ&usg=AFQjCNGi-ZzfRYp_qBVb84nSYLM_VAVU3Q

[6] Irving, 105, 106.

[7] Leaf, "Omega-3 Fatty Acids and Ventricular Arrhythmias."

[8] Alexander Leaf, *"Dietary Prevention of Coronary Heart Disease: The Lyon Diet Heart Study."* *http://circ.ahajournals.org/cgi/content/full/99/6/733#R9*

[9] This is a reference to a commercial made by actor Paul Hogan by the Australian Tourism Commission in the 1980s.

[10] Ingeborg A. Brouwer et al., "Dietary Linolenic Acid Is Associated with Reduced Risk of Fatal Coronary Heart Disease, but Increased Prostate Cancer Risk: A Meta-Analysis," *The American Society for Nutritional Sciences*, J. Nutr (April 2004), 134:919-922. ALA is the only omega 3 fatty acid found in vegetable sources. The studies were unable to determine if this alpha-linolenic acidcame from meat consumption or flax seed consumption. Another investigation revealed that five studies which examined alpha linolenic acid and found a prostate cancer connection were "extremely inconsistent." With advanced prostate cancer this report suggested an "association with total and saturated fat with advanced prostate cancer, but showed no associations with linoleic acid, alpha-linolenic acid, polyunsaturated fat, eicosapentaenoic acid, or docosahexaenoic acid fatty acids." It concluded that the "associations between dietary fatty acids and prostate cancer remain unclear." See Leslie K. Dennis et al., "Problems with the Assessment of Dietary Fat in Prostate Cancer Studies," *American Journal of Epidemiology* (2004), 160(5):436-444; doi:10.1093/aje/kwh243.http://aje.oxfordjournals.org/cgi/content/full/160/5/436. Another study showed that flax seed reduced prostate cancer risk. See Wendy Demark-Wahnefried, et al., "Flaxseed Supplementation (Not Dietary Fat Restriction) Reduces Prostate Cancer Proliferation Rates in Men," *Presurgery, Cancer Epidemiology Biomarkers & Prevention* (December 1, 2008), 17, 3577-3587,. Doi 10.1158/1055-9965.EPI-08-

0008,http://cebp.aacrjournals.org/cgi/content/abstract/17/12/3,
http://jn.nutrition.org/cgi/content/full/134/4/919577

Chapter 17

[1] Laura J. Snyder, "William Whewell," *Stanford Encyclopedia of Philosophy* (November 12, 2012), http://plato.stanford.edu/entries/whewell/
[2] Marc Bekoff et al., *The Cognitive Animal: Empirical and Theoretical Perspectives on Animal Cognition,* (Cambridge, MA: MIT Press, 2002), digitized at
http://books.google.com/books?id=TztyW8eTnIC&pg=PA105&lpg=PA105&dq=
Marc+Bekoff+et+al.,+The+Cognitive+Animal:+Empirical+and+Theoretical+Pers
pectives+on+Animal+Cognition&source=bl&ots=uHmbTAnmCk&sig=r8KsoLR
5fNJi4ut1jyvUQermZxk&hl=en&ei=gL4xSrvAGYSGtgfuyIyCQ&sa=X&oi=boo
k_result&ct=result&resnum=2
[3] Laura Tangley, "Animal Emotions," *U.S. News and World Report*, October 22, 2000,
http://www.usnews.com/usnews/culture/articles/001030/archive_010364_3.htm
See also Connie Garfalk, "Help, My Cat Loves Me," Offbeat Cats,
http://www.offbeat-cats.com/feature_feelings_e.html
[4] Ibid.
[5] Sara J. Shettleworth, "Spatial Behavior, Food Storing, and the Modular Mind," in Bekoff, *The Cognitive Animal,* 126.

Chapter 18

[1] The Bible, Isaiah 2:6, King James version.

Appendix

[1] The Bible., Acts 9:4 and Acts 26:18, King James version.
[2] Ibid., I Corinthians 13: 1-13.
[3] Phil Dowe, *Galileo, Darwin, and Hawking*: *The Interplay of Science, Reason, and Religion* (Wm. B. Eerdmans Publishing, 2005), 24, 25,
http://books.google.com/books?id=CJlmSpOpODoC&q=doggedly+literal+minde
d#v=snippet&q=doggedly%20literal%20minded&f=false
http://books.google.com/books?id=CJlmSpOpODoC&dq=Augustine,+scriptures+
can+be+taken+metaphorically&source=gbs_navlinks_s
[4] Michael Middleton, "Faith of our Fathers: Successors of the Apostles," http://trushare.com/0111AUG04/AU04MIDD.htm
[5] Mendelson, "Saint Augustine."

Made in the USA
Charleston, SC
19 December 2014